BEYOND FAMILY VALUES

A Call to Christian Virtue

CAMERON LEE

InterVarsity Press
Downers Grove, Illinois

InterVarsity Press
P.O. Box 1400, Downers Grove, IL 60515
World Wide Web: www.ivpress.com
E-mail: mail@ivpress.com

InterVarsity Press® is the book-publishing division of InterVarsity Christian Fellowship/USA®, a student movement active on campus at hundreds of universities, colleges and schools of nursing in the United States of America, and a member movement of the International Fellowship of Evangelical Students. For information about local and regional activities, write Public Relations Dept., InterVarsity Christian Fellowship/USA, 6400 Schroeder Rd., P.O. Box 7895, Madison, WI 53707-7895.

Scripture quotations, unless otherwise noted, are from the New Revised Standard Version of the Bible, copyright 1989 by the Division of Christian Education of the National Council of the Churches of Christ in the USA. Used by permission. All rights reserved.

Cover photograph: Jerry Gay/Tony Stone Images

ISBN 0-8308-1509-0

Printed in the United States of America ♾

Library of Congress Cataloging-in-Publication Data

Lee, Cameron.
    Beyond family values: a call to Christian virtue/Cameron Lee.
      p.   cm.
    Includes bibliographical references.
    ISBN 0-8308-1509-0 (paper: alk. paper)
    1. Virtues.   2. Christian ethics.   I. Title.
   BV4630.L44   1998
   241'.4—dc21   98-21900
                                                                        CIP

20	19	18	17	16	15	14	13	12	11	10	9	8	7	6	5	4	3	2	1
14	13	12	11	10	09	08	07	06	05	04	03	02	01	00	99	98			

Preface   7

Part I   The Current Debate

1   What Are Family Values?   *19*

2   The More Things Change   *44*

3   Family Values Go Postmodern   *68*

4   Moral Horizons   *88*

5   Until Culture Do Us Part?   *113*

Part II   Christian Virtue

6   From Values to Virtue   *143*

7   Indwelling the Story: *The Virtue of Faith*   *160*

8   Living Toward the Promise: *The Virtue of Hope*   *181*

9   The Mark of the Kingdom: *The Virtue of Love*   *204*

Postscript   *229*

Appendix A: Values Related to Marital Permanence   *232*

Appendix B: Values Related to Support for Divorce   *234*

Notes   *236*

Bibliography   *254*

Index of Names and Subjects   *261*

Index of Scripture   *264*

Preface

It was May 1992. Vice President Dan Quayle was on the campaign trail at the Commonwealth Club in San Francisco. His speech reflected the GOP's strategic decision to make values and the well-being of American families the central rhetorical plank of the party's campaign platform. Touching upon a range of commonsense concerns, much of the speech was regarded by both parties as expressing ideas that were unobjectionable and, at best, even laudable. The GOP hoped that such themes would have a broad emotional resonance with the voting public.

Then the vice president uttered the infamous sound bite that made the media go ballistic. In the midst of a jeremiad against fatherlessness and illegitimacy, Quayle leveled a broadside at a fictional TV character, an investigative journalist and anchorwoman named Murphy Brown, who had accidentally become pregnant and decided to bear the child out of wedlock. "It doesn't help matters," Quayle observed, "when prime-time TV has Murphy Brown—a character who supposedly epitomizes today's intelligent, highly paid professional woman—mocking the importance of a father, by bearing a child alone, and calling it just another 'lifestyle choice.' "

The press reacted immediately, and family values went prime time. The vice president had cannonballed into a media pool, and the splash drenched the month of June with sarcastic op-ed pieces and a proliferation of Dan Quayle jokes. John Leo, writing for *U.S. News and World Report*, called Quayle "a proven nincompoop."[1] Robin Knight, also writing for *U.S. News & World Report*, quipped that the fall season would bring the resolution of *two* cliffhangers: whether Republican family values rhetoric would win the election, and whether Murphy Brown would name her son "J. Danforth."[2] Lance Morrow, in an article for *Time* magazine, called the "Murphy Brown debate" that followed

Quayle's speech "amazingly stupid, obscurely degrading and somehow important at the same time."[3] In the pages of *Newsweek,* Eleanor Clift wrote that Quayle had not even seen the episode that he had criticized, and had taken the idea from speechwriter Lisa Schiffren. The controversial foray into the politics of family values must have seemed advantageous, Clift stated drily, else "Quayle would never have attacked a situation comedy with higher ratings than the one he's part of in Washington."[4]

It should not be thought, of course, that either the vice president or his speechwriters invented the notion of family values. The debate over the apparent waning of traditional family norms had already been simmering in academia for some time. What Quayle's speech did, in retrospect, was to create the media effect that planted the issue of family values firmly in the public square.

Looking back, one wonders whether the former vice president has not, in fact, managed to get the last word. The Democrats initially responded to the GOP values platform by touting their own family-oriented policies, but for the most part, they attempted to steer the election away from family values and toward issues of the economy. The strategy was successful, and to some, the campaign for family values seemed to stall. But the effect was only temporary. Articles and op-ed pieces, emphasizing especially the need for intact two-parent families, continued to appear. Barbara Dafoe Whitehead, for example, reenergized the controversy with a cover story in the *Atlantic Monthly,* provocatively titled "Dan Quayle Was Right."[5] President Bill Clinton himself publicly adopted the family values rhetoric, seeking to win the swing vote by speaking to issues that would appeal to suburban mothers. Looking back over the 1996 election, *Newsweek* observed, "In 1996 Bill Clinton . . . grabbed family values for the Democrats, and he's not about to give them back."[6] And as Quayle himself has recently noted, despite the furor over his speech, "things have turned around. . . . America has truly reached a new consensus—an understanding that when families are happy and healthy, communities thrive; and when families are battered and children neglected, communities fail. Now voices at all points on the political spectrum, from Bill Clinton to Bill Bennett, are calling for strong families."[7]

While broad and influential, the consensus to which Quayle refers still is not universal. Historian Stephanie Coontz, for example, questions the validity of many "new consensus" conclusions. She objects to the simple moralistic tone of much family values writing, worrying that we will overlook the strengths of families in favor of their moral deficits, minimize the concrete impact of economic factors and fail to develop the kind of realistic policies needed to help existing families.[8]

Part of the difficulty, of course, is that the language of "family values" itself seems infinitely plastic, capable of being used in ways that doubtless would make Quayle uneasy. Gay and lesbian groups, for example, condemn the way the term is used to promote traditional heterosexual family structures, and seek to redefine "family values" in a more inclusive way. Indeed, *Family Values* was the title given to a book by novelist Phyllis Burke describing her experience of lesbian motherhood.[9]

Some recent literature has tended to drift away from an exclusive emphasis on the language of "values," opting instead for the related notion of "virtue." Former secretary of education William Bennett's bestselling anthology *The Book of Virtues* uses an eclectic collection of fables and stories to teach virtues such as self-discipline, courage and loyalty. Bennett, himself a part of Quayle's new consensus on values, distinguishes between values and virtues in the following way:

> Today we speak about values and how it is important to "have them," as if they were beads on a string or marbles in a pouch. But these stories speak to morality and virtues not as something to be possessed, but as the central part of human nature, not as something to have but as something to be, the most important thing to be.[10]

The book has indeed struck a responsive chord, spawning not only a sequel entitled *The Moral Compass* but also a children's version, a cartoon series and a variety of imitative titles, including *The Book of American Values and Virtues.*[11] Other authors, such as Yale law professor Stephen Carter, have weighed in with their own books using virtue language.[12]

All of this raises a simple question: Is another book about "family values" or "virtue" really necessary? Indeed, one could look suspiciously upon both the title and subtitle of this book as an opportunistic combination of trendy words. What could such a book have to offer? Let me preview the thesis of this book by dealing with each term in turn.

The starting point of our discussion is the notion of "family values." Lance Morrow's comment, cited previously, seems to capture the ambivalence regarding the term itself. On the one hand, there is a sense that the term is a mere political codeword that bears little, if any, substantive content. On the other hand, the issues raised under that heading are far from incidental. Pundits and commentators of every stripe are in fact trying to address something important when they use the language of family values. The problem is the lack of broad agreement on exactly what that something is. The meaning of the term *family values,* and how it should be used, is itself open to debate.

Does the notion of "virtue" capture something less transitory? We might suppose that the movement toward such language shows a desire to find a more enduring basis for public discussion about what kind of a people we should be. We would do well, however, to notice the peculiarly modern backdrop to the suggestion that we move beyond values to virtue. As historian Gertrude Himmelfarb explains, the Victorian age of the premodern Western world, despite its shortcomings, understood the language of virtue well. It is in the modern period that such understandings were abandoned in favor of the more relativistic language of values. She writes:

> It was not until the present century that morality became so thoroughly relativized and subjectified that virtues ceased to be "virtues" and became "values." This transmutation is the great philosophical revolution of modernity. . . . So long as morality was couched in the language of "virtue," it had a firm, resolute character. . . . Values, as we now understand that word, do not have to be virtues; they can be beliefs, opinions, attitudes, feelings, habits, conventions, preferences, prejudices, even idiosyncrasies—whatever any individual, group, or society happens to value, at any time, for any reason. One cannot say of virtues, as one can of values, that anyone's virtues are as good as anyone else's, or that everyone has a right to his own virtues. Only values can lay that claim to moral equality and neutrality.[13]

Those who use the language of virtue today hope that it will provide a way for people of seemingly incommensurable values to find a common basis for dialogue about our social and moral concerns. But are the current uses of the word *virtue* any more successful at transcending the subjectification of which Himmelfarb writes? As we will see in the latter part of this book, the mere use of the term does not guarantee any improvement over the values language it seeks to replace.

This is particularly important for those concerned about the life of Christian families in a so-called postmodern society. The character of the postmodern age is in many ways an exaggeration of the modern tendencies that Himmelfarb describes, where the individual self becomes its own moral center, over against any and all received traditions. Some self-described advocates of postmodernity hold that families should decide for themselves what goods to pursue, and indeed, even the individuals within each family are not to be restricted by the dictates of the family itself.

But we may ask whether there should be anything particularly distinctive about families that go by the name Christian. The answer, of course, is a resounding yes, but one that requires some self-scrutiny. The thesis of this book is that Christian families are not exempt from either modernity or postmodernity and that our use of the language of values frequently betrays the very extent to which we are inextricably immersed in the thought-forms of our culture. Let it be said at the outset that this is not an argument for the church to be hermetically sealed off from the world, for that would be a betrayal of its mission. But neither should we be led unthinkingly to believe that the mere acknowledgment of the importance of values and virtues, nor any amount of head-nodding or hand-wringing, is in fact sufficient to make the church or its families "virtuous." The form of virtue put forth by this book is specifically *Christian* virtue, the development of dispositions and habits of thought, speech and action that befit the community that claims to be under the discipleship of Christ. What Christian families need most today is neither a clarification of their personal values nor a hearty reaffirmation of self-discipline and responsibility, even though these may be of use in themselves. What they need are local congregations that embody the spirit and character of the resurrected Christ.

The plan of the book is as follows. Part one analyzes the current debate about family values and sets the context for the alternative emphasis upon Christian virtue in part two. Chapter one examines how the term *family values* is used in public opinion and discourse, and suggests that the sense that America is experiencing a "crisis of values" will take on different meanings according to how values are understood. Do Christians agree that America is having a family-oriented values crisis? How do they understand this crisis? Some empirical evidence is used to demonstrate that Christians represent an American subculture, holding views regarding the family that are substantially similar to those of the general population.

Chapter two proposes that part of our contemporary concern about families is related to the symbolic role they play in our culture. Change in family structures and ideals is not a new phenomenon; striking shifts in family-related values have occurred from colonial times to the industrial period to the present day. What has remained constant is the importance attached to the family. Our beliefs about the family are tied to the understandable need to maintain a meaningful sense of cultural stability and continuity in the face of social and technological change. But has the family become an object of veneration, even for the church? Has the ideal become an idol?

The third chapter introduces the notion that we live in a "postmodern" era and considers the instability that this generates for any discussion of values. Authors promoting the new ideal of the "postmodern family" counsel us to develop a tolerant sense of irony, celebrating the diversity between individual family members, who must each choose his or her own way. But as this chapter suggests, even the postmodern view itself is but a logical extension of the values of modernism. This recognition leads us to reexamine some of our most cherished cultural assumptions and their impact upon our attitudes toward the family.

On the basis of these observations, chapter four suggests that the nature of our current "crisis" is indeed a moral crisis, but not simply one of behavior. As Alasdair MacIntyre has written, the very use of moral language in the modern world is in "grave disorder," and there is "no rational way of securing moral agreement in our culture."[14] I suggest that our contemporary American culture is dominated by three types of moral discourse, each imposing its own inherent logic: the language of individual rights, the language of the consumer marketplace and the language of psychotherapy. Such is the case both inside and outside the church: the three languages become mingled in practice and in some cases replace the biblical narratives as the functional moral logic of today's Christians.

Chapter five applies this to concerns about family values by examining Christian attitudes toward divorce as a case study. Whitehead and others recently have argued that we live in a "divorce culture," one in which it becomes increasingly difficult to articulate why one should put aside personal desires in favor of commitments to our marital vows.[15] Eighty Christian couples were interviewed as part of the background research for this book. Among several questions related to family values, they were asked to express their views on divorce. As this chapter documents, their responses indicate the extent to which the default moral traditions cited in chapter four have become intertwined in the language and practice of the church.

Part two presents the constructive alternative: rather than emphasize the effort to win the culture war over family values, the church should direct its attention to its primary function of embodying the reign of Christ in its corporate life. This entails the rediscovery of the meaning of Christian virtue. Chapter six examines the paradoxical nature of contemporary values language and argues instead for the restoration of the language of virtue. Chapters seven through nine, in turn, address the classical theological virtues of faith, hope and love and their relationship to the identity of the church.

Faith, as a virtue, is a continuing response of trustful obedience. Through faith we are granted the increasing ability to understand our place in the story of the kingdom of God. We "indwell" the narrative of God's redemptive action in our world, an imaginative vision that is normally transmitted from one generation to the next through the family. Hope is the virtue whereby we learn to live as pilgrims, not placing our ultimate confidence in anything created. By hope we look forward to the fulfillment of God's promises, and order our lives accordingly. Finally, love is the virtue in which we concretely manifest the very character of Christ, the mark of his kingdom. For Christians, sacrificial love within our families is sustained by the love we have for one another in the body of Christ. The virtue of love is grounded in the virtues of faith and hope, for it is these that make it possible to continue in love when love seems impossible.

These chapters seek to demonstrate that for the church, *virtue* denotes neither a catalog of vaguely desirable character qualities nor an impossible set of moral demands leading to sainthood. They are rather the real-world embodiment of our discipleship in all of our dealings and relationships, first and foremost in that body we call the church, and second in our families. A final postscript brings these arguments to their conclusion and points the way toward a virtue-conscious relationship between families and the local church.

Thus this book, especially part two, is obviously and intentionally theological in nature. Although I offer suggestions from time to time, this book is not intended to be a self-help or how-to manual on either family life or family ministry. My training is in family studies and theology; I teach the former and read both. I do not consider myself a theologian in the professional sense. But if I may offer an apologia for what I have done in the book, this is an exercise in theology in the sense that theology should be a task of the *whole* church—the task of learning to interpret our lives before God, both individually and corporately. The story of the reign of God is continually unfolding before us, and our stories unfold with it. But we must learn, as a group, to tell such stories rightly, because our culture supplies other narratives that compete for the role of ordering how we think and speak. I hope, with Christian hope, that this book will encourage thoughtful Christians to take up the task of theology in this sense, and that, in addition, ministers and seminarians will be called to remember that the primary ministry to families begins with learning to *be* the people of God.[16]

The book is based, in part, on my own research with church-attending Protestant Christians in the United States. The data, collected under the heading of the Religion and Values Project, consist of (a) responses to ten-page questionnaires mailed to congregations representing a variety of denominations, spread geographically throughout the United States, and (b) transcribed interviews with Christian couples in Southern California. The questionnaires contained items adapted from several sources, most notably from the General Social Survey of the National Opinion Resource Center in Chicago. The questions cover a range of measures of religious behavior and attitudes, as well as beliefs about family structure, values and the like. Over 500 completed questionnaires were collected over the period from November 1996 through July 1997, representing 44 congregations spanning 23 denominations and 21 states.[17] The interviews, which followed a structured format of standardized questions about family values, were conducted by my students at Fuller Seminary in the summers of 1994 and 1996. Altogether, eighty couples from Southern California were interviewed, and their comments were audiotaped and transcribed for analysis. The Religion and Values Project data provide direct insight into the actual beliefs of the Christian populace, and supply a benchmark for the arguments presented in this book.

As always, while books may bear the imprint of a single author's name, they are more truly the product of countless interactions, and the work of many. The interviews for the Project were conducted by students in my course Family as Faith Community, taught in both Pasadena and Menlo Park, California. I cannot, of course, list you all by name, but you know who you are. Your enthusiasm for the course and the quality of the interviews you conducted were a great encouragement to me. Thanks also to my two research assistants, Cheryl Dueck Smith and Lisa Carruthers, who volunteered their time to help with the distribution and coding of questionnaires. And I do mean *volunteered:* these two gave of their time and energy without a penny of compensation, over and above their already demanding course load in the seminary's marital and family therapy program.

I am grateful to all the pastors who agreed to distribute questionnaires in their congregations. I know that this is not as simple as it might first sound, and I appreciate both your willingness and time in helping with this crucial part of the project. And thanks, of course, to the hundreds of individuals who took the time to complete those ten-page monstrosities or who made themselves available for interviews. Your personalities shone through delightfully in both the marginal remarks on the surveys ("Yuck!" wrote one in response to several distasteful items) and the transcripts ("Who *wrote* these questions?" exclaimed one interviewee).

The Generations adult fellowship at Hillside Community Church in Alta Loma, California, has always been supportive of me in my role as their teacher. As iron sharpens iron, I have taught them from the same perspective as you will read here, and they, in turn, have challenged me to maintain and deepen my commitment to teaching and preaching from the riches of God's Word. A special thanks goes to one of the

Generations families in particular: Chun and Serena Chin, who graciously allowed me to use their home as a quiet place to concentrate on writing this book. Serena and the children were visiting family in Malaysia, and while Chun was off to work during the day, I took command of their study and computer. Thanks again. I hope I didn't leave too many doughnut crumbs behind.

Finally, one who writes about families would be sorely remiss not to remember the part that his own family has played. My wife Suha has always been my first and best conversation partner and editor; if anything I have written here is too abstruse, it will be because I have from time to time forgotten or ignored her counsel to come down from my academic mountaintop and use real English. And to my children, Jonathan and Randa: thanks for your understanding and patience while Dad put so much time and energy into writing another book (not to mention hogging the computer!). I have tried not to neglect those one-on-one driveway basketball contests or the cuddles on the couch. In the years to come, it is the two of you who will have to tell me whether or not what I have written in these pages has the ring of authenticity and integrity.

Part I

THE CURRENT DEBATE

. . . .

One

WHAT ARE
FAMILY VALUES?

. . . .

*"Family values means placing your family first.
It means to value the traditional family
and to uphold the morals of society."*

*"I somehow associate that term with Dan Quayle and Murphy Brown.
It seems like that's become the catchphrase of the nineties,
especially in the political arena, as if the politicians
could really teach us family values."*

*"I think it means whatever is important to the people who
live in your house, whether you're married or not,
just living together, gay or straight . . . it's all relative."*

THREE RESPONDENTS FROM THE RELIGION AND VALUES PROJECT,
defining what family values *means to them*

Considering how widely the term *family values* has been used in recent years, it is troublesome that there is little consensus on what the term actually *means*. While preachers and politicians, social critics and social scientists, debate their views in the public square, the attentive observer is not always sure that the parties to the debate are actually talking about the same thing. A broad range of issues are discussed under the one heading, and for each problem there is a further range of opinion on its severity and causes. If any consensus exists, it is that significant social change in the latter part of the twentieth century has greatly impacted family life. What is disputed is how we should interpret such change, and what we should do about it.

But if there is little consensus in public debate, neither are we unanimous within the church. Each of the three individuals quoted in the preceding epigraph, by their own self-description, have been Christians for at least a decade. Their comments illustrate the diversity of views that Christians express regarding family values. The first respondent holds what might be called a traditionalist view; the second expresses skepticism about the politicization of the language of family values itself; and the third expresses the relativism of what is known today as the postmodern view of family.

What do Christians believe about family values? Is there, or should there be, anything particularly distinctive about what the church professes in this area? The purpose of this chapter is to examine how Christians understand the meaning of family values, what values they actually hold and whether or not they agree that we are in the midst of a social crisis in this area. The interview and questionnaire data from the Religion and Values Project (hereinafter referred to as RVP) form a baseline for addressing these questions. First, however, let us create a framework for the discussion by looking at how family values have been debated in the public square. The purpose of the following section is not to present detailed arguments for the views represented but to create a background against which the specific views of Christians may stand out in greater relief.

The Nature of the Debate

The public debate over family values tends to organize itself along a continuum of viewpoints, with a tendency to polarize into opposing camps. At one end of the ideological spectrum are those who believe that we are awash in a bewildering flood of social problems, which must be resolved lest society as we know it perish. Terms such as *decline, crisis* and *breakdown* have filtered down from the media and academia to influence our perceptions and discourse, both within the church and without. The family as an institution is viewed as the key to maintaining American civil society. Crisis-oriented terms are therefore linked with *family* and *values,* so that the nature of the crisis is expressed alternatively as family decline, a breakdown of the family or even a crisis of family values. In short, those at this end of the continuum consider social problems and the current state of family relationships to be indissolubly linked to an underlying deterioration of values. The solution, in general, is to recapture a normative set of values, often through the proposed intervention of social policies. Such solutions, they hope, will not only revitalize the family but also renew the nation.

Consider, for example, the work of David Popenoe, a family sociologist at Rutgers University. Popenoe's advocacy of the intact two-parent family was thrust into public attention with a widely cited op-ed piece he wrote for *The New York Times* in December 1992, which was titled "The Controversial Truth: Two-Parent Families Are Better." The following year, the prestigious *Journal of Marriage and the Family* published his article reviewing empirical data regarding the state of the American family from the 1960s onward. Distancing himself from those scholars with a more sanguine outlook, Popenoe states clearly:

> Like the majority of Americans, I see the family as an institution in decline and believe that this should be a cause for alarm—especially as regards the consequences for children. . . . For whatever reasons, families are not as successfully meeting the needs of society as they once were. . . . The weakening of this unit is much more problematic than any prior family change.[1]

This is not a new emphasis for Popenoe, whose 1988 book *Disturbing the Nest* was already a central text in the argument for family decline.[2] He cites numerous trends that signal a weakening of the institution of the traditional modern family: fewer people are marrying, and those who do are marrying later and having fewer children; more marriages are ending in divorce; fathers are abandoning their commitments to their children.[3] In 1990 he wrote the following, which serves as an apt expression of the "decline" side of the family values debate:

> During the past 25 years, the institution of the family has weakened substantially in a number of ways. Individual family members have become more autonomous and less bound by the family group, and the group has become less cohesive. Fewer of its traditional social functions are now carried out by the family; these have shifted to other institutions. The family has lost more power and authority to

other institutions, especially to the state and its agencies. The family
has grown smaller, less stable, and has a shorter life span; people
are therefore family members for a smaller percentage of their life.
The outcome of these trends is that people have become less willing
to invest time, money, and energy in family life. It is the individual
him- or herself, not the family unit, in whom the main investments
are increasingly made.[4]

Taken together, the preceding two excerpts demonstrate the two sides
of the decline thesis. On the one hand, social trends of the last three
decades have weakened the institutional viability of the traditional
two-parent family; on the other hand, this weakening has a reciprocal
impact on society, since it is in the family that children first learn the
character qualities that make them good citizens. As Popenoe has
written, "If parents fail, society fails."[5]

Other writers make a similar link between the fate of the family and
the fate of the nation and take the rhetoric a step further. Jack Kemp,
in the foreword to a book by Jerry Falwell, writes about family decline
with language of nearly mythic proportions:

The American way is to make the family the beneficiary of our
economic prosperity. I am convinced that business and government
can only succeed when they are focused within the context of the
family. If the family unit collapses, or if this touchstone of personal
worth and ethical responsibility should somehow disappear, America's future will suffer irreparable damage. Our hopes for success in
every sphere of life will be affected.[6]

Some Christian authors also assert the causal relationship between
family deterioration and social decay. Robert Lewis, for example, asserts
the superiority of the so-called "traditional family" over against the
growing plurality of family structures: "Family diversity . . . does not
strengthen the fabric of society. . . . In fact, far from advancing social
progress, family changes in America have resulted in social regression."[7]
Unlike Popenoe, Lewis offers no empirical grounds for this assertion
but simply states it as fact. In the face of social change, he takes a
position on family values that links biblical Christianity with the
redemption of family life and the rebirth of the nation:

IF it is true that our world is in the midst of a great transition, and a
new world fundamentally different from the one we have known is

being birthed, THEN we can either surrender to the currents of change and let them take us wherever they will, or we can discern our times and set out courageously to reestablish *a biblical way of life that will first redeem our families and then our nation.*[8]

Lewis pictures American Christians standing courageously against the "currents of change." Falwell, for his part, adopts even more explicitly personal and adversarial language:

Be assured that, in the months and years ahead, one group or the other will define the American family. Either the social activists will do it, or we will do it. Let everyone who cherishes this nation's heritage of faith and purpose hereby resolve to engage the enemy, to stop the outrages, and to restore dignity and honor to the very first social organization created by God: the family.[9]

In summary, then, the changes of recent decades are interpreted as injurious to the family; conversely, threats to the family are threats to the national order; and those who honor God and country are called to take a stand for the family.

At the other ideological pole, scholars of a different bent tend to reject the language of "crisis" as overly alarmist. They, too, acknowledge the important changes of the last few decades and may even agree on the empirical indicators.[10] The difference, again, is in how such change is interpreted. Some of the major arguments may be briefly summarized, taking the recent writings of feminist family scholars Stephanie Coontz and Judith Stacey as representative.[11]

Both scholars argue against the implicit or explicit restorationist agenda of those at Popenoe's end of the continuum. Explicitly, some family values proponents bemoan the passing of the 1950s suburban family ideal embodied in television series such as *Ozzie and Harriet, Leave It to Beaver* and *Father Knows Best,* an approach that Stacey derogates as "sitcom sociology."[12] Coontz and others argue forcefully against an unjustified nostalgia for that decade.[13] They remind us that the bright optimism that attended falling divorce rates, rising birth rates and postwar consumer affluence had a darker side. The underside of the national pride of the 1950s was the xenophobic Cold War. We should not forget the image of the secure and happy suburban family who had not only a white picket fence around the yard but a bomb shelter buried beneath it. Nor should we overlook the extent to which middle-class prosperity, especially in pre-civil rights America, continued to depend on the urban lower class from which it fled. Feminist authors are particularly at pains to point out that while suburban housewives of the fifties may have seemed on the outside to be living the American dream, they were far from content, and many felt trapped. In short, the middle-class values of the 1950s were overly idealized in the popular imagination. These authors argue that simplistically to advocate a restoration of those values could well jeopardize the real social gains that have been made since then.

A second theme regards these scholars' uneasiness with the moralizing tendencies of the restorationist side of the spectrum. Why, they might ask, do more married women seem to be emphasizing their careers as over against their traditional family obligations? Is this an example of the kind of selfish individualism that has been eroding family commitments since the 1960s? No, says Coontz; the roots of the problem can be traced back at least to the 1950s, when families believed in the cultural dream that united upward social mobility with the male-breadwinner family form. The expectation was that each generation would enjoy greater prosperity than their parents had. But in the harsher economic realities of the 1970s, the dream became more like a nightmare. Coontz writes:

> In the 1970s, new economic trends began to clash with all the social expectations that 1950s families had instilled in their children. That clash, not the willful abandonment of responsibility and commitment, has been the primary cause of both family rearrangements and the growing social problems that are usually attributed to family changes.[14]

Women work for many reasons, one of which is that they *must* work, in many cases, if their families are to embody the materialistic ideals that are widely shared in our culture. One could, of course, respond that this too is a moral issue; but it is one that applies equally to both men's and women's work. At any rate, the underlying point is that moralistic arguments often fail to do justice to the concrete realities with which today's families must live.

An extension of this point can be applied to the plight of the inner-city poor. Jonathan Kozol, for example, observes that there is a popular tendency to attribute family breakdown to the moral failings of those who live in ghetto neighborhoods. Such generalizations are particularly offensive to those who live in these areas. Kozol, who spent many hours interviewing inhabitants of the severely beleaguered South Bronx neighborhood of New York, notes that residents there are fully aware of the fragility of their families. The problem is that people who live outside the ghetto tend to be ignorant of the more general fragility of life in that environment: the danger of drug-infested and crime-ridden streets; the unreliability of social services, including hospital care; the shortage of work, even for those who want jobs. Thus Kozol's interviewees are offended by the language of family breakdown "not because they think it is not true, but because those who repeat the phrase, often in an unkind or censorious way, do so with no reference to the absolute collapse of almost every other form of life-affirming institution in the same communities."[15]

Thus in the public debates over family values, there are two general poles of argument. At one pole are those who decry the erosion of traditional family structures and their associated values, proposing ways in which they may be restored, encouraged or even enforced. At the other pole are those who worry that such proposals are too moralistic and nearsighted, neglecting other social causes and leading us away from policies that would help the families that actually exist in the present.

Who is right? The truth is probably not just somewhere in the middle but to be found in part at many points on the continuum. It is easy, in so short a space, to caricature the positions represented here, ignoring subtle differences and the nuances by which authors attempt to grapple with substantive issues. Even the most divisive of disagreements may sometimes be differences more of emphasis than of substance, and one can find points of agreement between the poles. Popenoe, for example, even while arguing the decline thesis, recognizes some positive gains of recent decades. He cites the improved status of women and minorities, the likelihood that the marriages that actually last are probably more rewarding than in the past, and the improvements to health care and the standard of living as indicators of positive aspects of social change. He also recognizes that it would be culturally and economically impossible for women to leave the work force in favor of a male-breadwinner ideal.[16] Moreover, far from holding to a simplistically traditional ideal, he defines *family* as "a relatively small domestic group of kin (or people in a kinlike relationship) consisting of at least one adult and one dependent person."[17] This definition inclusively embraces single parenthood, stepfamilies, unmarried couples living together and same-sex unions—with the only proviso being that the group contain a dependent member. Not all scholars who argue for the family-decline thesis assume automatically that the traditional family structure is normative.[18]

On the other side of the spectrum, sociologist Edward L. Kain has argued that the "prophets of doom," the scholars who insist that the American family is in decline, often do so on the basis of a faulty understanding of the history and demographics of family change. Nevertheless, in his closing comments he makes the following concession to the more conservative family values argument:

> In and of itself, more privacy and freedom may be viewed as positive, but there are costs as well as benefits. . . . An increase in individual choice has often led to an increase in concern for the self over others. Freedom without responsibility is anarchy, and critics of the modern family fear that the individual has come to be more important than relationships and family life, that self-interest has replaced commitment. This is a powerful argument, and I would suggest that while it may overstate the case, it must not be ignored.[19]

Thus even a scholar who stands firmly against the decline thesis may recognize there is in fact a moral dimension to the discussion. These comments represent merely two examples of the fact that disagreements over the current state of the American family cannot be neatly dichotomized into opposing camps, creating an "us versus them" mentality. At best, for each relevant issue we may be able to identify a continuum of opinion, and each argument must be weighed on its own merit.

The lack of clear-cut distinctions brings us back to the matter with which we began. What are family values? How can we sort through the jumble of ways in which the term is used? Can certain family values be identified, and if so, are Christians any different from the general population in the values that they hold? These are the questions to be addressed in the remainder of this chapter.

The Meaning of Family Values

It does not take long before a person reading on the topic of family values must confront a question: exactly what does the phrase mean? We know that a *value* is anything, including beliefs, customs and institutions, to which a group assigns a certain worth. But what makes a value a *family* value? The language of family values is not invoked purely in the abstract, independent of current real-world events. Rather the term functions to some degree as a code word that serves as shorthand for two broad assumptions. The first is that the state of the culture at large is inescapably bound up with the state of its families; the second and related assumption is that a key aspect of assessing the state of either has to do with what we value. In general usage we may observe that a "family" value is one that possesses one or more of the following characteristics: (1) it is a value about what defines a family, (2) it is a value whose exercise indirectly impacts families or children, or (3) it is a value that should be taught to children by their parents. Put differently, the language of family values is used to discuss what family is or should be, what values a society should hold to support family life, and what values should actually be embodied and passed on within the family sphere.

Thus one way of assessing the family values of Christians is to begin with their views of what families are or should be. The traditional view is that a family is composed of two individuals of opposite sex, married to one another and raising children. Many alternative living arrangements, however, also exist in our culture. A Roper survey conducted in 1992 presented 1,000 Americans with a list of fourteen different types of households. Respondents were asked, yes or no, if they considered each to be a family.[20] Not surprisingly, the highest rating went to "a married couple living with their children"; 98 percent of respondents agreed that they should be considered a family. Only 20 percent, however, agreed that "two gay men committed to each other and who are living together" deserved that label, the lowest rating of the fourteen options.

The Roper poll was addressed to a representative group drawn from the general population. Would the results for Christians be the same or different? To what extent are Christians willing to assign the label "family" to these various arrangements? To answer this question the same list of fourteen household arrangements was given to the national sample of Christians who participated in the RVP. Table 1 shows the comparison.

"Is this a family?"

Living arrangement	Percentage responding yes	
	Roper (1992)	RVP (1997)
Married couple living with their children	98	98
Married couple living with children from a previous marriage	93	95
Married couple with no children	87	95
A divorced mother living with her children	84	93
An unwed, never-married mother living with her children	81	73
A divorced father living with his children	80	91
A man and a woman who live together for a long time, are not married, but are raising children together	77	36
An unwed, never-married father living with his children	73	69
A man and woman who live together a long time but are not married	53	14
Unrelated adults who live together and consider themselves a family	28	14
Two lesbian women living with children they are raising	27	8
Two gay men living with children they are raising	26	8
Two lesbian women committed to each other and living together without children	21	6
Two gay men committed to each other and living together without children	20	5

Table 1. Values Regarding Living Arrangements

A close examination of the results reveals several patterns common to both groups. First, the Roper and the RVP groups agree that the traditional model is the norm. Second, both groups agree that of the three criteria of heterosexuality, marriage and the presence of children, heterosexuality is the most important. Both groups rank the four same-sex alternatives at the bottom of the list. Third, marriage is a more important criterion than the presence of children. Respondents were more likely to accord the status of family to a married couple without children than to an unmarried couple with children. Even in the case of single parents, a divorced single parent (that is, one who was at least *formerly* married) is more acceptable than a single parent who has *never* been married. Fourth, the presence of children is a positive factor, even if not as important as the presence of a marriage relationship; all of the living arrangements that include children are rated more highly than the same arrangements without the children. Fifth, there is a slight bias toward women. In single-parent families, single mothers with children are somewhat more likely to be deemed families than are fathers. This distinction virtually disappears, however, in the case of same-sex unions.

Thus where family structure is concerned, Christians share the same hierarchy of values as the general population. The traditional family is most likely to be considered the norm. More specifically, the element of heterosexuality appears to be the most important criterion, followed by marriage and finally by the presence of children. We should note that this differs from Popenoe's definition of the family, cited previously, in which care for a dependent member was the primary criterion of family.

There are, however, differences of emphasis. First, the RVP sample is far less accepting of same-sex arrangements than the general population surveyed by the Roper poll. Second, the relative value given to the institution of marriage as over against the presence of children is far more striking among Christians. On the one hand, deleting the children from the traditional family arrangement results in a drop of 11 percentage points in the general population but only 3 points in the RVP sample. On the other hand, deleting the marriage relationship and retaining the children yields a 21 percentage point decrease in the Roper survey but a 62 point decrease among the RVP participants.

We can make a similar observation by starting with the cohabiting childless couple instead. Adding children to the mix improves the ratings by only 24 points in the general population and 22 points in the RVP group. Adding a marriage, however, yields increases of 34 and *81* points, respectively. A possible corollary to this difference is that Christians appear to be more accepting of divorce than the general population, where the definition of family is concerned. They are slightly more accepting of blended families, in which all three traditional elements are present, despite the background presence of a divorce. There is, moreover, a clear hierarchy between divorced single parents (with ratings of 91 to 93 percent), never-married single parents (69 to 73 percent) and cohabiting couples (14 to 36 percent). One possible interpretation is that given the importance assigned to marriage, Christians may view divorced individuals as "previously married," never-married parents as being at least "marriageable" but somehow blocked from marriage, and cohabiting couples as flouting the marital institution by choice.

On the matter of structural norms for the family, then, Christians should be considered a *subculture*, which shares an overall pattern of values with the surrounding culture but differs in emphasis. The largest differences are twofold: (1) Christians are less willing to define same-sex arrangements as families, and (2) Christians place more stock in the importance of the marital union.

Another approach to evaluating the family values of Christians is to ask what family values are important to them. As already noted, while many have seemed eager to use the language of family values, the meaning of the term itself often has remained vague. Mark Mellman, Edward Lazarus and Allan Rivlin, however, have attempted to give an empirical answer to that question. They conducted four focus-group discussions in Baltimore and Denver, in order to explore how Americans understood family values, and then presented their findings in survey fashion to a sample of 1200 participants.[21]

Mellman and his colleagues found that Americans consider the family a primary source of fulfillment. Asked what in life gave them the greatest pleasure, nearly two-thirds of the respondents pointed to their families, while over three-fourths of the parents specifically answered that their children did. Conversely, when asked which of several items best explained the incidence of crime and other social problems, respondents also pointed to the family: the most common responses were "parents failing to discipline their children" (20 percent) and "declining family values" (17 percent).

What are these family values? Presented with a list of twenty-eight values identified in the focus-group research, respondents were asked both to indicate whether or not they considered it a family value and how important each value was to them personally. The researchers found a very close correspondence between these two categories: the values that were ranked most highly as family values were also those that were held to be of the greatest personal importance. The first column of table 2 shows the ten family values that participants in the Mellman study rated as the most important to them personally.

Mellman, Lazarus and Rivlin (1990)	Religion and Values Project (1977)	Ranking in Mellman study
1. Being responsible for your actions	1. Having faith in God	(8)
2. Being able to provide emotional support to your family	2. Being responsible for your actions	(1)
3. Respecting your parents	3. Being able to provide emotional support to your family	(2)
4. Respecting other people for who they are	4. Respecting your children	(6)
5. Having a happy marriage	5. Respecting your parents	(3)
6. Respecting your children	6. Having a happy marriage	(5)
7. Being able to communicate your feelings to your family	7. Being married to the same person for life	(13)
8. Having faith in God	8. Respecting authority	(9)
9. Respecting authority	9. Being able to communicate your feelings to your family	(7)
10. Leaving the world to the next generation in better shape than you found it	10. Following a strict moral code	(14)

Table 2. Ten Family Values Identified as Most Important

Even a casual examination of the list reveals that these values do not all relate to the family in the same way. The content of some of these values is directly related to family relationships, while others are more general. One might infer that some of the values become family values because of the expectation that they should be embodied in family relationships and taught by parents to their children.

Do Christians share similar values? The RVP questionnaire presented the same list of twenty-eight values, in random order. Participants rated how important each value was to them, using a four-point scale that ranged from "not very important" to "absolutely essential."[22] The ten top-ranked items for this multidenominational Christian sample are shown in the second column of table 2, again in descending order. For ease of comparison, how the participants in the Mellman study ranked these items is shown in the third column of the table. The similarities and differences are instructive. First, there are striking parallels between the two lists. On seven of the ten items that Christians rated as the most important, the difference in ranking between the two groups was two points or less. This suggests that Christians agree with the general population on some key family values.

But important differences exist. First, while faith in God is an important value in the Mellman sample, it is the supreme value for Christians, outranking all others. Second, while the two groups agree on the value of marital *happiness,* the RVP sample also values "being married to the same person for life," or marital *permanence.* This suggests once again that Christians greatly value the institution of marriage itself, which is not reflected as strongly in the general population. Similarly, whereas the simple value "being married" was ranked twenty-fourth out of twenty-eight in the Mellman study, it was ranked sixteenth in the RVP.

As an aside we might note that an examination of the eighteen values rated lower by Christians demonstrates far less similarity with the Mellman study than the top ten. Only five of these eighteen show a difference in ranking of two points or less; this represents only 28 percent congruence, as opposed to 70 percent for the ten highest values. Two highly politicized values were given greater emphasis among Christians: "opposing abortion" ranked fourteenth, as opposed to twenty-seventh in the Mellman study, and "being in favor of prayer in school" ranked nineteenth, as opposed to twenty-fifth. Several values also received *lower* ratings in the RVP group. The following were ranked five or more points lower than in the Mellman study: "being physically fit" (twenty-second versus twelfth), "being independent" (twenty-fifth versus fifteenth), "being well-educated and cultured" (twenty-sixth versus seventeenth), "earning a good living" (twenty-fourth versus eighteenth), and "having a rewarding job" (twenty-first versus sixteenth).

It is important to read each of these similarities and differences in the context of the entire list of twenty-eight values. It is not surprising that Christians would rate faith in God as the surpassing value. We should not, however, understand this to mean that faith in God is *not* a value in the general population. It is more a matter of priority and emphasis than an absolute, black-and-white distinction. As we have seen, there is substantial similarity between the two groups in terms of their most cherished values; most of the differences are found in values that are less central by comparison. To put the matter again, Christians appear to represent a value *subculture,* rather than an alternative culture. Earlier we observed that members of this subculture might be tentatively distinguished by their lower acceptance of same-sex relationships and their greater emphasis upon the value of marriage. The latter observation is repeated here: marriage as an institution is valued over and above its psychological benefits. To these we may add the following: Christians value faith in God above all else; they give greater importance to the social issues of abortion and school prayer; and they tend to deemphasize some of the culturally accepted markers of success.

The RVP also offered a third, less structured method of evaluating the family value orientation of individual Christians. The people interviewed for the present study were asked what the phrase *family values* meant to them but were not presented with a prescribed list of possible answers. Their responses were instructive.

The most straightforward and basic response was that family values are simply *values that families hold,* whatever they may be. As one respondent put it, family values are those "that a family has established, that they all agree to. . . . They could be good, they could be bad." Similarly, another woman defined family values as "what a family is committed to in their lives, not just in their words, but what they actually do in acting on what they believe." These are, in essence, *descriptive* definitions of the term: family values are those values that family members hold in common and demonstrate in their behavior, "a set of morals that you live by as a family—values that you hold to govern how you operate as a family." There is no evaluative or *prescriptive* element in these explanations, nor any sense of what the "right" values might be. This does not mean, of course, that these respondents therefore adopted a relativistic stance whereby all values are held to be of equal value. The first respondent, while observing that families could hold either "good" or "bad" values, stated unequivocally that her own values are "based on laws that God has set up in his word" and judged that "America is not really doing very well as far as family values." Far from being a relativist herself, the woman who defined family values as simply a set of morals a family lives by also believes that America has a "spiritual problem" in the area of values, because "people are just winging it—they don't have guidelines." She interpreted this as a lack of "spiritual awareness," of not understanding "who God is, or what he intended."

But if these women exemplify those who avoided including a prescriptive element in their definitions, many others displayed no such reticence. One man, asked what family values meant to him, responded simply, "Tradition, commitment, rugged individuality, and personal responsibility." Asked by the interviewer to elaborate on what he meant by tradition, he said, "I would have to say it is more of a loyalty. That would be a better way to define it—loyalty. Loyalty to a family as well. The stereotype of a family . . . two people of the opposite sex—the opposite sex, and children." Regarding "rugged individuality" he added: "It is your job to take care of yourself and your family the best that you can. Without having to ask for handouts, try to approach the world [as if] it would not owe you anything. . . . You have to go out and do things yourself. That is what I mean by rugged individualism, as opposed to where our society is moving now [where] the government owes you everything." For this man, therefore, *family values* meant a particular set of values, embodied in the traditional family structure and a cultural ideal of self-reliance, extended from the individual to cover one's family.

Others emphasized values that they understood as more explicitly Christian. A respondent spoke of "Judeo-Christian values that are absolute, not relative, as in some of the more Eastern religions," and gave as examples "purity before marriage, no fornication; homosexuality as being sin." Others were more tentative, searching for specifically Christian responses. One woman blended two themes already observed, namely the idea of "Judeo-Christian" values and the valuing of a traditional family norms: "Family values? I guess that it sort of implies those traditional Judeo-Christian kinds of values—things such as two parents, of the opposite sex, with kids." More specifically, this respondent, who seemed to grope for an answer, cited the Bible: "Family values mean to me? I don't know . . . just what the Bible says . . . like the Ten Commandments and stuff." One interviewee took the question further, applying it more narrowly to the Christian home, and defined family values as "living life according to God's commandments and his rules—going by what he taught us in Scripture on how to live."

Thus while some of the interviewees defined family values descriptively, others defined them prescriptively, giving specific content to the values that families *should* have. In some cases prescriptive responses reflected values more endemic to the culture at large, and in others specifically religious values were identified. It is worth noting, in addition, the *rule-oriented* way in which Christian values were applied, suggesting that the Bible provides Christian families with a set of moral standards along the lines of Ten Commandments. Are there other ways to understand how the biblical texts might shape the lives of families? We will return to this question in later chapters.

We should also notice that while some values seemed to apply directly to family relationships, others were more general, as with the values cited in the Mellman study. Indeed, when interviewees were asked for specific examples of the values they considered most important to their marriages and families, they gave a diverse assortment of responses. Some described character qualities that they assumed would benefit family relationships but that were not specific to families. These included, in no particular order, loyalty to God and country, personal integrity, honesty, maintaining a sound financial base, going to church, being a good citizen, being involved in the community, kindness, mutual respect, hard work and a commitment to open communication. Other values, however, were more directly related to family life. Two themes at least deserve mention.

One theme had to do with the ordering of commitments and priorities. Several respondents defined family values as *valuing the family,* making family life a priority. The following response was typical in this regard:

> I think family values means valuing the family. I think that is where we fall short today, because as much as we say we love our family, we love our children, it is not priority. . . . Valuing the family means the family is priority. . . . The media, and the problems in our society, reflect that the family is not priority. Second jobs, two cars, vacations, clothing—you name it—career, power, success, attention. . . . Family values is valuing the family to the degree that it is the priority in your life, above all other human experiences.

Putting priority on the family means striving to keep the family together, as another respondent commented:

> Family values means that the family is important. I don't think that
> morals in general are any more screwed up than they ever have
> been, but . . . families fall apart more than they used to. That is what
> I think of when I think of family values . . . keeping the family
> together.

Many of the interview participants, however, stressed that the family is
not to be considered a higher priority than one's relationship to God.
As one woman said:

> The value that I hold most important is the value of my relationship
> to God. . . . Second to that is trying to maintain, as healthy as possible,
> a good relationship with my husband. That's a lot of hard work, but
> that is an important family value that I feel very strongly about. And
> third to that is the raising of my children. . . . After that comes my
> career, and ministry in the church and things like that.

For these Christians family values meant prescriptively that commitment to one's spouse and children should take precedence over all
other commitments, save that to God alone. We demonstrate the
priority of marriage in different ways, including sexual fidelity and
the refusal to consider divorce as a solution for marital difficulties.
For these respondents, rightly ordered priorities included an understanding that marriage is a lifelong commitment, as the following
comments demonstrate:

> I think family values would mean being committed to one spouse
> for your life. . . . It means sticking with it, no matter what it takes.
> And when you make that decision, that means you're with one
> husband or one wife for the rest of your life. And I think it means
> underneath God [is] . . . first priority, spouse second priority, and
> your children would be third priority, and everything else would
> come after that.

While some respondents seemed to value characteristics such as good
communication and conflict resolution skills almost as ends in their
own right, others appeared to hold these as means only, as practical
skills needed to sustain the more fundamental commitment to a lifelong
marital union.

    The commitment of parents to children raises a second theme: that
family values involve the *transmission of values from parents to their*

spouse before children.

children. The values that are transmitted may be specifically Christian or not; some are related specifically to family norms, and others are not. In this view what makes them *family* values is that they are taught in the family, perhaps even best learned in that environment. One woman told the interviewer what comes to her mind when she thinks of family values:

> I think of what parents teach their children in terms of life, in terms of being a person and how to relate to people in our society in general. And I think a lot of it does revolve around the values that parents have that they want to pass on to their children in terms of marriage, [and] being the kind of person that they want their kids to be.

In a similar vein, other participants defined family values as "things you teach to your children . . . so that they get along with everybody," or, from a different vantage point, values that "are instilled upon you through your parents." One man gave a more specifically Christian response: "Family values, in my opinion, has to do with teaching your kids what is right and wrong, teaching them about what is in the Bible." Taking this theme even further, one woman observed that parents are to transmit these values in both word and deed:

> [Family values] means the things that are important to you, what you want to instill in your children and what you would want them to carry on as citizens. . . . It's definitely the moral, spiritual things that you would want to teach your children; it is also the lifestyle. It means living a lifestyle you would want to show your children.

Or, to use another's language, "you need to show outwardly what you are trying to teach inwardly."

Such themes should by now be familiar. The family values espoused by Christians fall along similar content and context dimensions as those of the general population. In terms of content, Christians define family values in ways that would be affirmed by a broad array of citizens, even while occasionally attempting to ground these values on a more specifically Christian basis. The differences, again, are mostly a matter of priority.

Are We Having a Crisis?

In the RVP questionnaire, participants were asked if they agreed with the statement that "there is a crisis of family values in this country." An overwhelming majority did: over 96 percent were in agreement, with 78 percent responding "strongly agree." This clear consensus, however, begs the question of how they understand the nature of the crisis, given the wide variation in how family values itself is defined. In this section we briefly survey the different markers of the crisis, as perceived by interview participants.

Before we begin, however, it is useful to ask the question: what about the 4 percent that did not agree? Can we know the reasons for their response? There was no place for survey respondents to explain their disagreement, but we may draw some clues from the interview participants, since they were able to give more detailed answers. A few of the interviewees also disagreed that we are facing a crisis of family values. What they questioned, in general, was the accuracy of the term *crisis*. There were two ways in which this was done.

First, there were those individuals who took a longer view: they stated that families had always experienced various kinds of problems and stressors in the past, and were reluctant to judge present problems as constituting a crisis. Note that this does not mean that they viewed present-day families as problem-free. Rather they viewed *crisis* as an inflated term, reflecting two related characteristics of the information age. To begin with, we know more than we used to, so we are more aware of problems than before. Beyond this, however, interviewees suggest that the media intentionally exaggerate the facts, especially during recent election years. Thus we should be realistic about our present difficulties but not make more of them than necessary. As one schoolteacher commented wryly, "*Every* generation thinks the younger generation is sending us off to hell in a handbasket."

A smaller number of interviewees disagreed for a second reason. If the first group could be considered the historical realists, the second were pluralists. These individuals viewed the word *crisis* as indicating an unwillingness to change, a symptom of the difficulty of living in a multicultural climate. As one man stated:

There are people who use the word *crisis* in family values, because it's not as homogeneous . . . as it used to be. These people have a set idea of what they think all families should aspire to, what all family values should be, but that's not the case because a lot of these families come from other cultures now. When America was first founded, the range of cultures was far more limited, and therefore the range of family values far more uniform. So what we have now is a different set of family values that is much broader. . . . Is there a crisis in family values? No, I don't think so. I think, if anything, there might be a crisis in the fact that we no longer have a standard family, and a lot of the families have very difficult times because of that.

This response demonstrates what Richard Mouw has called *descriptive pluralism,* a practical recognition that we live in the midst of a kaleidoscopic array of cultures, traditions and values.[23] This falls short of the kind of *prescriptive pluralism* that characterizes the young man who was quoted in the epigraph: "[Family values] means whatever is important to the people who live in your house, whether you're married or not, just living together, gay or straight . . . it's all relative." Asked if he believed that we are facing a crisis of family values, he predictably demurred:

No, no, I think that we're having a crisis of some people's idea of family values, but not mine. . . . I think what's happening is that people's values are just changing, and for those people who are more conservative, they're having a crisis—but for those of us with more liberal points of view, we're not having a crisis.

This type of pluralism goes beyond the recognition and acceptance of the fact of value diversity, toward a more fully "postmodern" claim: if it's all relative, then crisis is only in the eye of the beholder.

In summary, while the vast majority of participants agreed that we are experiencing a crisis in the area of family values, a few did not, citing either realist or pluralist reasons. These justifications, of course, are not mutually exclusive. Both would probably agree that even if families have always had difficulties, so that social strains upon family life are nothing new, the degree and extent of value pluralism in our culture *is* new. As we shall see in the next chapter, a great deal may be said for this thesis, based on what recent historical scholarship informs us about Western family life in the past.

For the present, however, let us examine how Christians perceive the nature of the crisis. Interviewees who agreed that we are having a crisis of family values were asked how they understood the crisis itself.

Interviewees as a group illustrated the crisis by reference to a wide array of topics; some individuals gave interviewers long litanies of social ills. For convenience let us call these problems *crisis markers.* The markers they identified varied greatly in the degree to which they directly relate to families. Some respondents, for example, cited issues such as alcoholism and pornography; clearly while these may be disruptive of family relationships, they do not apply to families alone. Other markers were more directly related to family relationships and norms, such as child abuse, family violence, illegitimacy, infidelity and surrogate motherhood. By far the most commonly cited sign of crisis was the prevalence of divorce, a finding that becomes even more striking if we add to it the related issues of single parenthood and father absence, which were often cited in tandem with the mention of divorce.

Interviewees, perhaps unintentionally, also distinguished between values held inside the family and those held outside the family. The values of the outside world were seen as threatening those inside the family. They tended, in other words, to adopt what might be called a *siege mentality:* there is a crisis because my family, and all good families like mine, are surrounded by social problems "out there" in the culture or in somebody else's family. No doubt interviewees would resist such a starkly phrased summary, but the indicators are there.

For example, the most commonly cited crisis marker, after divorce, was the fact that respondents' children were exposed regularly to values other than their own: at school, in the mall, around the neighborhood, at the supermarket. These parents are concerned that their kids are confronted with children from families who hold and live by different values, making it more difficult to maintain firm value standards in their own households. Even respondents who were not yet parents expressed this perception, as this young woman's comments illustrate:

> It is hard to teach your children values; they get values from you and the culture that they live in, and sometimes those might completely conflict. It's hard to teach kids values if they are getting a totally different message from society.

The media, the third most oft-cited crisis marker, is often blamed as the conduit of these alternative values.

It is not merely the exposure to other values that constitutes the problem, however: the deterioration of traditional family values has made the world a less safe place to live in. Respondents did not explain the connection but took it as almost axiomatic. As one husband stated simply: "I don't feel safe with my wife going out at night, because of the breakdown in family values." A father of two gave a lengthier response:

> The climate in which you raise your children is less safe as a direct consequence of the disintegration of families. . . . I will look for ways to . . . make sure that we seek out safe places—be it school systems, or the neighborhoods we live in, the places that we go. I think it makes us a lot more aware of the dangers that our children will be facing as they grow up, particularly in terms of peer pressure and societal influence. For all intents and purposes, it is going to be a hostile environment to family values in which they are growing up—that respects marriage and the sacredness of marriage, the sacredness and priority of the family.

This is the notion of the family as a "haven in a heartless world" with a vengeance.[24] The family is perceived as a safe shelter to be protected against the onslaught of the world. As one mother of young children stated, "Our children live a rather sheltered life—we spend time with parents who are like minded." Or in the words of one woman, defining what she meant by family values; "The family takes care of each other and defends itself against the outside."

As a father of two children myself, I am also concerned about the values promoted in our culture and about the safety of our streets. Regarding the former, for example, we closely monitor the content and limit television viewing time in our home, and not just for the kids. Regarding the latter, my wife and I have been the victims of both burglary and armed robbery; although we currently live in a reasonably quiet middle-class suburb, two drive-by shootings have occurred within three blocks of our home. Needless to say, we maintain a certain amount of vigilance where our children's safety is concerned.

What I am after, however, is a more fundamental observation: there appears to be a self-serving aspect to our perceptions of social crisis. We may readily admit that we are not perfect; to not do so would be sheer arrogance. By and large, however, it is other people's values that have deteriorated, rather than our own. The bad influences, the crisis markers, are mostly "out there," to be defended against. When interviewees explained the nature of the crisis in family values, they seldom, if ever, showed concern over their own values. As John Gillis has written, "although most Americans do not believe their own family life to be in immediate danger, they are quick to perceive their neighbors as being in total disrepair."[25] In other words, there appears to be a distinctively heroic element to how many of us would tell the story of our families: we are beleaguered captains, holding fast to the wheel of the ship in the midst of a stormy sea.

Christians, of course, are not alone in this. A single example, taken from the Mellman study, should suffice. When the researchers asked participants to tell them the most important reason for the perceived decline in family values, the most popular response was that parents do not spend enough time with their children. Family togetherness was seen as being in conflict with the economic necessity of working more hours. The researchers then presented participants with a hypothetical scenario: Imagine that you are thirty-eight years old and are offered a job in a field that you enjoy. On the negative side, the job will require more hours and leave you with less time to spend with your family. The researchers then offered three different versions of the positive side of the scenario. In the first version the job is more prestigious but does not involve a raise; the second and third versions involved 15 percent and 35 percent raises, respectively. How likely would participants be to take the job?

Despite the fact that participants cited a lack of time together as the chief cause of the erosion of family values, the majority of them said that they would take the job anyway. Even in the case of the no-raise scenario, nearly two-thirds responded that they would be at least likely to take the job, and over one-third said that they would be *very* likely to take the job. For these individuals, it would appear, occupational prestige is the higher value.[26] Where family values are concerned, we must ask if the oft-quoted words of Walt Kelly's comic strip character Pogo apply to us: "We have met the enemy, and he is us."

In summary, Christians generally agree that we are in the midst of a nationwide crisis of family values. Christians have a profound respect, sometimes bordering on reverence, for the family as an institution. *Family values* is an umbrella term for any and all values that have the capacity to support or undermine the stability of families, or values that are important to civic order that should be taught within the family circle. While these values may be expressed either by families themselves or in the culture at large, there is a tendency to draw a line between the two realms. Problems with values are located largely in the world outside one's own family, and potential or actual value conflicts within the family itself are overlooked or ignored.

I have argued that, at present, the church should be understood as a subculture, sharing many of the same values as the surrounding culture, albeit with differences of emphasis. If this is the case, then the siege mentality suggested by the comments cited in this chapter is understandable but wrongheaded. The contentiousness of the public debate over family values, I suspect, only exacerbates this tendency to divide the culture into us versus them, the good guys versus the bad guys, my family versus other families.[27]

Does this mean that the church has no moral distinctive? No, not at all; indeed it is the burden of this book to describe that distinctiveness, particularly as regards the family. But we should not settle for a deceptively black-and-white understanding of the church's relationship to the world. Nor should we adopt too quickly the associated strategy of lining up good values versus bad values, identifying the good values with the church and calling down fire from heaven on the bad ones. Our first task is to discover the extent to which we are not only *in* the world but also *of* the world: the ways in which our values are conformed to the mold inherited from the culture in which we live.

TWO

THE MORE
THINGS CHANGE

. . . .

Never before has family taken on a greater cultural significance. . . .
Finding no other location for such values as cooperation,
enduring loyalty, and moral consideration, modern Western culture has
mapped these exclusively onto the families we live with. . . .
What sets the culture of contemporary family life apart and
accounts for our obsession with family myths, rituals, and images
is the fact that we no longer have access to other locations
onto which we might map our deepest moral values.
JOHN R. GILLIS, *A World of Their Own Making*[1]

There is wisdom in the well-known French proverb "The more things change, the more they remain the same." The one thing that both sides in the family values debate agree upon is that in the space of only the last few decades, our social landscape has changed dramatically, and our values and expectations are not keeping pace. Where they disagree is in how they evaluate these changes. On one side, broadly, are those who use the language of decline, often interpreting changes to the family as evidence of moral dissolution and advocating policies to shore up traditional values and structures. Opposing them are those who view recent changes in a more positive light, as progress rather than decline. For them the problem is not that we have lost values that need to be restored, but that their transformation is incomplete; we are trying to cling to outmoded values, which prevents us from making the changes needed for families living in our current social and economic climate.

It is important, however, that we not allow the changes of the last thirty to forty years to eclipse a longer historical view. Cultural values and social structures have always been fluid, adapting to changes in a wide variety of factors. Ever since the first Pilgrims landed on the North American continent, norms and expectations regarding family life have been subjected to an unending process of change. Families, as social institutions, are not immune to political and economic currents. Indeed as we shall see, contemporary concerns about the impact of government policy on the family are grounded in peculiarly modern assumptions, which tend to downplay the family's role as a public institution. Such a view would have distressed our colonial forebears, for whom the family constituted the fundamental political unit of society.

Change, it seems, is a constant in the history of American families. To use a phrase coined by Steven Mintz and Susan Kellogg, in the last three centuries American values and practices regarding family life have been transformed by a series of "domestic revolutions." These authors cite three fundamental factors that account for much of the change. First, the *economic* relationships between families and family members changed dramatically as we moved away from self-sufficient agrarian households toward industrialization. As we shall see, there is a reciprocal relationship between economic assumptions and family arrangements. Such relationships are difficult to discern when economic assumptions are taken for granted. Second, family change is shown by crucial *demographic* shifts. Two stand out among these: the decreased role of childbearing within marriage and the "graying" of the population that comes with greater life expectancies. Taken together, these shifts signal smaller families and more years of adult life without the responsibilities of caring for dependent children. Finally, the *role of women* has changed profoundly, especially since the rapid entry of women into the labor force during and after World War II.[2] These three interlocking factors represent one way to understand the ever-present currents of change that have been a part of the American social landscape for centuries, with important implications for family norms and behaviors.

But if change is constant, it is not the only constant. We have always valued the family as a social institution; from colonial days to the present Americans have insisted on the foundational role of families in training each successive generation in the values important to society. There is also, however, a persistent tendency in our history to go beyond valuing the family to *idealizing* it, a tendency that has become more pronounced as the family has retreated into its own private sphere.

This has great significance for the life of the church and its relationship to the institution of the family. Over the last several years I have taught a parent education course to seminarians preparing for ministries as counselors and pastors. One of their assignments has been to interview a local pastor, to determine what ministries to parents and families exist in that congregation and what rationale, if any, is used to justify the ministry. Where such ministries exist, the typical pattern has been simple and straightforward: someone in the church, whether staff member or parishioner, has expressed the desire for a ministry to parents. A brief period of casting about for parent education materials ensues, and a program is selected, often on the strength of a personal recommendation, and the program is implemented. When asked how the program fits with the mission of the church, pastors tended to respond along the following lines: the mission of the church is to minister to the needs of people in the name of Christ; parents have needs; these needs have been concretely expressed; we have implemented this program to meet these expressed needs. When asked if they were aware of the assumptions behind each program, pastors often confessed their ignorance, referring either to another staff member who knew the program better or to some other trusted individual who gave the program high marks. In short, it was the rare congregation or pastoral staff that actually took the time to critically evaluate materials or even concretely articulate how the program related to the mission of the church.

I wish neither to criticize overworked pastors nor to deny the needs of contemporary Christian parents. The question is this: Have we too easily assumed that valuing families means that any ministry that seems to help them is for that reason worthy of our time and effort? It is a matter of priorities. As we have seen in chapter one, Christians recognize the importance of placing God first in their lives. But how do we put this into practice? Does our concern for family life, in our day-to-day ministry practice, take precedence over discipleship? One could argue, of course, that the two are not mutually exclusive, and rightly so. But if the preceding observations about parent education in the church are at all valid, then the relationship of family ministry to Christian discipleship is poorly articulated, if at all. If so, does the presence of such ministries indicate a theologically uncritical devotion to family?

Certainly this is *not* to say that our concern for families is theologically indefensible. Again, it is a matter of rightly ordering our priorities. To borrow a theme repeatedly emphasized by Stanley Hauerwas, the church's first order of business is to *be* the church, to be the community whose life and habits are uniquely formed by the Christian gospel.[3] Only within this broader context of discipleship do our values regarding the family have their rightful place. Our tendency to idealize the family is part of our cultural inheritance, shaped by Christian ideals, but also modified by currents outside the church. If the church is to fulfill its primary mandate, this will entail "the recovery of habits of the mind that give us the skills to understand the world in which we live on our terms and not on the world's terms."[4] As this chapter argues, much of how we understand the current plight of families derives from our cultural mythology and the symbolic role that families play in the public consciousness. Only when we understand this can we begin the constructive process of revisioning the church's relationship to the family, and vice versa.

We will begin by surveying key changes in family life throughout our history. If our concern for family values is driven by the perception of change, then we must understand these changes as soberly as possible. Many excellent histories of American family life have been written in recent years, and the reader is referred to the endnotes for representative sources. It will not be possible, of course, to do more than paint this historical portrait with exceedingly broad strokes. The goal, however, is to illustrate a single point: there is no ideal family of the past that embodies all of the values that we wish to maintain in the present.

With this as a basis we may explore the extent to which the church as a subculture embodies the family mythology of the larger culture.

Have we, as some have argued, carried this to the extremes of idolatry? Such considerations in turn lead to a more constructive examination of the relationship between the church and the families that compose it.

Domestic Revolutions, Domestic Ideals

What do we think of when we use the word *family?* As we have seen in chapter one, the typical picture is of a heterosexual couple raising children, with heterosexuality the primary criterion, the presence of marriage second and the presence of children third. Christians, as a subculture, share the same hierarchy of values, with two differences of emphasis: they are even less willing than the general population to ascribe family status to same-sex partnerships, and they place a higher value on lifelong marital union.

In the popular imagination, however, the notion of the "traditional" family goes beyond these simple structural criteria. Additional characteristics include the father's role as the sole breadwinner, the mother's role as the caretaker of the home and children, and the sovereignty of the parents' authority over their own children without interference from outside the family. This image is further developed in the icons that are still a part of the baby boomers' cultural repertoire: the families portrayed in popular television sitcoms of the 1950s. These white, middle-class families lived on quiet, tree-lined suburban streets behind white picket fences. The episodes were typically driven by the escapades of the children. Their adventures were generally both amusing and harmless, and could always be turned into a lesson in good character by the wise and patient father. For some these television families provide a compelling image of a more stable and predictable time, when everyone knew their proper roles and could be counted on to fulfill them.

As historian Stephanie Coontz and others have forcefully argued, however, these *Father Knows Best* families were less an objective portrayal of reality than the construction of a new social ideal.[5] To be sure, after the two long decades of hardship that families had endured through the Great Depression and World War II, there were reasons for optimism. After an unprecedented postwar peak, the divorce rate fell sharply. People were marrying earlier and having more children. A new ideal of the good life was needed. We enshrined this ideal in the image of the suburban family, a place where growing postwar affluence could be directed toward comfortable living, supported by all the modern conveniences that American technology had to offer. Elaine Tyler May cites the example of the "kitchen debate" between President Richard Nixon and Soviet Premier Nikita Khrushchev in 1959 at the opening of the American National Exhibition in Moscow. Sparring over the superiority of American capitalism as contrasted with communism, Nixon and Khrushchev ended up comparing the merits of American versus Soviet washing machines and other appliances. Nixon put forward the suburban ideal of the male breadwinner and the housewife surrounded by a wide choice of American-made consumer goods:

To us, diversity, the right to choose, . . . is the most important thing. We don't have one decision made at the top by one government official. . . . We have many different manufacturers and many different kinds of washing machines so that the housewives have a choice. . . . Would it not be better to compete in the relative merits of washing machines than in the strength of rockets?[6]

Summarizing, May writes:

So Nixon insisted that American superiority in the cold war rested not on weapons, but on the secure abundant family life of modern suburban homes. In these structures, adorned and worshiped by their inhabitants, women would achieve their glory and men would display their success. Consumerism was not an end in itself; it was the means for achieving individuality, leisure, and upward mobility.[7]

From our contemporary vantage point there may be a certain quaintness to the ideal, yet in our own way we still cherish it. What Coontz and others would have us remember is that there is a dark side to the fifties as well. As the preceding quote reminds us, the context of Nixon's praise of the suburban consumer ideal was the Cold War. We must remember that the 1950s were a pre-civil rights era of racial and cultural anxieties that brought us lynchings, McCarthyism and bomb shelters. Nor were men and women as happy in their suburban roles as they were supposed to be. Books like William Whyte's *The Organization Man* (1956) and David Riesman's *The Lonely Crowd* (1958) expressed doubts about the mindless economic treadmill that characterized the male half of the gender ideal, while Betty Friedan's *The Feminine*

Mystique (1963) reflected the discontent of 1950s women with their suburban role. The scenario, of course, is not unremittingly negative:

> Happy memories of 1950s family life are not all illusion, of course—there were good times for many families. But even the most positive aspects had another side. One reason that the 1950s family model was so fleeting was that it contained the seeds of its own destruction. . . . Many of the so-called rebels of the 1960s were simply acting on the values that they had internalized in the bosom of their families.[8]

In other words, the 1950s found Americans in need of a new social ideal on which to center their postwar reconstruction of national identity. They found it in the suburban family. As in any era, the social arrangements of the decade contained both positive and negative aspects, and there was much for which families could feel genuinely grateful. Nevertheless, the symbolic role of the family in fulfilling a national ideal made it difficult to assess the disadvantages realistically. It seemed ungrateful and nearly antisocial to express discontent. Not only were the fifties not idyllic, the values promoted in service of the ideal would later serve, ironically, to undermine family commitment. To this subject we will return.

But if the era of the fifties is not a suitable candidate for family nostalgia, then neither is any other period in American history. We may admire and even wish to emulate certain characteristics of a particular period. Each era, however, represents a unique combination of sociocultural, political and economic variables that cannot simply be reproduced in another time by either force of desire or a sheer act of will. At our own point in history we embody values that may be invisible to us, since they operate at the level of assumptions. The characteristics of other times, which embody different values, cannot simply be grafted onto our own.

Consider, for example, the family arrangements of colonial America. There is much that present-day Christians might find admirable about the Puritans' commitments to God and family. They had emigrated from an England they viewed as barbarous, and hoped to establish a more godly "New" England that would "avoid the disorder of English family life through a structured and disciplined family."[9] Cotton Mather, writing in 1699, asserted that "Well-ordered Families naturally produce a Good

Order in other Societies."[10] They honored the marital commitment, viewing love between spouses as a Christian duty and not mere sentiment. Moreover, they took literally the biblical image of marriage as a union of two individuals into one flesh, both enriching and complicating the network of kin relationships in the community:

> Puritans felt the obligations of minor relationships only slightly less than those of their immediate families. . . . Puritans addressed as brothers, sisters, parents, and cousins individuals with whom they were connected only by the more remote ties of marriage. . . . The death of a spouse and remarriage of the remaining partner further enlarged and complicated the web of relationships; for although a man might gain a whole new set of relations by a new marriage, he did not lose his first wife's relations by her death: he still addressed her kin as his own and still treated them with the same deference.[11]

They treated childrearing responsibilities just as seriously. Because children bore the evil of original sin, they were to be trained early and diligently in the Bible and Christian morality. Although Cotton Mather's famous phrase "Better whipt, than Damn'd" may characterize our image of Puritan parental discipline, Edmund Morgan argues for a more balanced and humane view:

> There is no proof that seventeenth-century parents employed the rod more freely than twentieth-century parents. . . . In fact, if [the Puritan parent] listened to his religious advisers, he employed bodily punishment only as a last resort; for the ministers who wrote and spoke on the subject almost always counseled their readers and listeners to win children to holiness by kindness rather than try to force them to it by severity.[12]

And whereas we tend to view our attention to a child's unique characteristics as the insight of modern psychology, the Puritans were also aware of this and shaped their educational goals accordingly:

> Children were not subjected to a preconceived discipline without reference to their individual needs and capacities. A parent in order to educate his children properly had to know them well, to understand their particular characters, and to treat them accordingly. . . . Puritan education was intelligently planned, and the relationship between parent and child which it envisaged was not one of harshness and severity but of tenderness and sympathy.[13]

Thus the Puritans of colonial America represent an attempt to found a godly society on a well-ordered family, characterized not only by moral discipline but by love and an authentic commitment to kin relationships.

There is no question that colonial husbands and wives loved each other, nor that parents loved their children. Our modern minds are likely to find two characteristics of the colonial family alien, a reminder of the disjunction of values between their time and ours. First, the family was a public rather than a private institution, in ways that moderns would find intrusive. Second, and related to the first, is the extensive role that economic considerations played in the formation of families and the maintenance of parental authority.

To begin with, colonists would have understood *family* as synonymous with *household,* a collection of relatives and nonrelatives organized for economic purposes. As Beatrice Gottlieb reminds us, the word *family* is derived from the Latin word for *servant* and in its original use did not denote kinship in the way it does today.[14] Households, headed by male property holders, were usually organized around a nucleus of kin relationships but also included a continually shifting membership of nonkin servants and apprentices.

The family household, as a public institution, was considered the fundamental unit of social governance. Local communities expected heads of households to keep order among their children and servants alike. This was particularly true among the Puritans, who acted on the assumption that "the state is made up of families rather than individuals."[15] Thus, for example, with regard to marriage,

> Puritan governments did not always wait for marital troubles to reach the point of divorce without endeavoring to restore harmony and enforce a performance of marital duties. . . . Since marriage was an ordinance of God and its duties commands of God, the Puritan courts enforced these duties not simply at the request of the injured party but on their own paternal initiative.[16]

The Puritans did not assume that all property holders were automatically qualified to keep good order in their households. Community officers known as selectmen and tithingmen were empowered to represent community interests, monitoring families and carrying out the wishes of the court. The authority of the community extended to every area of colonial life:

The laws of New England reveal a society in which village and church officials regulated all aspects, from sexual conduct to prices of goods to whether a person could build a fence or take up a trade. Town and church determined where people should live, what they should wear, how long they could put up strangers in their homes; neighbors constantly intervened to report departures from the norm.[17]

Households were so central to the good of the commonwealth that colonists went as far as to enact legislation that made it illegal for single people to live on their own—that is, outside the good order of a well-governed household. The judgment of the Essex County Court, in the 1672 case of one John Littleale, illustrates this:

> Court being informed that John Littleale of Haverhill lay in a house by himself contrary to the law of the country, whereby he is subject to much sin and iniquity, which ordinarily are the companions of a solitary life, it was ordered . . . he remove and settle himself in some orderly family in the town, and be subject to the orderly rules of family government. . . . If he did not comply with this order, the selectmen were ordered to place him in some family, which if he refused, a warrant was to be issued to place him in the house of correction at Hampton.[18]

Thus while households might represent the commonwealth in microcosm, they were not independent monarchies. Communal order was enforced in ways that might prove offensive to modern families who take for granted the sacrosanct nature of their private lives, as free as possible of government regulation.

Related to the matter of the public nature of family life was the extent to which economic considerations played a pivotal role. Although love and affection were important to a marriage, the marriage itself was not understood as the expression of personal sentiment but as the establishment of a new household. Communal order required that some assurance be made that the new household would be stable economically. As Gottlieb writes,

> For most people, marriage was in large measure an economic relationship, no matter how they felt about the people they married. . . . Marriage was closely associated in people's minds with economic independence.[19]

Where more money was at stake, parents became more involved in the wedding plans. Wealthier New Englanders wielded more power over their children's choices of mates, and the fathers of the betrothed children frequently engaged in a preliminary bargaining process "with all the enthusiasm they might have devoted to a horse trade."[20] In 1764, when John Walker and Elizabeth Moore wished to marry, their respective fathers had to negotiate the financial details, as appeared to be the custom. Thomas Walker, in a brief but direct letter to Bernard Moore, wrote:

> My son, Mr. John Walker, having informed me of his intention to pay his addresses to your daughter, Elizabeth, if he should be agreeable to yourself, lady and daughter, it may not be amiss to inform you what I feel myself able to afford for their support in case of a union. My affairs are in an uncertain state, but I will promise one thousand pounds, to be paid in 1766, and the further sum of two thousand pounds I promise to give him; but the uncertainty of my present affairs prevent my fixing on a time of payment. The above sums are all to be in money or lands and other effects, at the option of my son, John Walker.

A day later, Elizabeth's father replied:

> Your son, Mr. John Walker, applied to me for leave to make his addresses to my daughter, Elizabeth. I gave him leave, and told him at the same time that my affairs were in such a state that it was not in my power to pay him all the money this year that I intended to give my daughter, provided he succeeded; but would give him five hundred pounds more as soon after as I could raise or get the money, which sums you may depend I will most punctually pay to him.[21]

The money involved in an upcoming wedding might even be stated in newspaper announcements of the event. Thus in 1737 the *Virginia Gazette* described one bride-to-be as "an agreeable young Lady, with a Fortune of upwards of 5000 pounds" and another as "a very genteel accomplished young lady of great merit and considerable fortune."[22]

Such matters were important, because the passing of wealth through inheritance, especially landed property, was key to consolidating a family's fortunes and thereby their standing in the community. Typically children did not receive full title to the property until the father's death, and even at this point, parents may have established legal contracts beforehand to control the disposition of the estate. We might chafe today at the idea of parents controlling their children by manipulating their access to an inheritance, but this was common practice in colonial America and would not have been viewed in the same way then as it is now.

Such values and practices indicate how our family ideals are more historically conditioned than we normally may recognize. We may applaud the Puritan recognition of the moral and religious role of the family and its foundational role with respect to civil society. But we occupy a different point in history, in which we have grown used to thinking of the family in private rather than public terms. Such a transformation was already beginning in the eighteenth century, as the possession of landed property became less critical and the parental authority that accompanied it began to wane:

As parents lost the ability to pass on their "status position" to their children by distributing land to each of their sons, relations between parents and children were transformed and the emotional character of family life began to change. A new conception of parental responsibility appeared that centered on the care and proper nurture of children. . . . As the family lost its earlier position as society's primary social and economic unit, it began to acquire new emotional significance as a place of peace and a repository of higher moral and spiritual values, a haven in a heartless world.[23]

This movement toward a more privatized and emotional interpretation of the family would be reinforced by the separation of work and family spheres during the period of industrialization and hallowed by the postwar ideology of the 1950s. Is it possible for inhabitants of a postindustrial world to truly understand, much less embody, the public nature of the colonial family? If we agree with the Puritans as to the pivotal moral and civic role of family life, must we then also subject families to public scrutiny and control? This is the same conundrum that stands behind the controversies surrounding the legislative proposals of profamily-values groups: how do we meaningfully affirm and support the value of the family and its contribution to society, while not violating its right to privacy and self-governance?

It is questionable whether we can expect any past form of family life to be able to contain all the multiple and conflicting values that we hold. But there is a larger issue here. Should the family itself be the sole bearer of our most cherished values? Jan Dizard and Howard Gadlin use the term *familism* to describe a "reciprocal sense of commitment, sharing, cooperation, and intimacy that is taken as defining the bonds between family members."[24] They recognize that familism was at one time more a part of public life, especially during the colonial era, when the lines between the community and the household were not so exclusively drawn. With the increasing dominance of the values of the marketplace and the thickening of the barrier between the public and the private spheres, familism came to reside almost exclusively with the family. Dizard and Gadlin put the question sharply:

> Our desire to form families may remain strong, and in that sense the abstract idea of the family may be secure, but our capacity to sustain real families, and with them a sense of familism, is clearly questionable.

In this sense the crisis of the family is less about the trials and tribulations of individual families, or even the form the family takes, than about the steadily shrinking range of social contexts that call forth our capacities to cooperate, love and make sacrifices for one another. If families, conventionally conceived, cannot be depended on to nurture familism, where might familism be fostered?[25]

To put it another way, the crisis facing families today may be less about families per se and more about their moral context. Do individual families possess within themselves the moral resources to sustain familism? From what social contexts should such resources derive?

Christians should have a ready answer for this question. The ideals of love and self-sacrifice are to characterize the church in every age. The apostle Paul, for example, wrote to his beloved church in Philippi, to encourage them to lead lives reflective of the gospel that knit them together:

> If then there is any encouragement in Christ, any consolation from love, any sharing in the Spirit, any compassion and sympathy, make my joy complete: be of the same mind, having the same love, being in full accord and of one mind. Do nothing from selfish ambition or conceit, but in humility regard others as better than yourselves. Let each of you look not to your own interests, but to the interests of others. (Phil 2:1-4)

Paul grounds his exhortation in the story of a self-emptying and glorified Christ:

> Let the same mind be in you that was in Christ Jesus,
>> who, though he was in the form of God,
>>> did not regard equality with God
>>> as something to be exploited,
>> but emptied himself,
>>> taking the form of a slave,
>>> being born in human likeness.
>> And being found in human form,
>> (he humbled himself)
>>> and became obedient to the point of death—
>>> even death on a cross.
>> Therefore God also highly exalted him
>>> and gave him the name
>>> that is above every name, *Jesus becoming Christ?*
>> so that at the name of Jesus
>>> every knee should bend,
>>> in heaven and on earth and under the earth,
>> and every tongue should confess
>>> that Jesus Christ is Lord,
>>> to the glory of God the Father. (Phil 2:5-11)

It is this story, as found in various forms throughout Scripture, that forms the basis of the church's identity. The question, however, is whether or not the church itself has also unwittingly embraced another story, namely the cultural identification of familism with the family. Is our concern for families legitimately derived from our commitment to the gospel? Or is it a religious subspecies of the quest for the American dream?

Ideals and Idols

"The more things change, the more they remain the same." From era to era in American history, family arrangements and many of the values associated with them have been in flux. As suggested earlier, however, the tendency to idealize the family, to make it the repository of our fondest cultural aspirations, has been present from the beginning.

The Puritans, as we have seen, left England with the dream of establishing a God-fearing society on the new continent. The family or household was to be the key building block of the new society. At the start their priorities regarding God and family were clear. In Morgan's words, "They had fixed their eyes on a heavenly goal, which directed and informed their lives."[26] This meant that all earthly loves, including the love for one's spouse and children, were to be kept in proper proportion vis-à-vis the supreme love for God.

But not all of the emigrants who crossed the ocean with them could be counted among the elect. It was not only freedom of religion but also opportunity that drew people to America, and not all shared the Puritans' divine vision. It was not long before Puritan writers, in a manner reminiscent of the "siege mentality" observed in chapter one, began counseling parents to protect their children from the wrong kind of influence. As one writer sharply asserted: "If you would not have your Sons and Daughters destroyed, then keep them from ill company as much as may be."[27] Similarly, Cotton Mather wrote: "Often repeat this Charge unto them, That if there be any Vicious Company, they shun them, as they would the Plague or the Devil."[28] The first generation of Puritans had intended to "make New England a beacon to the world, not a refuge from it."[29] Finding their hopes for a new society difficult to attain, however, they increasingly focused their attention on the maintenance of their own tribal loyalties, such that they eventually "translated 'Love thy neighbor' as 'Love thy family.' "[30] Thus despite the Puritans' early emphasis on keeping their earthly affections rightly ordered, Morgan observes that they had "committed the very sin that they so often admonished themselves to avoid; they had allowed their children to usurp a higher place than God in their affections."[31]

Have we fared any better in our era? Many of my students come to the seminary from other countries and quickly conclude that much of American Christianity is more American than Christian; our values and goals are shaped more by cultural visions of the good life than by the radical challenges of the gospel. Tim Dearborn tells of his enlightening conversation with a Malaysian man while bumping along in a taxi in Bangkok. The Malaysian, an avowed Marxist, declared, "You American Christians don't stand a chance against us Marxists." Asked why, he replied,

Because for you, the integrating value in your life is self-interest. You become a Christian because you want to have your sins forgiven and be sure of going to heaven. You pray because you want God to do things for you. You go to church because you think it will make you more successful and happier and keep your family together. Everything you do, you do for yourself. But everything I do is for the revolution.[32]

Set aside for the moment the question of how accurate the generalizations are: certainly not all American Christians are equally self-absorbed, and somewhere in the world there must be at least one self-interested Marxist. But there is a ring of truth in the observation made by those who stand outside our culture and are therefore more likely to see things about ourselves that we take for granted.

Everything I do is for the revolution. The Puritans certainly would have rejected Marxism, but equally would have rejected today's capitalist excesses in favor of their "revolutionary" vision. The family played an important, even crucial, role in that vision, but family affections were not of ultimate significance. Children were routinely given over to other households, to be suckled by a wet nurse, to learn a trade by being apprenticed to a craftsman for several years or simply as servants. Children were therefore under the care and tutelage of some household, even if not the one into which they had been born. The household served the public order, not the sentiments of families.

Over time, however, the family itself moved to center stage. We have already seen the tribalistic impulses that began to emerge as the Puritans discovered the obstacles to achieving their political and religious ends. Subsequent centuries would bring further changes. By the mid-eighteenth century the communal bonds of colonial America were already loosening substantially. The growth of the colonies brought an inevitable diversification that would make it difficult to maintain the kind of like-minded small community the colonists had previously enjoyed. With land available on the western frontier, the solution became to find one's own way. The pioneers of westward expansion exhibited what we would today consider a truly independent and entrepreneurial spirit. Families became less bound to communities, and individuals also began to be seen as more independent.

The growth of a more individualistic ethos can be found in the ideals of the American Revolution of the latter part of the century. Those who framed the founding documents of the nation, for example, viewed the pursuit of happiness as an inalienable right of individuals, an idea that would have strained the patience of the Puritan divines. But the revolution itself already embodied an abandonment of patriarchy, as the colonists sought to extricate themselves from British rule. The proposed alternative was to create a new nation founded on the principle of voluntary cooperation among citizens of equal standing. This political break from patriarchy paralleled the move away from the older, patriarchal household and toward a newer understanding of the family in terms of its emotional bonds.

The key change of the nineteenth century was the advent of industrialization. Economic production had already begun to move out of the household with the rise of wage labor. But the major impact of industrialization on the family was to institutionalize this shift, creating the separate spheres of work and home and transforming the family from being "a unit of production to being a unit of consumption."[33] Work, the aggressive and demanding sphere of the marketplace, became the province of the husband/father. The home, in contrast, became the private sphere where the man retreated from the world of commerce to seek emotional and spiritual renewal in the presence of his family. The home was the woman's domain; it was her responsibility to maintain the family haven.

It was particularly during this century that the family and home took on mythic dimensions. Formerly the house had served a largely pragmatic role, as a place where people slept, ate and worked. People did not seek private spaces within the dwelling, and furnishings tended to be spare and functional. With the separation of the spheres of work and family life, however, the house now had to become a *home,* a place of symbolic and emotional significance. In particular it became the woman's mission to create and sustain the rituals of this domestic sanctuary, in essence to become a "homemaker." The passion with which the wife and mother's proper spiritual role was proclaimed has led some historians to speak of the creation of a "cult of domesticity," and with it a cult of "True Womanhood":

> In a society where values changed frequently, where fortunes rose
> and fell with frightening rapidity, where social and economic

mobility provided instability as well as hope, one thing at least remained the same—a true woman was a true woman. . . . If anyone, male or female, dared to tamper with the complex of virtues which made up True Womanhood, he was damned immediately as an enemy of God, of Civilization, and of the Republic.[34]

But this mythic portrait of womanhood was but a reflection of the sacralizing of home itself: "The home had never before been sanctified in the way it was in the nineteenth century. . . . Home had become a sacramental site, complete with the redemptive qualities previously associated with holy places."[35] Family members had always had affection for one another, but they had understood the family itself as a flexible unit that served the public order. With the separation of the public and private spheres of life, however, the family became a private institution, imbued with spiritual and emotional significance like never before.

From the industrialization of society onward, the family has become the locus of the fulfillment of the American dream. Our contemporary pessimism regarding the future of the family makes more sense against the backdrop of failed expectations and disappointed hopes.[36] The 1950s family ideal, building on the model of separate spheres, promoted an ethic of self-fulfillment against a mythic backdrop of endless upward mobility. This implicit social contract floundered in the economic instability of the 1970s. Today's youth are no longer assured that they will be able to maintain a standard of living equal to or better than what their parents had. In the 1950s the traditional male-breadwinner model was seamlessly wedded to the goal of the family's economic success. Since the 1970s, however, it has become increasingly difficult to keep these values together:

American families were facing a *conflict* between two values they had dutifully absorbed in the 1950s. On the one hand, experts told them that the best way to have a happy family was to have the husband work and the wife stay home. On the other hand, the media's descriptions of happiness had revolved around mother using the latest cooking and cleaning appliances, dad washing the car with the kids, and the kids hanging out in the comforts and spaciousness of an up-to-date home. By the mid-1970s, maintaining the prescribed family *lifestyle* meant for many couples giving up the prescribed family *form*. They married later, postponed children, and curbed their fertility; the wives went to work.[37]

Thus it is not simply that people with "bad" values are encroaching upon people with "good" values; rather, we are all heir to conflicting values and desires regarding the family, and it is not possible to embody all of them at our particular point in history. Concretely, as the preceding quote suggests, middle-class Americans have grown up with the expectation of—indeed almost the sense of entitlement to—being able to live in their own home. In previous decades it was more feasible to do this on a single income, and therefore it was also possible to maintain *both* the values of homeownership and a male-breadwinner structure. Even where wives worked, the pretense could be maintained that her income was purely supplementary, supplying the additional cash needed to further the family's standard of living. In recent years young couples have had to deal with a more complex reality. It may not be possible, for example, to purchase a home on the salary of a single young adult. If the lifestyle ideal is to be maintained, then the economic contribution of both spouses is *necessary*, and inevitably the values associated with women's work will change accordingly. Surely to blame the erosion of family values on the entrance of women into careers of their own begs the question. One could just as easily ask, and should ask, whether as a society our economic lifestyle commitments have become the dominant motive force behind our most important family decisions.[38]

Gillis makes a helpful distinction between the families that we "live by" and the families that we "live with."[39] The former refers to our cultural family ideals, the family as it should be, the bearer of our hopes and dreams. The latter refers to the people with whom we must actually live. Compared to the families we live by, the families we live with often disappoint us with their fallibility, fragility and selfishness. The question for society and the church is whether we have become so captivated by the families we live by that we soon cease to deal compassionately and realistically with the families we must live with.

The Family and the Church

Janet Fishburn has argued that the church exhibits a "domestic captivity," the uncritical adoption of the cultural idealization of the family and its pivotal role in the American dream. She uses the term "religious familism" to describe the domestic folk religion whereby we adapt Christian language and symbols to reinforce commitments to the family. To Fishburn this constitutes a form of idolatry and has important consequences for the church:

> Americans tend to uncritically identify loyalty to family with loyalty to church. Congregations in which loyalty to church and family are virtually synonymous are engaged in an American form of religious familism. . . . The captivity of Protestant congregations in visions of a domesticated church leads to a severely truncated vision of the nature and mission of the church. It threatens to reduce the role of a pastor to that of family chaplain.[40]

Dizard and Gadlin's use of the term *familism,* discussed previously, differs somewhat from Fishburn's notion of *religious familism*. The former denotes a set of values that have been historically associated with the family, but need not be. The latter, by contrast, assumes that the association is taken for granted and then given further religious sanction. Fishburn thus joins with those scholars who view the family as important but not of *ultimate* significance for the Christian. It is the church itself, as the "household of God," and not the so-called "Christian home" that is of greater consequence:

> It has been typical of the Protestant tradition to believe that "the Christian home" can or should be a little church. This reverses the biblical expectation that the power of "the love of Christ" is known through participation in "the household of God." . . . God's blessing can also be experienced in the family relationships of Christians; but "the Christian home" is not the source of blessing. . . . There is no sociological entity that can accurately be called *the Christian home.* The family is not essential to the Christian life. People can become Christian through participation in a congregation of Christians whether they were born into a Christian family or not. Only the church is essential to the Christian life.[41]

Fishburn seems to skate a little too lightly over some potentially important questions here: even if the family is not "essential" to the Christian life, what role does it play, if any? We return to this question in a later chapter on the virtue of faith. For the present, however, her point is well taken. To use Gillis's terms, the church's adoption of the culture's idealization of the family we live by has led to a split between church life and our daily existence in the families we live with.[42] Has the church, in so doing, sabotaged its own role as the bearer of familism?

The New Testament places eschatological limits on our devotion to family. The Sadducees attempted to confound Jesus with an apparently apocryphal story about a man who had six brothers and who died childless. Fulfilling the obligations of levirate marriage, the next brother took the widow as his wife, but also died before she could bear him any children. The same unhappy sequence was repeated down to the seventh brother. "In the resurrection, then," they asked, anticipating their victory, "whose wife of the seven will she be?" His answer astounded all those within earshot: "You are wrong, because you know neither the scriptures nor the power of God. For in the resurrection they neither marry nor are given in marriage, but are like angels in heaven" (Mt 22:23-30). What exactly Jesus meant by his response cannot be known with certainty, but he does set temporal boundaries around the institution of marriage itself.

Recently a conversation among the members of our adult fellowship turned to the death of a much-beloved couple from our congregation. Cancer had rapidly claimed the husband, and some months later, after a valiant struggle and much care and prayer from her friends, the wife died of cancer as well. "He's in a much better place now," my wife commented, receiving several approving nods. "Yes, and they're together again," I added unthinkingly, again to nods of assent. I had to sit back and ask myself: Just how much do we need to believe that marriage and family relationships are so divinely ordained that they must be eternal?

Jesus emphasized discipleship, not family devotion, in such a way that the former radically qualified the latter. Luke tells of two men who received this lesson directly. To one Jesus commanded, "Follow me." The man replied, "Lord, first let me go and bury my father." We do not know if the father was already dead or if the man's response meant something akin to "Lord, my father will die soon, and then I will be free to follow you." In either case the response would have seemed reasonable in light of Jewish custom and filial duty. But Jesus' response is curt: "Let the dead bury their own dead; but as for you, go and proclaim the kingdom of God" (Lk 9:59-60). I. Howard Marshall interprets the response as meaning "Let the spiritually dead bury the physically dead," implying that not to follow Jesus is akin to spiritual death, and therefore following him is to be considered of greater importance than any human duty.[43]

Likewise, the second would-be disciple would seem to have made an even more reasonable request: "Let me first say farewell to those at my home" (Lk 9:61). He could have cited the prophet Elisha as precedent; when Elijah came to anoint him, he granted Elisha's request to return home to bid his parents farewell (1 Kings 19:19-21). But this man, too, received an equally terse response: "No one who puts a hand to the plow and looks back is fit for the kingdom of God" (Lk 9:62). In both cases Jesus sets aside what others of that time and place would have considered not only acceptable but important duties to family, in favor of the call to discipleship. "Whoever comes to me," Luke reports Jesus saying on another occasion, "and does not hate father and mother, wife and children, brothers and sisters, yes, and even life itself, cannot be my disciple" (Lk 14:26). Hauerwas, reflecting on how difficult these words are for present-day Christians, points to the larger social issue behind our reaction, namely the idealization of the family and the cultural captivity of the church:

> We have been led to believe that Christianity is good for the nation because Christianity is good for the family. We therefore fail to stand under the authority of the word because the word is captured by practices and narratives that are more constitutive of that entity called America than that community called Church.[44]

The church, in other words, is captive to the cultural narrative that assigns primary importance to a privatized notion of family life. In the biblical narrative, however, it is the church, and not the family, that is the primary site of discipleship. The church, not the family, is "God's most important institution on earth."[45] In a memorable phrase, Rodney Clapp describes the church as "first family":

> With the coming of the kingdom . . . Jesus creates a new family. It is the new first family, a family of his followers that now demands primary allegiance. In fact, it demands allegiance even over the old first family, the biological family. . . . Allegiance to the kingdom *precedes* the family. It does not destroy the family.[46]

The families we live with are neither abandoned nor dismissed, but a biblical view recognizes the primacy of the church. Hauerwas, again, makes a similar point:

> The blood of the cross has forever qualified the blood of the family. . . . This new eschatological family we call the Church which now has our fundamental loyalty, makes peace possible even among families. . . . If we are to love one another well in the family . . . we need a sense of a love that is as nonviolent as it is truthful. Such love cannot be real without our families' loves being fundamentally qualified by the love that we learned in the Church.[47]

Finally, Mark DeVries, reflecting on his experiences in youth ministry, also emphasizes the primacy of the kingdom. He argues that youth who remain in the faith in later years are not necessarily the products of the biggest, flashiest or most entertaining youth programs, but those who worshiped and ministered side by side with the adults in the congregation. Thus true ministry occurs when the church properly orders its priorities:

> Though important, the preservation of the family and "family values" is not of ultimate importance for the Christian. . . . Our primary allegiance is to God and God alone, not to any human institution. The family is a good gift from God. . . . But for the Christian, nothing, no matter how noble or good, must be allowed to take the place of God or the priorities of God's kingdom.[48]

Our concerns about the changes that confront the family are legitimate, and to some extent, at least, the substance of those concerns may be unique to our time. We must remember, however, that people have raised similar concerns in every era of our history. Whenever the currents of social change seemed to threaten the stability of society as we knew it and wanted it to stay, someone would predict the impending demise of the family. This is because the *idea* of family has always occupied an important place in the public imagination, even while our concrete commitment to actual families has waxed and waned. Just how serious today's changes may be and what should be done about them is a complex topic that reaches well beyond the scope of this book and the author's wisdom. But we should be reminded, as Christians, not to let our unquestioned devotion to the culturally defined families we live by eclipse either the centrality of the church or the charity and commitment due the families we live with.

It is the Christian story that shapes our identity, and in this narrative
the family does not play the fundamental role. As Gilbert Meilaender McWilliam
has written, "God has given his Christ, and nothing decisively new is
to be anticipated within our history."[49] In this light no political or social
achievements, including the establishment or reestablishment of particular forms of family life, are to be accorded "the status of events in
the history of salvation."[50] There will always be change. Whether we
should interpret this change as decline and crisis involves many
considerations, and the question of how to respond is more complicated still. But where such language betrays a sense of paradise lost,
the church must begin to reevaluate its allegiances and the stories that
generate its life and vision. In Meilaender's words, we should view the
current social crisis

> as an occasion to rethink now in the present the significance of what
> has always been true: that we live every moment of our life
> equidistant from eternity; that nonetheless, we must walk—moment
> by moment—the pilgrim's way toward God, and that, always, we
> must struggle to find a way to do both.[51]

In one sense all points in our history are equidistant from God. There
is no era that is either more or less deserving of the scandalous grace
of God than any other. There is no period of our history that represents
the reign of God in its fullness, and therefore all periods are in need
of redemption. Nevertheless, the pilgrim church does not abandon its
mission to embody that reign in this world, in these families with which
we live. For disciples of the risen Christ, the family we live by is in fact
his body, the church itself. But this is not merely the church as a ragtag
collection of individuals in all their worldly imperfection. These are
people called to live by the spirit of the resurrected One; they strive to
see themselves and their world through lenses of faith and hope, and
to manifest the love of Christ in the present age.

But does this actually describe the church's, or any particular local
congregation's, self-understanding? When it comes to matters regarding
the family, can we expect that the church will have anything unique to
say? Or is it only a subculture that maintains relatively minor differences
of emphasis? The purpose of the next three chapters is to explore these
questions by examining the cultural narratives that inform our understanding of the family.

Three

FAMILY VALUES
GO POSTMODERN

• • • • • • • • • • • • • • • • • • • •

We careen along the uncertain arch that bridges
the modern world and the postmodern.
LARRY RASMUSSEN, *Moral Fragments and Moral Community*[1]

The demise of modernity, like the demise of the modern family,
has been announced somewhat prematurely.
BRIGITTE AND PETER BERGER, *The War over the Family*[2]

T he matter of family values goes well beyond what we believe about the moral acceptability of divorce, teenage pregnancy and the like. In this regard, as chapter one attempts to show, Christians are not all that different from the general population. Their priorities, in terms of what they list as important values, and their definitions of what does and does not merit the designation *family* are substantially similar to those of the general population. Christians represent more of a subculture than an alternative culture. This should not be surprising, although it is important to keep this in mind, given the tendencies of the participants in the contemporary "culture wars" to paint debates in stark black and white.

One aspect of the adoption of cultural narratives is in the valuation of the family itself. As chapter two points out, the family has always held an honored place in the public imagination. What has changed from colonial times to the present is the understanding of the relationship between the public and the private. For the Puritans there was no clear distinction between the private interior governance of households, on the one hand, and the public good, on the other. The community had covenanted together to create a new polity, a godly civic order that would necessarily be founded on well-ordered and godly households.

If the extent to which Puritan legislation seemed to intrude on the liberties of families and individuals is offensive to us today, it is partly because we have taken on the values of a later age. For us the family has become a private sphere, invested with emotional rather than public significance. An indication of this is found in the siege mentality adopted by many who decry the moral breakdown of our culture. Such attitudes are far from new, representing an almost predictable response to periods of rapid social change. When Christian families feel besieged from without, this may be a distant echo of Puritan tribalism. We must begin to ask how culturally transmitted narratives may implicitly define the church's self-understanding and mission. Many of our modern values, including those related to the family, are like the air we breathe: we depend on them, but they go unnoticed until disturbed. They are so integral to the way we understand our world that they have the character of "oughtness." To challenge them would seem like attempting to contradict the laws of gravity.

Such understandings, however, profoundly shape how Christians perceive their role and ministry. There are many layers of cultural assumptions about the family that influence both our rhetoric about family values and our preferred methods of response. Consider, for example, the different ways in which the church may respond to abortion. Richard Hays quotes Presbyterian minister Bill Tibert, who states the alternatives sharply:

> Let me ask you: Which has the greater power? Ten thousand people who fill the streets in front of abortion clinics and shame those seeking abortions, or ten thousand people in California who take to the state capital [sic] a petition they have signed stating they will take any unwanted child of any age, any color, any physical condition so that they can love that child in the name of Jesus Christ?[3]

For the moment let us bypass the pastor's question as to which strategy might have the greater impact. Notice instead the background assumptions that might inform each strategy. The goal of the first approach is to change the behavior of the mothers by publicly declaring their values unacceptable. It attempts to exert public pressure on what many would consider under normal circumstances to be a private decision. The use of public coercion, however, does not mean the abandonment of the value of privacy altogether. The protesters return to their own private residences after their work is done, and would greatly resist anyone who attempted to tell *them* how to make family decisions. The goal of the second response, in contrast, is to extend care directly to the children. Instead of insisting that others make appropriate private decisions while simultaneously maintaining one's own right to privacy, this approach opens up one's own home in the name of love.

Similarly, Hays also relates a story told by William Willimon in his 1985 book *What's Right with the Church?* A group of pastors were debating abortion, and one member of the group justified abortion by asserting that young teenagers cannot raise children by themselves. One black minister, however, told of a fourteen-year-old girl whose child was to be baptized in the church the following Sunday. He agreed that a girl that age could not raise a child by herself. But when asked, therefore, what his church does with the babies, he responded:

> Well, we baptize them so that *we all raise them together.* In the case of that fourteen year old, we have given her baby to a retired couple who have enough time and enough wisdom to raise children. They can then raise the mama along with her baby. That's the way we do it.[4]

What values undergird these radically different approaches? The first pastor represents what many of us would consider a valid argument: a young girl does not have the resources to raise a child by herself; to attempt to do so would likely be detrimental to the child; therefore abortion is a morally justifiable alternative. But there is an unquestioned assumption that is brought out in bold relief by the second pastor's response: who says she has to raise the child *by herself?* In a world in which families are considered private and personal domains, it is easy to regard teenage pregnancy as an individual moral failing. The consequences redound to the girl and her child, to the boy who fathered the baby or perhaps to the girl's parents. Our notion of moral responsibility here is limited: you made the baby, you raise it. If I didn't make the baby, it is not my responsibility, although I may decide somehow to extend myself in Christian charity—a gift from my private household to yours.

Contrast this with the second pastor's response: *We all raise them together.* At the risk of reading too much into the phrase, let me suggest an interpretation of what this pastor is saying. *We:* for this pastor baptism is the induction of the child into a family—not the adoptive family alone, but the church family. *Them:* the teenage mother is not left to her own private resources, to deal with the consequences of her own decisions. Nor is she treated as an individual who must reform morally before she is accepted. Rather, a particular family opens their home to receive both her and her baby, the child-mother together with her child. *Together:* the retired couple is merely one family of many within the congregation. The couple represents not only a corporate identity but a corporate sense of responsibility. This is not simply the admirable charity of two individuals acting on their own initiative, but the all-encompassing embrace of the first family, the body of Christ. It is that embrace that gives meaning to the selflessness of the couple and a context of hope for the child.

The measure to which the first pastor's argument seems both reasonable and obvious indicates, in part, how easily we take for granted our modern values. The extent to which the second pastor's response seems radical shows how far we have come from a truly communal understanding of the church and familism. One of the goals of this book is to demonstrate that if there is a family values crisis, it is not simply "out there" but "in here" as well. As Christians, we are not simply God's children but children of modern culture. The latter inheritance entails values that are so axiomatic to us that we fail to notice when they clash with the former.

The Slide into Postmodernity

We live in a peculiar time of cultural contradictions. On the one hand, we have inherited modern understandings that are generally taken for granted as aspects of our social world. Who seriously questions, for example, the family's right to privacy in their own home? On the other hand, we are told that the age of modernity is passing and postmodernity has come. The purpose of this chapter is to examine how some scholars have applied postmodern perspectives to the contemporary family. A balanced view of postmodernism allows us to learn from the cultural critique of modern values while simultaneously renewing our appreciation of the role of communities of faith. But first, what *is* postmodernism? Different authors give varied readings of the meaning of *modern* or *postmodern,* and the latter has become a fashionable catchall adjective in pop culture. Nevertheless there is generally a common thread.

In brief: Modernity was the age in which human reason was glorified. Over against the received traditions and meanings of both religion and the rising middle class was set the image of the enlightened individual. The philosophy of the Enlightenment was already in place by the time of the American Revolution and was a distinctive force in shaping the individualism that has come to characterize the United States. The idea of free and rational individuals acting on their own self-interest, for example, is foundational to capitalism. This, combined with technical rationality, later give birth to the Industrial Revolution. Overall, modernism had a dual religious nature. On the one hand, moderns denigrated revealed religion as either prerational or even irrational, and thus promoted a wide trend toward secularization. On the other hand, the Enlightenment proposed what should be considered its own "faith"—faith in human reason and our ability to achieve rational solutions to the world's problems.

Postmodernity, by contrast, is the era in which even faith in universal reason has failed. Modernism, again, meant a radical challenge to religion and inherited values. The Enlightenment preached a gospel of liberation and progress, in which truth was discovered rather than received. In the age of postmodernity, however, the corrosive effect of liberated, individual reason turns back on itself. If all authority is to be questioned, why not the authority of scientific rationality? The truth is not something to be *discovered* by objective and neutral methods or the application of right reason. Rather, truth is something *constructed* by particular groups, for particular purposes, in particular times and places. The *facts* of reason become the *artifacts* of culture.[5] As Maureen O'Hara and Walt Anderson write: "A society enters the postmodern age when it loses faith in absolute truth—even the attempt to discover absolute truth."[6] This has the practical effect of making belief more tentative; right belief is replaced by a pluralism of possible beliefs. Again to quote O'Hara and Anderson: "People do not so much believe as have beliefs."[7]

How well does this describe our current experience? Pollster George Barna's research shows that a majority of Americans no longer believe in absolute truth. The percentages of such disbelief are lower among Christians and older adults, but the differences from the general population are slight.[8] We are more apt to be tentative about our beliefs than in the past. Even where we may not be entirely willing to surrender the transcendent truthfulness of our beliefs, we are still conscious of living in a multicultural, global society. The homogeneous values of village life are gone, and the multiple perspectives of the global village are here to stay.

It is important, however, to distinguish between the features of the world that we live in and the values that we hold, even if they are difficult to sort out in practice. The term *postmodern* is bandied about rather freely, often invoked whenever someone stumbles across a new cultural oddity (of which there appear to be plenty). The mere ubiquity of the term itself is almost enough to convince people that there is substance behind it, even if they are not certain what it means. Let us therefore begin by clarifying some terms.[9] To speak of *postmodernity,* as opposed to *modernity,* is to suggest that society has entered a new epoch or age. If modernity is characterized by the technologies and organizing principles of industrial society, then *postmodernity* refers to the postindustrial global society of the Information Age. *Postmodernism* refers less to social structures and more to the cultural shifts of meaning and value that accompany these societal changes. It is, in the words of Stanley Grenz, "an intellectual mood and an array of cultural expressions."[10]

There is a chicken-and-egg question here. Do the mood and values of postmodernism precede and give rise to the structures of postmodernity, or is it the other way around? As with the chicken and her egg, the answer may be equally unsatisfying: it is both/and. When social structures change, there are often underlying values driving these changes. But structural changes, in turn, influence values in ways that cannot always be anticipated.

To writers like social psychologist Kenneth Gergen, for example, the chicken is first: he tends to place greater emphasis on the impact of new technologies on our self-understandings.[11] What would once have been considered insurmountable distances, separating worlds of experience and belief, have been bridged by automobile and air travel. Communication with any and every part of the globe is virtually instantaneous by television, telephone, facsimile and the Internet. The result is that we are exposed to a multitude of cultural images and values that are difficult to integrate into a coherent whole. Gergen calls this phenomenon "social saturation":

> Through these technologies, we are now, whether indirectly or directly, significantly connected to vastly more people, of more varied ways of life . . . than could scarcely be imagined in any other historical time. . . . We ingest myriad bits of others' being—values, attitudes, opinions, life-styles, personalities—synthesizing and incorporating them into our own definition of self. . . . We have gathered so many bits (or bytes) of being to create ourselves that the pieces no longer mix well together, perhaps even contradict each other.[12]

As we shall see shortly, such an understanding also shapes his view of family life. What Gergen does not address here is the extent to which technological advance not only shapes values but is shaped by them. To follow the argument of Daniel Bell, for example, the egg may be first. The parochial limitations of small-town life were not simply altered from without, but new technologies were invented to serve an emerging emphasis on the values of consumption.[13] Technology made the transformation possible, but the impetus comes from a value system that seeks to democratize material wealth. As former president Ronald Reagan once said, representing the moral tone of the 1980s: "What I want to see above all is that this country remains a country where someone can always get rich. That's the one thing we have and that must be preserved."[14]

Postmodernity and postmodernism, therefore, are reciprocally related. When it comes to the postmodern, we are talking about phenomena that are still taking shape, and all such distinctions are incomplete at best. So why is this important? Because some writers seem to take the existence of postmodernity for granted, and with it the pragmatic necessity of adopting the values of postmodernism. We may grant that elements of postmodernity are surely with us, as undeniably as the industrial society of a century ago. A full-blown postmodernism, however, is no more historically or logically necessary than the modernism it supposedly replaces. Indeed, in many respects postmodernism is an exaggeration of modernism, not its contrary. If this is so, then we may rightly ask whether or not a critique of modern values might also apply to postmodern conclusions. We can and should recognize, with Gergen and others, the difficulties posed by postmodernity for our understanding of family relationships. This does not require, however, that we capitulate uncritically to the postmodern ethos.

What does it mean, then, when the adjective *postmodern* is applied to the family? Some write of the implications of postmodernism for how we understand and work with the family but do not apply the term directly to the family itself. Other speak more directly of the "postmodern family," a pragmatic ideal occasioned by the supposed arrival of a postmodern epoch. What can we learn from such approaches? The following section explores three representative views, drawn from the works of family sociologist Judith Stacey, psychotherapists Alan Parry and Robert Doan, and social psychologist Kenneth Gergen.

Families in the Age of Postmodernity

In 1990 sociologist Judith Stacey published a book entitled *Brave New Families*, based on a three-year study of working-class families in California in the 1980s.[15] The families she profiled were struggling to creatively balance work and family concerns, experimenting with new family arrangements. In portraying these families heroically, Stacey incurred the ire of family values advocates, including James Q. Wilson, David Popenoe and Christopher Lasch.[16] Six years later, she published *In the Name of the Family: Rethinking Family Values in the Postmodern Age*, partly as a response to her critics.[17]

In the latter book Stacey notes that it was Edward Shorter who first used the term *postmodern family* back in 1975.[18] Shorter had coined the phrase to describe the confluence of three structural changes in family life: the increased influence of adolescent peers, the instability of the marriage relationship and the massive entrance of women into the workplace. Stacey accepts these as facets of contemporary family life but shifts the definition of the term "to signal the contested, ambivalent, and undecided character of our contemporary family cultures."[19] She writes:

Like postmodern culture, contemporary Western family arrangements are diverse, fluid, and unresolved. Like postmodern cultural forms, our families today admix unlikely elements in an improvisational pastiche of old and new. The postmodern family condition is not a new model of family life equivalent to that of the modern family; it is not the next stage in an orderly progression of stages of family history. . . . [It] incorporates both experimental and nostalgic dimensions as it lurches forward and backward into an uncertain future.[20]

Although she occasionally uses the term *postmodern family,* Stacey seems to prefer the phrase "postmodern family *condition.*" The advantage of the latter, as shown in the preceding excerpt, is that it steers away from the paradoxical suggestion that there is *a* postmodern family.

To use an earlier distinction, Stacey accepts that postmodern*ity* is here and thus advocates postmodern*ism* as the appropriate stance toward our families. She argues rightly that what we consider the traditional nuclear family arrangement is built on economic and gender assumptions that are no longer possible for many families to sustain. Stacey declares the modern norm of the married male breadwinner and female homemaker raising their own children to be "dead," and resists any attempt to resuscitate this ideal that fails to deal squarely with the economic realities involved.[21] Instead, she advocates a postmodern "get used to it" pragmatism that appreciates contemporary diversity and refuses to devalue alternative family forms.[22]

Feminist authors like Stacey and Stephanie Coontz have done us a service by reminding us forcefully of the gender and economic logic behind our traditional family values. Postmodernity, in part, may be interpreted as the coming together of social and economic changes that make modern family ideals seem like the quaint remnants of a not-too-distant past. Under such conditions it is counterproductive simply to charge our social crisis to the moral laxity of those who live in nontraditional arrangements.

This said, however, one may ask if all family forms are the result of courageous attempts to cope with social change. In her chapter titled "Backward Toward the Postmodern Family" Stacey notes that if there is any household arrangement that can lay claim to being "a new cultural and statistical norm," it is the two-income family, with a heterosexual couple at the helm raising children.[23] This modifies the traditional norm by spreading the breadwinning role between both spouses.[24] A postmodern attitude would allow us to recognize and accept the necessity of such an arrangement in today's world. But are *all* alternative forms a response to economic constraints? Again, Stacey's argument suggests that postmodernity is characterized at least in part by a changed economic landscape, and postmodern tolerance is the prescribed response. Should we then extend that postmodern attitude to all possible family forms? And if all family arrangements are morally equivalent, would the economic argument even be necessary in the first place?

To press the point in a somewhat different direction: what makes it possible to appreciate the struggles of the heroic postmodern families of Stacey's work is that we can identify with their goals of intimacy and economic independence. The diversity of form is due, in large part, to social conditions that block traditional avenues to these goals. But the more fundamental question regards the goals themselves. In effect Stacey's argument draws us away from criticizing our differences by resting on these shared values. Could it be, however, that it is the *shared* values that are most in need of critique? If so, then it would seem that the postmodern condition still retains modern characteristics after all. Neither intimacy nor economic independence is a "bad" value—that would be a misstep in the argument. But to use Dizard and Gadlin's notion, cited in chapter two, to what extent do we continue in the modern overidentification of familism, of the values of mutual cooperation and sacrifice, with the nuclear family? Stacey notes that family systems were more stable under earlier conditions of economic *inter*dependence, when households were "embedded in, supported, and sanctioned by wider sets of kinship, community, and religious ties."[25] She rejects this historical arrangement, however, because of its patriarchal tendencies toward coercion and inequality. But must it be so? Is it possible to sustain a wider network of familism *without* patriarchal excesses? The historian's skepticism is, of course, warranted; but it is also wiser to let skepticism temper vision rather than to thwart it.

Many among the current generation of family therapists have also adopted postmodern perspectives. Those in the intellectual vanguard of the movement emphasize newer theories of knowledge as either determined by the organism's biological structure or else socially constructed through language.[26] Some, like psychologists Alan Parry and Robert Doan, herald the demise of modernity and the rise of postmodernity. They recognize, for example, that Christian habits of mind were once dominant in our culture:

> As long as the Christian story was dominant in the Western world, people were able to live their lives intentionally by experiencing themselves as characters within that story and interpreting events in their lives in terms of the meaning provided by Christianity's dramatic and cosmic events.[27]

That story, however, becomes but one example of a *metanarrative*, or *grand narrative*, a comprehensive and authoritative story that brings together important questions about our human existence. It was Jean-François Lyotard who defined the postmodern stance as "incredulity toward metanarratives."[28] In a similar vein, Parry and Doan write that the postmodern world is "a place without any single claim to a truth universally respected, and a growing realization that no single story sums up the meaning of life."[29] While they observe that modernism is "still alive and more or less well,"[30] they nevertheless write as if postmodernity were an accomplished fact: "In the demise of all grand narratives, we now live in a world in which personal narratives essentially stand alone as the means by which we pull together the text of our own lives."[31] The task of the therapist, therefore, is to help clients to become more involved in the creation of their own meanings, "reminding them that there are no other yardsticks of stories or persons against which to measure the legitimacy of their own stories."[32]

At first blush this sounds highly individualistic, as if each individual were to be free to create his or her own meanings, regardless of what anyone else thinks. But the authors also assert:

> No one ever fully becomes the author of her/his own story; any such assumption can only lead back into the illusions of control, individual autonomy, isolated selfhood, and single truth. The person goes forth instead to join with others in the universal human action of multiple authorship.[33]

In other words, we are not isolated beings creating our own worlds. If truth cannot be centered in grand narratives, neither can it be located in any particular personal narrative. "Personal story" does not mean sole authorship. In true postmodern fashion, any and all contributions are potentially welcome. The difference is that there is no transcendent criterion by which individuals must gauge the adequacy of their creations. The individual may not be the sole author, but he or she is the only critic that really matters.

What does this have to do with the family? Parry and Doan hold that children are born into a world of socially accepted meanings.[34] Children begin in a state of biological dependency, and they gradually learn to adapt to their social surroundings. This happens when they acquire language. With language comes the internalization of stories, as they learn descriptions and explanations of the world and their place in it from their parents. Such stories form a natural part of "making sense of and coping with the adult world."[35] Parry and Doan, as psychotherapists, naturally address the darker side of this process: for children in abusive or otherwise unhealthy family settings, narratives can take on survival value. Love, acceptance and even safety may be contingent on internalizing and expressing the "right" stories and meanings. Not everyone, however, is "terrorized" by childhood narratives. Some may find them merely "constraining" and "unhelpful."[36] When dependence is outgrown, individuals may be helped to deconstruct childhood stories that are experienced as too constrictive. The view presented here poses a fundamental challenge to traditional family structures, since the authors hold that there can be "no legitimizing metanarrative that intrinsically gives the family any more than the individual a special claim on the lives of its members, or parents authority over their children."[37] The authority of parental stories, terrorizing or otherwise, is a function of the child's biological state of dependency, not of any characteristic of the stories themselves.

But might not a story be compelling because of its truthfulness? We may grant the importance of recognizing the power that socially constructed meanings exercise over individuals. Since it is a fundamental role of social institutions, including the family, to transmit these meanings, some skepticism toward institutions is wise. Some postmodernists, however, elevate this to the level of principle, suspecting every metanarrative simply because it is a metanarrative, and granting authority to none. The irony is that this postmodern therapeutic worldview ends up simply substituting another authoritative metanarrative, the human as independent moral agent:

> When people author their own stories, they clearly express their own moral perspective; they honor their own thinking, feeling, and doing with respect to what is right and wrong; they assume responsibility for their own moral actions. . . . Such a therapy will help people address the central issues of their lives—that is, *how they can live in a manner that, to a reasonable degree, gets them what they want and need.*[38]

This is a modern therapeutic metanarrative in its distilled form: that the "central issues" of one's life are defined by wants and needs. As a postmodern statement, this text is obviously no tribute to Enlightenment rationality. Ironically, however, the background image of the free moral agent, standing over against externally imposed grand narratives, has a peculiarly modernist hue.

Before passing to the views of our third and final family scholar, we should note that not all professionals in the field of family therapy are equally buoyant about postmodernism. As William J. Doherty writes: "If postmodernism has taught us anything, it is the critical importance of analyzing the context of a field's thinking and work. . . . We are swimming in a sociocultural river whose waters can both nourish and drown us."[39] Postmodernism has the positive effect of revealing to us our idolatrous attachment to modern ideals, including the metanarratives that we so transparently take for granted. But postmodernism by its very nature cannot tell us if there *are* any grand narratives to which we *should* submit ourselves; it can only sneak them in through the back door. The argument here is that not even a resolute postmodernist can avoid assuming some metanarrative context for her arguments, and a closer look will often reveal this context itself to be quite modern indeed.

If Stacey and Parry and Doan avoid delineating a specific new model of postmodern family life, not so Kenneth Gergen. We have already seen his notion of "social saturation," a condition of cultural overload brought on by technologies of travel and communication. Gergen's focus is on the experience of postmodernity and the effects on identity and selfhood.[40] More than two decades ago, Gergen was already challenging the assumption that healthy development entails the creation of a coherent sense of identity. In an article written in 1972 for

Psychology Today, he presents empirical evidence of the plasticity of our self-concept. Given the variety of lessons we learn about ourselves from parents, friends and others, Gergen asserted that "the value that society places on a coherent identity is unwarranted and possibly detrimental."[41] Clearly the postmodern tolerance of diversity and even incongruity provides a fitting framework for his earlier work.

Although he makes a brief reference to marriage in the 1972 article, it is later that he lays out the implications of postmodernity for the family more fully. In his 1991 article titled "The Saturated Family" Gergen draws the direct linkage between social saturation and the changing experience of family life. Whereas modern ideals portray a more unified family with members sharing common goals, the technologies of saturation

> have made it possible for any member of the family to be in virtually any state of mind or motion at one time. The ordinary, daily confluence of multiple lives within one household makes for a sense of fragmentation, as if the members of the family were being scattered by the centrifugal force of postmodern life.[42]

Thus the modern traditional family was more clearly defined, but under the condition of social saturation the boundaries of the family have become more ambiguous. Individual family members have their own schedules and interests. They have their own circles of friends and acquaintances. They form ties with others that may be far removed from the family itself, today including virtual relationships in cyberspace. Family life becomes more chaotic, and members seem to share less and less in common. Gergen coins the term *floating family* to describe the feeling of being adrift amidst a sea of shifting definitions and allegiances, "a relatively formless array of familial relationships in a continuous state of flux."[43]

It is not only the experience of diverse and scattered relationships that characterizes this postmodern scenario. Gergen observes that technologies of social saturation have contributed directly to the "blurring" of the traditional family ideal.[44] Television plays a special role here, not only by portraying a range of family options but also by intentionally exploiting a market demand for the new and different. Producers "explore the marginalized and parody the mainstream," undermining the credibility of the modern traditional family and its values.[45] Thus in the condition of postmodernity, neither the ideal nor the reality of the clearly defined traditional family is maintained.

The question naturally arises: Can there be any shared meanings in the floating family? Yes, but Gergen is not optimistic on this point. He asserts that "the greater range and intensity of outside relationships" make for a "smaller potential for mutual and shared definitions of the true and good." The behavioral consequence of this is that

> family life becomes contested ground between incommensurable perspectives—my values, my way of life, my way of seeing things against yours—and your failure to recognize the rightness of my views is only evidence of your own ignorance or wrongheadedness.[46]

Nor can such differences be resolved by parental fiat. Here Gergen echoes a theme already observed in our earlier examination of Parry and Doan's narrative approach to therapy. With the coming of social saturation, parental authority loses its privileged place. Because children are already immersed in multiple realities, "parental voices are likely to be only two thin reeds piping in a roaring wilderness of contending opinion."[47] Here, too, television plays a role, as it gives children an insider's view of adult foibles and undermines the sense that parents may occupy any higher plane of wisdom.

Does Gergen view this saturated, floating family as a new family form, as a new norm or standard? In a sense, yes, but for pragmatic reasons. Again, to use the distinction introduced earlier in the chapter, he assumes that postmodernity has arrived and that therefore postmodernism is the proper response. We must grant, with Gergen, that the technologies of saturation are here and are not going away and that new technologies will continue to be developed. As their influence in our lives grows, traditional family ideals will become increasingly out of step with the times.

Then how should we respond? If postmodernity is unavoidable, Gergen would say, then we must learn to adapt our expectations accordingly. That we carry the fragments of multiple identities is taken as a given; to expect coherence between these fragments is a modern ideal that should be left behind. To further expect coherence between the multiple individuals within a family is even less realistic. To paraphrase a 1960s slogan, Gergen advocates that we should simply relax and let all of our multiple selves hang out: "To relax in the floating family is to feel free to express the range of voices within—to allow space to all the mixed fragments of identity without worrying about appearing consistent, sensible and well put together."[48] Families that learn to tolerate ambiguity and diversity in this way can move beyond the conflicts engendered by expectations of unity and coherence:

> Varied expressions of diverse selves can generate in the family a communal, friendly and tolerant sense of shared irony. The family that sees each of its members in all their plenitude of possible beings recognizes and accepts the incoherence of personality necessitated by the world, and even learns to appreciate the startling capacity for *contradiction* within human nature.[49]

Gergen is aware of the starkness of this portrait of postmodern incoherence, as are other authors. O'Hara and Anderson, for example, try to balance the implications of postmodernism and end with a pragmatic bit of advice:

> The bad news about postmodern life is the serious despair, emptiness and social disintegration that sometimes follow the disappearance of all certainties. The good news is the freedom it offers, the great wealth of opportunities to explore life. . . . If this is postmodernism, let us make the most of it.[50]

For his part, Gergen gives us his own version of the good news and the bad news. With a droll touch he notes that acceptance of the floating family will at least avoid absolutism and tyranny: "For all the accusations of moral vacuity, emotional aridity and intellectual flabbiness aimed at postmodernism and the floating family, at least they're not likely to engender a Fourth Reich."[51] This is true enough; such a political resurgence would require that a large number of people commit themselves wholeheartedly to a common story. But is a common commitment to a metanarrative impossible in the socially saturated world of postmodernity?

Two responses must be made. First, we should ask why the practical implications of Gergen's version of postmodernity differ so markedly from Parry and Doan's. Like Gergen, narrative therapy recognizes that clients bring a multiplicity of stories to the consulting room. The client is not told, however, that an incoherent assemblage of competing stories is all that she can hope for (so "make the most of it"). In principle, rather, the therapist assumes that it is possible to attain narrative coherence through the process of conversation. In this case two individuals of differing histories and experience may come together in a relationship and leave with *greater* coherence than when they began. Thus, although it is understandable that the identity of saturated families would fragment from lack of consensus, such agreement is not impossible.

A second, and more telling, question is this: If multiplicity is all that can be expected in a postmodern world, why even attempt to move beyond conflict? Because it is assumed that at least some form of consensus is still possible. The "communal, friendly and tolerant sense of shared irony" of which Gergen speaks is premised on the possibility of a shared metanarrative: that of the saturated family afloat in a postmodern world. *This* grand narrative, it would seem, is still available to families. Though it may differ drastically from the modern traditional ideal, it provides a common set of meanings around which a family can construct a sense of identity. It is coherence of a different order, but it is coherence nonetheless. But if this metanarrative can be invoked, why not others?

How then should we understand the implications of postmodernity for the family? Important insights can be drawn from these three authors. First, whatever decline of modern ideals we are experiencing today, they are not due solely to a lack of personal morals among some subset of the population. There are a host of concrete socioeconomic factors that should come into the discussion. When these have been recognized, we might find that it is not the peculiar values of certain individuals and families that constitute the problem, but the assumptions of modernism that we have in common. Unless these issues are fully addressed, we should continue to expect families to exhibit a multitude of arrangements as they struggle to meet their goals in diverse circumstances.

Second, we must learn to recognize the metanarratives that we take for granted as more or less objective descriptions of a concrete reality. The ways we define and value the family in particular are social constructs, however much we may attempt to ground our beliefs with references to biology. Our culture provides a limited set of options for how we should understand the family as a social institution. Moreover, we must recognize that parents are more than merely nurturing care-takers; they are agents of this culture, purveyors of its meanings. Through the process of socialization, parents transmit narratives that shape their children's understanding of the world and their place in it. Sometimes these narratives need revision, and as with all change the process may be threatening. Even if we are willing to grant, intellectually, that many of our assumptions about family life are relative to our history and culture, this may not make it any easier to question them with any seriousness. But question them we must, if we hope to move beyond the present crisis of confidence.

Third, we must come to terms with the nature of the technological world that we have created. Parents complain about the difficulty of teaching their children values in today's world. We are exposed to a far broader array of ideas and values than ever before. With an expanding range of choice in every area of life, family members need not center their sense of identity on the family itself. It is possible that this may lead to fragmentation, but this is not necessarily the case. Families are still capable of shared meaning; the question is simply which meanings they can and will share.

In all of this we may recognize that the *post* in *postmodern* does not mean that modern values have evaporated. They are still present in the shared values that allow us to view the working-class families of Stacey's research as heroic. They assert themselves through Parry and Doan's therapeutic version of the narrative of the independent moral agent. They stand behind the development of the very technologies that Gergen takes for granted. One lesson of postmodernism, therefore, is that we have not yet finished with modernism. These postmodern authors critique some modern values by letting others stand.

Modernism Unchained

As the designation for a new cultural epoch, then, postmodernity is decidedly ambiguous. It points less to the birth of a whole new age than the signs of the ill health and eventual demise of an old one. The signs themselves are not equally present everywhere. For example, readers from different geographical regions of the United States will probably react somewhat differently to the foregoing discussion. Within these regions, rural, urban and suburban families will notice, and have to contend with, different issues. Furthermore, the postmodern attitude is far more likely to be found in the places where culture is produced, rather than consumed. Denizens of the media and academic institutions are probably more directly concerned with such matters than the family down the street. This said, the signs posted by scholars such as Stacey and Gergen cannot be lightly dismissed. We do see change; we are exposed to more alternative points of view. Whatever stance we may adopt toward various family issues, we know that cultural consensus has eroded. What once was taken for granted can be so no longer.

The question "Has the age of the postmodern arrived?" deserves an appropriately postmodern paradoxical response: yes, no and maybe. Postmodernity, as a cultural era, may have more of a negative existence than a positive one. In a sense it is the name we give to the burned-out husk of modernity before we know if something definite has arisen from the ashes. In this state of anticipation it is not certain that the normative pluralism of postmodernism is the only adaptive response. But neither is it certain that modern values have been incinerated altogether.

At issue here is the meaning of the prefix *post-* in *postmodern*. The prefix denotes something that comes after: but after what? The suggestion to be made here is that while some important facets of the modern world view have changed, much of the core remains intact. The *post-* thus refers not to the passing of modernism *in toto* but to the abandonment of the Enlightenment project and its rationalistic faith. Postmodernity is modernity unchained, modern values shorn from the quasi-religious narratives of progress that supported them. It is, to use a different term, *hyper*modernity, an exaggerated form of modern tendencies.[52] As we have seen in chapter two, the contemporary scene is not all change; there are important continuities. We stand in a period of transition in which some modern values are passing away while others are as dominant as ever.

There is a delicate balance to be struck here. We should become postmodern to the extent that we recognize the markers of modernism and refuse to worship at its shrines. This means, in part, examining the ways in which modern assumptions about the family continue to invisibly assert themselves, even within the discourse of the church. But we need not capitulate to a relativism that views all metanarratives as equal and relegates them to the private sphere of individual conscience. Instead, transcending the limitations of our modern values may help us to renew our commitment to living as a *community* of believers. As Robert Bellah writes:

> Once we take the measure of the limitations of modern consciousness we may begin to look at Christianity in a new way. . . . Christianity is the living practice of the Christian community, a way of educating simultaneously our intelligence and our feelings so that our actions may be rightly guided in accordance with the example of the one whose life is the basis of all that we do. . . . To make Christ manifest, to disclose the truth for our lives of what was incarnate in him, we must show what he was and what he means for us now.[53]

We can now come back full circle, to the question asked by Pastor Tibert at the beginning of the chapter: Which is the more powerful approach—people protesting in front of an abortion clinic or people expressing their commitment to take unwanted children into their homes? The latter is, but not because of its political efficacy. It is powerful because a postmodern world that is insecure about the status of truth needs to see a people who can *live* the truth. It needs the example of a people who can transcend the limitations of our inherited modern perspectives and demonstrate the possibility of a living alternative. But how far have we come in questioning our modern presuppositions? If the church is to navigate the present times better, it must first find its location on the cultural map. How might we "take the measure of the limitations of modern consciousness"? This is the task of the next two chapters.

block grants

or

relativism?

Four

MORAL HORIZONS

• •

*One reason that the church has become so bitterly divided over moral issues
is that the community of faith has uncritically accepted the categories
of popular U.S. discourse about these topics,
without subjecting them to sustained critical scrutiny in light of
a close reading of the Bible.*
RICHARD HAYS, *The Moral Vision of the New Testament*[1]

We inhabit a socially constructed world, a set of ways of understanding the world that are passed on to us throughout our childhood and even later. These habits of thought become as natural to us as inhaling and exhaling; accordingly, it is probably as awkward to pay sustained attention to these cultural assumptions as it is to concentrate on our breathing. What is transparent to us, however, often can be spotted easily by others who have different habits of vision. The realization can be striking. Philip Yancey, for example, tells of a lesson learned in the midst of a small whale-watching expedition off the New Zealand coast. Afloat in a rubber dinghy, Yancey and his group watched as a royal albatross sailed overhead. He listened attentively as their guide, a Maori biologist, waxed eloquent about the wonders of this magnificent creature, including its ability to process the salt out of seawater. His imagination stimulated, Yancey pushed for more information. He wondered aloud if the same "technology" could be used to construct desalinization plants in arid regions around the globe. After a moment's silence and a blank stare the guide finally responded: "You're an American, aren't you?"[2] Indeed, and a *modern* American at that.

Yancey's point is to encourage us to see the created world for once through the eyes of worship rather than science. My point is the obverse: to notice how natural it is, even for a Christian, to see with the eyes of science, even when confronted with an expression of worship. But what is true of scientific rationality is also true of other modern habits of thought. Over the history of our culture we have learned to understand ourselves in ways that are particularly characteristic of our society. Christians are "multilingual," using the various discourses of the secular society side by side with religious language. As Lesslie Newbigin writes, contemporary Christians do not simply inhabit a sacred world, separate from the secular; rather, "the boundary between two realms runs through each of us."[3] Nor is it as simple as having two utterly distinct realms of the sacred and the profane within us. Our culture is permeated with religious images; we can still see a strong tradition of civil religion in the United States, for example, as illustrated in our recitation of the Pledge of Allegiance's credo that we are "one nation, under God, indivisible, with liberty and justice for all." Conversely, most of us have not even begun to understand the ways in which our culture's means of construing the world determine how we express our faith. Newbigin's point is not that the boundary is clear and distinct but that we must begin to differentiate the realms and recognize our dual citizenship.

It was sociologist Robert Bellah and his colleagues who popularized the nineteenth-century French social philosopher Alexis de Tocqueville's phrase "habits of the heart."[4] By this Tocqueville meant the central social ideals that shaped the character of a nation. His observations of American life, more than a century ago, led him to conclude that "individualism" was paradoxically both a great strength and a great weakness of the American character. Tocqueville saw with clarity how individually oriented habits of the heart could eventually corrode the very institutions that cemented a common concern for the well-being of society.

The progress of modernism, as we have seen, emphasized individualistic ideals over communal and traditional standards. Postmodernism

has radicalized this trend, yielding a *hyper*individualism that emphasizes "the individual over against every collective entity, including the
family itself," and in which "the search for individual identity in isolation
from all communal definitions becomes a central concern of life."[5]
Postmodernism is not the eradication of modern narratives. The moral
images of modern society and the individualistic habits of thought
associated with them are still very much with us. But in the absence of
any common metanarrative to unify and contextualize them, these
images develop a life of their own. Our moral imagination becomes
fragmented. We alternate between different ways of perceiving and
speaking about the good, sometimes without even noticing the lack of
coherence.

Bellah, for example, tells of an undergraduate seminar offered by a
doctoral student who was writing a dissertation on the sociology of
divorce. A majority of the students in the course either were children
of divorced parents or had themselves divorced as married adults. As
might be expected, the course took a personal turn, as the students
eagerly discussed their own experiences. Bellah observes an internal
contradiction between the ways in which these students spoke of
divorce:

> When they speak in what the seminar leader calls their child-iden-
> tified voices, they are quite angry at their parents. . . . And yet, when
> these same students speak in their adult-identified voices, they
> apparently believe that anyone ought to have the right to walk out
> of any marriage at any time. . . . In other words, they think of the
> parent-child relationship in terms of responsibilities and the hus-
> band-wife relationship in terms of rights. They have implicitly split
> apart the spheres of marriage and parenthood, and see no logical
> contradiction in this position.[6]

A more coherent moral perspective would have to recognize that one
set of values sets limits on the other. Either the parents' rights are limited
by their parental responsibilities or else the child's expectations of
nurture are bounded by parental freedom. But underlying the instability
of the students' ambivalence is a more fundamental belief: a conviction
that each *individual* member of the family should simply have what
he or she desires, whatever this may mean for the family as a group.
In a just world, it seems, the child must have the parents' care. But each

Berlin - not possible?

parent must also be equally entitled to his or her personal freedom, and the students lack a more comprehensive narrative by which to reconcile the two sets of moral demands. Welcome to the hyperindividualism of postmodernity.

The values of hyperindividualism within our culture are often expressed through the languages of three overlapping moral domains: individual rights, consumerism and therapy. Each of these supplies a way of thinking and speaking that reinforces the logic of American individualism, encouraging and embodying mutually reinforcing cultural ideals such as freedom from constraint, unlimited opportunity and choice, and self-fulfillment. These forms of discourse and habits of the heart have permeated the way we understand life in general and family relationships in particular. They represent the *moral horizons* of our culture: background assumptions that guide how we perceive and act on our commitments. We are normally only tacitly aware of such horizons. The purpose of this chapter is to understand better the nature and limits of modern consciousness by examining these domains of discourse. Lingering debates about family values cannot be resolved by fiat. Substantive change requires that we first explore the modern assumptions that shape how we understand both our selves and our relationships. With this in mind, let us begin with an examination of the rhetoric of individual rights.

The Horizon of Individual Rights

Imagine the following scenario. A young girl is celebrating her tenth birthday, surrounded by brightly wrapped presents and attentive friends and relatives. Her two-year-old brother stands nearby, his eyes agog as she reaches for the last gift, the biggest of all. It is only with difficulty that the parents have restrained the eager boy from tearing open the presents himself. Everyone knows that he is still too young to understand fully what is happening—after all, what good has it been to tell him, "But dear, your birthday isn't for another six months"? He only senses that his sister is getting something good out of this, and he wants a piece of the action. Sympathetically the parents offer him a compromise. "Would you like to come over and help your sister open the last present?" they say sweetly, patting the mysterious box. This much he understands. The two children together grab at the paper, and

the guests make the appropriate sounds as the gift inside is revealed—
an electronic keyboard. Both children smile delightedly: the girl
because it is what she wanted, and her brother because everybody else
is smiling. After a few moments cake and ice cream are served, and the
children all run off, leaving the presents behind. Later, however, the
girl returns to carry them to her room. The two-year-old sees her pick
up the keyboard. He has no idea what the keyboard is; he only knows
that this is the package that *he* helped to open. With a cry of fury and
dismay little brother charges across the room and tries to snatch the
box away from her. "No!" he wails. "Mine! MIIIIINE!"

How would you explain the situation to this screaming two-year-old?
Here is the process of social construction in action: whatever the
particulars of your explanation, you will have to school the hapless
child in the cultural rules regarding personal possessions. "This is hers,
not yours," you say firmly, pulling him away. "You can't have it." For
her part, the girl knows the rules of the birthday ritual: these things are
now *hers*, with the rights of ownership that go with them. Her parents
might encourage her to share the keyboard, to make her brother happy
(or perhaps to keep him quiet). She can, out of compassion, do so, but
she knows that she doesn't really have to, and her parents have against
them the weight of all the social conventions they have already taught
her if they try to force her to share. "But he'll *break* it!" is probably all
the objection she will need to repel their suggestion. They may suggest
that she share something else, and the game can go on for several
exchanges, but in the end it is her property rights that will carry the
day. The brother's consolation is that he, too, has property rights, and
when his birthday comes, he will have his chance to assert them
appropriately.

What we teach our children about rights reveals how axiomatic these
assumptions are. Our present understanding of rights is the culmination
of a long history of emphasizing the value of the individual. The
Constitution of the United States, of course, is premised on a notion of
the natural and inalienable rights of individuals. This reflects a fundamental Enlightenment perspective, a foundational philosophical principle of the new democracy, necessary to articulating the moral
rightness of freedom from the British monarchy. In emphasizing
individual liberty, however, the founders of the American experiment

tended to take for granted the existence of moral communities that would nurture the sentiments of concern for the common good.

Individualism, in a sense, was a political ideal, a respect for individual liberty that functioned as a hedge against totalitarian rule. Constitutional principles were meant not only to establish a new government but to limit its influence. But the power of such images and values could not be contained solely within the political sphere. As Bruce Hafen reminds us, "The concepts embodied in the Bill of Rights were originally intended to define the political relationship between individual citizens and the state—not the domestic and personal relationships of the citizens themselves."[7] We live, however, in an age in which the language of individual rights, or what Mary Ann Glendon has called "rights talk," has come to pervade every area of our lives.[8] Tocqueville, visiting the United States in the 1800s, had already noted with concern the extent to which American discourse was permeated with legalisms.[9] His observation, it seems, was prescient. It is not simply a matter of how legal trends have influenced family life, as important as this is. Rather, the language of individual rights has penetrated popular discourse, providing an important moral framework for our thought and speech about social issues. Writes Glendon:

> This "legalization" of popular culture is both cause and consequence of our increasing tendency to look to law as an expression and carrier of the few values that are widely shared in our society: liberty, equality, and the ideal of justice under law. With increasing heterogeneity, it has become quite difficult to convincingly articulate common values by reference to a shared history, religion, or cultural tradition. . . . Legality, to a great extent, has become a touchstone for legitimacy.[10]

Nowhere is this more clearly seen than in the history of the right to privacy. Glendon notes that the background of such a right had already existed in the notion that it was not within the purview of the government to regulate individual conduct, so far as such conduct did not infringe the rights of others.[11] The right itself was first formulated in the nineteenth century, when the developing technologies of photography and communication made it possible for industrious paparazzi to invade the privacy of public figures by splashing their likenesses across the mass media. In 1890 attorneys Samuel Warren and

Louis Brandeis cowrote a *Harvard Law Review* article in which they sought a legal principle that could be used in a court of law to protect people from intrusions. They noted legal precedents in which property rights were used to prevent the publication of personal effects such as private letters and lecture notes. The underlying principle, they thought, was in actuality a personal right rather than a property right: the right to privacy, fundamental to the autonomy of the individual. In a now-famous turn of phrase, Warren and Brandeis interpreted this as the "right to be let alone."[12]

At the time the principle was not interpreted as a constitutional right. In 1928 this began to change. The Supreme Court ruled that a federal wiretapping operation had not violated a criminal defendant's rights regarding unreasonable search and seizure. Brandeis wrote the dissenting opinion, interpreting the right to be let alone as "the most comprehensive of rights and the right most valued by civilized men."[13] This time Brandeis attempted to ground his argument in a reinterpretation of the Fourth and Fifth Amendments. In this way the right to privacy was introduced into the realm of constitutional law. This principle was not formally invoked by the Supreme Court until 1965, when a Connecticut law prohibiting married couples from using contraceptives was ruled unconstitutional. But it is best known, perhaps, as the basis of the 1973 Supreme Court decision in *Roe v. Wade* that a specifically individual right to privacy included a woman's decision to have an elective abortion.

It was not until 1986, in the unusual case of *Bowers v. Hardwick,* that the Court seemed to recognize a need to set boundaries on the limitless potential of the privacy right. A Georgia policeman, investigating a minor offense, had inadvertently discovered one Mr. Hardwick engaged in homosexual intercourse. After a hearing on whether or not Hardwick could be tried for violation of the sodomy law, the state dropped the charge. Hardwick, however, challenged the constitutionality of the law in federal court. The appeals court, as could be expected, ruled the statute unconstitutional, citing the right to privacy as grounds. The Supreme Court, however, reversed the decision by a narrow margin, concerned that the right to privacy not be used as a pretext for the creation of new rights, such as the right to engage in sodomy—rights that themselves would be beyond the limits of the constitutional text.

Justice Harry Blackmun, who had written the majority opinion in *Roe v. Wade*, wrote the dissent in the Hardwick case. In it he argued that Hardwick's sexual conduct fell under his "right to be let alone." Whereas the majority had adopted the perspective that new rights should reflect a social consensus about society's deeply rooted values, the dissent made individual autonomy the higher principle. Despite the Supreme Court's decision in *Hardwick,* Blackmun's dissent now represents the dominant perspective. In effect, constitutional protection is given to matters of private conduct.

Why should the church care about such legal matters? Because these trends both reflect and produce culture. On the one hand, the logic of Supreme Court decisions reflects the hyperindividualism that is already embedded in our social history. On the other hand, the romance with constitutional law since the civil rights era has given it greater prestige than ever before. As important cases are tracked and reported in the media, they become public knowledge, to be debated over coffee by both legal specialists and armchair culture-watchers. In this way the relevant perspectives and issues, whether accurately represented or not, enter popular discourse.

By now the habits of mind that originate in legal discourse are so familiar to us as to be almost transparent. It has become quite natural for us to frame clashes of need or interest in terms of a conflict of rights. Abortion becomes a conflict between the rights of the mother and the rights of the fetus. Child custody often becomes less a decision about what is best for the child and more a battle over the parents' rights. Litigation on behalf of minor children pits their rights against those of their parents. Hafen, observing such trends, writes:

> In a subtle but pervasive sense, adults and children now seem increasingly liberated from one another, heading for a kind of contractual egalitarianism. . . . To liberate children is also to liberate adults. To liberate adults is to distance them from their familistic sense of unlimited commitment to their children.[14]

This is *not* to say that any of the concerns about rights listed in the preceding paragraph are misguided or unimportant. It is difficult to draw any consistent and clear line between basic human rights and others that some might deem less essential. The question is whether the language of rights is too limiting a horizon for our moral conversations. Is rights talk a sufficient basis for familism? Or even further: does an exaggeration of rights talk thwart familism? It is one thing to speak of rights when someone has been deprived of worth and dignity (as in the civil rights movements of the 1960s) or basic and fundamental freedoms (as in the work of Amnesty International). In such cases we are talking about protecting the individual against the very real oppression sometimes evidenced in our social and political structures.[15] But are all limitations of individual freedom of this nature? Is the language of oppression equally valid in every case? Do we, like the majority justices in the Hardwick case, look for public criteria by which we judge the legitimacy of such language? Or is the individual the only judge? Rights language, in fact, can be an extremely limiting basis on which to build consensus about truly public goods:

> Rights talk encourages our all too human tendency to place the self at the center of our moral universe. . . . Saturated with rights, political language can no longer perform the important function of facilitating public discussion of the right ordering of our lives together. Just as rights exist for us only through being articulated, other goods are not even available to be considered if they can be brought to expression only with great difficulty, or not at all.[16]

The responsibilities of living in a civil society, or in any relationship of commitment, entail mutual and voluntary boundaries to individual freedom. But as with the students in the divorce seminar, tipping the scales toward rights makes it more difficult to discern, discuss and act on these responsibilities.

We severely impoverish the very concept of freedom itself if we understand it only along the lines of Brandeis's "right to be let alone." Freedom, in the biblical sense, is not freedom from the demands of others in order to pursue our self-chosen ends, but freedom from the law of sin in order to serve God (see Rom 7). In this regard, freedom of religion is an important locus for the discussion of rights in any age. But those who serve a crucified Savior may need to learn to question the ways in which rights talk has eclipsed sacrifice in the Christian moral imagination.

The Horizon of the Consumer Marketplace

In 1776, the year the United States of America declared their independence, the Scottish moral philosopher and economist Adam Smith published a work that was to have enormous influence on the identity of the fledgling nation. Smith's *Inquiry into the Nature and Causes of the Wealth of Nations* (or, as it's more commonly known, *The Wealth of Nations*) became the authoritative text on capitalism. It is still studied today as a classic work in social philosophy. In both *Wealth* and his earlier work, *Theory of Moral Sentiments* (1759), Smith assumed that the moral universe is intrinsically social but that virtues and values needed to be learned in intimate communities. While he envisioned a capitalist economy that ran on the principle of enlightened self-interest, he "never imagined the possibility of a society that could run on self-interest alone."[17] Capitalism itself was not to provide the moral foundation for society; nonmarket values had to be nurtured in communities of moral formation. Unfortunately, as Rasmussen writes, this assumption "took the processes of moral formation utterly for granted and badly underestimated their vulnerability to the acids of modernity."[18]

Daniel Bell, examining what he calls the "cultural contradiction" of capitalism, locates the corrosiveness of modernity in the hedonism that arises from "the idolatry of the self."[19] The impulses of early capitalism were balanced by a Protestant ethic that viewed work itself as a calling and encouraged virtues such as industriousness, thrift and delayed gratification, all essential to the accumulation of capital. This ethic largely survived until the coming of industrialization, when it contributed to a considerable paradox. The conversion to an unstable early industrial economy was founded in large part on the availability of cheap factory labor, people who embraced thrift and self-denial and who could rely on kin networks to see them through the lean times.[20] But the expansion of the capitalist economy required higher levels of consumption. The idea of consumption was still too closely tied to a limited perception of need. Families who believed they had enough money to live on could not be counted on to work more hours or to purchase greater quantities of manufactured goods. The resolution of this paradox has many sources, but for illustrative purposes we will here examine only two key factors: the role of advertising in inducing people to buy and the invention of the installment plan to make it possible.

Susan Strasser writes: "The creation of modern American consumer culture involved not only introducing new products and establishing demand for them, but also creating new domestic habits and activities."[21] A product might be promoted for its superior capability to meet an existing need. Sometimes, however, the potential customer had to be convinced that there *was* a need. Early forms of advertising had concentrated on merely providing information to consumers, but a new breed of advertising professionals was trained to view the marketplace as a battlefield to be conquered, ready to "influence buyers by whatever means possible."[22]

Strasser cites as an example the strategy used by Eastman Kodak to create a market for its new compact camera. George Eastman, a bank clerk in Rochester, New York, had revolutionized photography by patenting an early prototype of roll film in 1884. Previously, photographs had to be made on heavy glass plates coated with a light-sensitive emulsion, making photography the exclusive and cumbersome domain of the professional. The new technology made it possible to take one hundred pictures in a pocket-sized box weighing just over two pounds. For twenty-five dollars a customer could purchase the new "Kodak" camera, including the first roll of film and the processing and printing of all one hundred pictures. In effect, what Eastman had created was a "democratic highway to art": anyone with the purchase price in hand could now be a photographer, capturing everyday experience for visual repetition whenever he or she desired.[23]

But how could consumers be convinced to buy the product? One of the company's strategies involved direct appeals to private family affections, a strategy that Kodak still uses today. The camera was shown in advertisements being used by women to capture family history. The ads themselves shaped family habits by offering instructions on what to photograph and how.[24] In essence the camera was marketed as one of the devoted wife and mother's important tools; it would enable her to record the "evidence" of a happy and healthy domestic haven. A moment's reflection reveals that we still use our cameras in the same way. We photograph family members playing, having parties, doing something exciting or being affectionate with one another. How often do we photograph one another doing chores, watching television or having an argument? We refuse to press the shutter release button until everyone smiles, because everyone is *supposed* to be happy, or at least look happy, since that is what the domestic myth requires. The camera, in short, became the instrument of family mythology, because the advertiser could exploit these ideals to make the sale. Advertisers, therefore, sell more than just products: by creating markets for new products, they sell consumption itself as a way of life. Advertising both appeals to preexisting values and shapes their expression: *if* this is important to you, *then* buy and use our product.

Try an experiment. The next time you watch television, study the commercials. Ask yourself: what is the advertiser really trying to say here? A recent commercial, for example, begins with a close-up of a daily planner. There is only one item written on the day's agenda: "Watch sunset." As the camera pulls back, a breeze riffles through the pages, revealing every day's schedule to be identical. The mythical owner of the planner has nothing to do, it seems, other than to enjoy a beautiful sunset each evening.

Is this a commercial for a travel agency? For a Club Med vacation? No, it is an advertisement for the bottle of beer now shown standing next to the planner. More and more, what is being sold is much less the product than the lifestyle visually associated with it. The commercial just described says absolutely nothing about the beer itself. You are not told to buy the beer because it tastes better, is less expensive, less fattening or even more environmentally responsible. You are certainly not told that it will get you drunk, which would be a blatant violation of political correctness. So why should you buy it? Because it represents both a lifestyle and an attitude, vague in its contours, but highly suggestive nonetheless.

The commodity is not the beer itself but the personal characteristics that are directly or indirectly associated with it. Commercials portray people who possess a wealth of culturally desirable attributes: they may be independent, beautiful or handsome, intelligent and shrewd, comfortably affluent, or irresistibly attractive to the opposite sex. The implication is that consumption of the appropriate products, buying items with the right labels, marks you as a particular kind of person:

> The modern individual within consumer culture is made conscious that he speaks not only with his clothes, but with his home, furnishings, decoration, car and other activities which are to be read

and classified in terms of the presence or absence of taste. The preoccupation with customizing a lifestyle and a stylistic self-consciousness are not just to be found among the young and the affluent; consumer culture publicity suggests that we all have room for self-improvement and self-expression whatever our age or class origins.[25]

It is not that anyone necessarily believes that using the right mouthwash or deodorant will immediately and directly make one more attractive. We see through the sham but participate in it nonetheless. I may know absolutely nothing about either of two competing brands of the same product. How do I decide between them? All else being equal, I will lean toward the one with the more attractive packaging or the one that I have seen in a commercial.

Lifestyle is a matter of image, of self-presentation. It is not simply a matter of who I believe I am but of what I *want* myself or others to believe about me; it is not just about what I may enjoy naturally but also about what I *should* enjoy if I want to be a person of a particular status. Teenagers are acutely aware of such social rules and are all too ready to accept the guidance of the advertising industry as to how to belong. Entering what is often a painfully self-conscious phase of life, they know clearly the social consequences of wearing the wrong clothes or the wrong shoes. They know implicitly that buying the right product admits you to what Daniel Boorstin calls a "consumption community":

An advertisement was, in fact, a form of insurance to the consumer that by buying this commodity, by smoking this brand of cigarette, or by driving this make of car he would not find himself alone. The larger the advertising campaign . . . the more the campaign itself offered a kind of communitarian seal of approval. Surely a million customers can't be wrong! An advertisement, then, announced that . . . some kind of consumption community probably existed. Won't you join?[26]

In the modern world, then, consumption becomes the avenue of what Bellah and his colleagues call "expressive individualism," the way in which an individual expresses his or her self-made identity.[27] Lifestyle itself becomes a moral good, and brand loyalty becomes a substitute form of community. Bell argues that this represents an expansion of unlimited individual desire:

What defines bourgeois society is not needs, but wants. Wants are psychological, not biological, and are by their nature unlimited. Society is not seen as a natural association of men—the polis or the family—ruled by a common purpose, but as a composite of atomistic individuals who pursue only their own gratification.[28]

But what must be recognized here is advertising's very capability to *redefine* wants as needs by tapping into cultural values and creating new markets for their expression.

Advertising alone, however, cannot account for the growth of a capitalist system of values. Advertisers could create the desire for a product but not the means to buy it. Consumers could save for an item, but the expansion of industrialism required a more immediate and steady flow of cash. Thus was installment credit invented, which Bell judges to be the "greatest single engine in the destruction of the Protestant ethic" of self-denial and delayed gratification.[29]

The notion of consumer credit already existed even in the face-to-face economy of the local general store; there credit was extended to customers of good character who could be depended on to settle their bills as promptly as possible. This understanding of credit was still tied to a personal relationship between buyer and seller and did not undermine an ethic of thrift. It was the advent of mass-produced automobiles that transformed consumer credit.[30] Henry Ford's dream was to democratize the automobile; he saw the need for a new form of transportation and set about revolutionizing production techniques to make cars as affordable as possible. Even so the price of a Model T was too high for many families. Ford was willing to innovate in the area of production but not in the area of buying and selling. He held to a strict morality of thrift and opposed the idea of people's buying items that they did not actually have the cash to purchase. His only "financing" plan was in actuality a savings plan, where customers regularly paid into an account until they had accumulated the cash price of a new Ford.

General Motors, however, had no such compunction, seeking ways to challenge Ford's dominance in the industry. In 1919 General Motors became the first major car manufacturer to establish its own financing plan. Ford was forced to follow suit in 1928. Over the ensuing years, installment buying became an increasingly common way of purchasing consumer durables. Whereas the older morality required that credit be extended only to those of proven character, the democratizing forces of the market drove the qualifications for credit downward until they all but vanished.

The massive spread of automobiles across the American landscape further necessitated gas-station credit and the innovation of what we now know as the credit card, whose applications quickly extended beyond the filling station. Consider for a moment the shift in values represented by the ubiquity of the credit card. As Boorstin writes:

> When installment credit became universal, the old thrift ethic had less meaning than ever. For the American Standard of Living had come to mean a habit of enjoying things before they were paid for. And that habit was becoming an industrial necessity.[31]

Here again we come up against the ambiguity of want versus need. Many desires in our consumer culture seem needful: we "need" new cars, bigger houses, more powerful computers. But often, when we simply decide that we cannot afford the car, the house, the computer, we manage with what we have. The question is what the word *afford* means when one can buy virtually anything on credit. More than one person has related to me the story of an interaction with a child who asked if she could buy something she had seen on television. "We can't afford it" was the parent's familiar and automatic response. Undaunted, however, the child retorted, "You have a credit card, don't you?" What would you say next? The answer may indicate the extent to which the moral horizon of consumerism dominates our lives.

To borrow a phrase from Bellah, the family has been "colonized" by the market and its values.[32] Not only has the family become the primary locus of consumption, but, barring a transcendent ethic, consumption has become the family's most tangible shared goal. Moreover, as Arlie Hochschild suggests, in some places a curious transposition has occurred. The workplace has become home, the bearer of familism, while the home has become a place that must be managed by the technical rationality of the office. She writes, for example, of middle-class working mothers who have difficulty finding the time to fulfill all of their responsibilities and must therefore hire others to fill the void:

> The time-starved mother is being forced more and more to choose between being a parent and buying a commodified version of parenthood from someone else. By relying on an expanding menu

of goods and services, she increasingly becomes a manager of parenthood, supervising and coordinating the outsourced pieces of family life.[33]

And the church is not a refuge from the totalitarianism of the market. The commercialization of Christmas into an "American Festival of Consumption" is a case in point.[34] It was the Catholic Church that originally set the date of December 25 to celebrate the birth of Christ, in contradistinction to pagan celebrations of the winter solstice. But local customs were not thereby eradicated. John Calvin objected to the syncretistic holiday, and following his example, so did the New England Puritans.[35] Boorstin records that in 1659 the General Court of Massachusetts passed an act that anyone found observing Christmas in any special way was to be fined five shillings.[36] Not all the colonies, however, were so strict. By the late nineteenth century Christmas was a legal holiday in every state, and increasingly under the influence of the marketplace. R. Laurence Moore writes:

> The cries that churches carried to the Protestant-founded department stores of Macy's, Wanamaker's, and Marshall Field's to "put Christ back into Christmas" only served to stir up a market for manufactured creches, cards with religious messages, and recorded sacred music. Merchandising in the twentieth century gave Christ a more visible role in Christmas than he ever had before, even if the same could be said for Bing Crosby and Rudolph.[37]

It may be worth noting, in passing, that the perennial favorite "Rudolph the Red-Nosed Reindeer" was a promotional gimmick written by an employee in Montgomery Ward's advertising department.[38]

Moreover, a study by sociologist Robert Wuthnow suggests that religious belief may make little if any difference where values related to consumerism and materialism are concerned. After an extensive interview study with over two thousand full- and part-time representatives of the labor force, Wuthnow concludes that

> there is no reason to think that religious teachings have, as some critics suggest, encouraged us to admire the rich and to seek riches ourselves. These orientations are already pervasive in American culture, among both the religious and nonreligious. However, it also appears to be the case that religious teachings do little to prevent us from adulating the rich.[39]

Part of the explanation for this, he surmises, is the "psychologization" of money that is apparently promoted by the Bible itself. "For the *love* of money is a root of all kinds of evil," Paul wrote, not the mere *possession* of it (1 Tim 6:10, italics added). As Wuthnow observes, however, love itself has become such a vague and subjective notion that "the love of money" becomes an extremely ambiguous criterion for greed.[40]

James Davison Hunter similarly concludes that the older Protestant ethic of self-denial is virtually dead in the generation of evangelicals that is currently coming into leadership. Ascetic values have given way to the cultural emphasis on a private sphere of economic well-being. He writes: "Far from being untouched by the cultural trends of the post World War II decades, *the coming generation of Evangelicals, in their own distinct way, have come to participate fully in them.*"[41] Hunter documents in detail the cultural capitulations of the evangelical world. But where the horizon of consumerism is concerned, it may be Wuthnow who has said it best:

> There is thus enormous synergy between religion and economic life in our society. We have kept the spiritual realm distinct, even separate. . . . But we have domesticated it, stripping the sacred of moral authority and allowing it to break through only occasionally . . . such as helping us out of a jam or salving our conscience when we succumb to the appeals of Madison Avenue. . . . Our religious impulses, therefore, caution us against becoming too materialistic, but their prompting is limited because we are thoroughly embedded in a world of material goods.[42]

What this suggests is that even for Christians, who believe that greed and the love of money are evil, the horizon of the marketplace has come to direct our moral habits of thought. Economic goals predominate. The "good life" ceases to be defined by religious ideals and becomes instead a life saturated with the finest of consumer goods. Those who do not have the money for lavish levels of consumption nevertheless aspire to similar ideals, and the credit card gives the illusion of a democratized access to wealth. When market logic begins to dominate our vision, life itself becomes a supermarket, an endless array of consumerlike choices, including what church we attend and what relationships we keep.

The Horizon of the Therapeutic

My family and I are avid basketball fans. In 1997 the National Basketball Association witnessed a first. The Utah Jazz, perennial contenders for the Western Conference championship, finally won the conference title, earning their first trip to the finals, against the Eastern Conference champions, Michael Jordan and the Chicago Bulls. The Jazz had achieved the second-best regular season record in the league, led by the play of their two veteran all-stars, point guard John Stockton and power forward Karl Malone. Malone entered the finals carrying the honor of being voted the league's Most Valuable Player. Expectations ran high for Malone, who played with an injury to his shooting hand, sustained during an earlier playoff game. Utah stayed close with Chicago throughout the series; neither team clearly dominated the other. In the end, however, Malone and the Jazz lost, to the bitter disappointment of their fans, old and new. In an emotionally charged interview after the final defeat, sportswriter Peter Vecsey pressed Malone with questions about his seeming inability to deliver an MVP-level performance when it was most needed. Agitated but attempting to keep his composure, Malone replied tersely that it didn't matter what anybody else expected of him. What mattered, in his words, was that "I didn't play the game *I* wanted to play."

This is not meant as a moral indictment against Malone, a true team player who loves his fans and has a solid reputation for community service. What the story illustrates, rather, is a key dimension of the modern therapeutic worldview: my life is to be judged only by standards that I myself generate. It also demonstrates that one need not be a therapist to participate in this understanding of the self.

In 1966 Philip Rieff described what he called "the triumph of the therapeutic," the ascendancy of a self-oriented worldview in the vacuum of meaning produced by the modernist project. "The death of a culture," Rieff asserted, "begins when its normative institutions fail to communicate ideals in ways that remain inwardly compelling, first of all to the cultural elites themselves."[43] Rieff viewed the church as one such normative institution, providing both communal purpose and corporate identity. But when the Christian metanarrative lost its capability to morally address our culture in a binding fashion, what institution stepped in to fill the gap? "What binding address now describes our successor culture?" Rieff pondered. "In what does the self try to find salvation, if not in the breaking of corporate identities and in an acute suspicion of all normative institutions?" But this is only a negative definition. He continues:

> Western culture has had a literary canon, through which its character ideals were conveyed. What canons will replace the scriptural? None, I suppose. We are probably witnessing the end of a cultural history dominated by book religions and word-makers. The elites of the emergent culture—if they do not destroy themselves and all culture with a dynamism they appear unable to control—are being trained in terminologies that have only the most tenuous relation to any historic culture or its incorporative self-interpretations.[44]

What terminologies are these? Those of the emerging culture of therapy, in which new terminologies are being created all the time. What Rieff probably could not have envisioned thirty years ago is the explosion of the therapeutic and self-help markets, a proliferation of books, tapes, workshops and conferences in which people pursue the latest answers. The late Christopher Lasch once wrote that mental health has become the "modern equivalent of salvation," but one that comes from within rather than without and results in a preoccupation with self:

> Therapy has established itself as the successor both to rugged individualism and to religion; but this does not mean that the "triumph of the therapeutic" has become a new religion in its own right. Therapy constitutes an antireligion . . . because modern society "has no future" and therefore gives no thought to anything beyond its immediate needs. Even when therapists speak of the need for "meaning" and "love," they define love and meaning simply as the fulfillment of the patient's emotional requirements. It hardly occurs to them . . . to encourage the subject to subordinate his needs and interests to those of others, to someone or some cause or tradition outside himself.[45]

We have already seen this exaggerated modern emphasis, for example, in Parry and Doan's version of narrative therapy, but the same theme is repeated across the spectrum of therapeutic approaches.

The therapeutic vision of selfhood is typified by Margaret Oldham, the therapist interviewed by Bellah and his colleagues in their study of American individualism. She is interested in people, accepts them for who they are, and views them as constant sources of stimulation. Ultimately, however, her moral center remains within herself. Bellah quotes her statement of the meaning of life:

> I tend to operate on the assumption that what I want to do and what I feel like is what I should do. What I think the universe wants from me is to take my values, whatever they might happen to be, and live up to them as much as I can. If I'm the best person I know how to be according to my lights, then something good will happen. I think in a lot of ways living that kind of life is its own reward in and of itself.[46]

Following Lasch, this is certainly not religion in any institutionalized sense, but it is not strictly *anti*religion either. The notion that there may be something that "the universe wants" from her indicates a form of faith, however subjective it may be. But the language of transcendence is ultimately reappropriated into the self. The therapeutic vision thus yields its own individualized religion. This is best illustrated by Bellah's oft-cited interview with Sheila Larson, a nurse who had been in psychotherapeutic treatment and who describes her own private faith as "Sheilaism." "I believe in God," she tells the interviewer, but quickly qualifies that statement: "I'm not a religious fanatic. I can't remember the last time I went to church." Here she expresses the modern suspicion of institutional forms of religion. Whether she herself is personally leery of the church is difficult to tell; at the very least her comment shows that she knows she should be. She describes her alternative: "My faith has carried me a long way. It's Sheilaism. Just my own little voice." What does Sheilaism entail? "It's just try to love yourself and be gentle with yourself. You know, I guess, take care of each other. I think He would want us to take care of each other."[47] Here both therapist and therapy client evoke an ethos in which the healthy self-directed individual is the moral center of the universe.

Similarly, a longitudinal study of changes in American attitudes revealed that in 1976 people were more likely to frame their lives in psychological terms than they had twenty years earlier. A sense of meaning in life was no longer to be defined by social criteria but by internal criteria:

> When religious authority waned, the autonomous, well-internalized moral code no longer seemed to guide behavior. The individual,

then, looked to others for direction, and finally, recognizing the relativity of all judgment, came to measure all things by their ability to provide individual gratification, narcissistic pleasure.[48]

Such gratification need not be interpreted crudely, as the earlier reference to Daniel Bell's notion of consumer "hedonism" might suggest. What is important is the shifting locus of both identity and moral authority. Margaret Oldham is running by her own "lights," and Sheila Larson is listening to her own "little voice." In the absence of an authoritative tradition to be first internalized and then lived out, the modern individual must supply her own moral framework, and in all likelihood the less articulate the framework, the more it will rely on simple desire.

As Charles Taylor has pointed out, the problem is not with an emphasis on the self as such but with a simplistic ethos of self-fulfillment. He summarizes this cultural ethos as follows:

> Everyone has a right to develop their own form of life, grounded on their own sense of what is really important or of value. People are called upon to be true to themselves and to seek their own self-fulfillment. What this consists of, each must, in the last instance, determine for him- or herself. No one else can or should try to dictate its content.[49]

For Taylor this narcissistic ethic of self-fulfillment sacrifices both transcendence and relationship on the altar of the individual, making others instrumental to the development of the self. To quote once again the longitudinal study cited previously, such an ethos

> actually increases distance between people by insisting that they turn inward for the derivation of meaning and self-definition, by placing the burden of self-definition entirely on the individual—and making it a matter of individual achievement rather than a consensual and shared reality.[50]

Rieff, too, notices the impact of the therapeutic ethos upon relationships:

> In its reasonableness, the triumph of the therapeutic cannot be viewed simply as a break with the established order of moral demand, but rather as a profound effort to end the tyranny of primary group moral passion (operating first through the family) as the inner dynamic of social order. Crowded more and more together, we are

learning to live more distantly from one another, in strategically varied and numerous contacts, rather than in the oppressive warmth of family and a few friends.[51]

As Rieff notes, the modernist tone of the therapeutic ethos is shown not in the mere substitution of a new ethic but in the challenge to the social basis of any ethic. The modern individual seeks freedom from the oppressive influence of others, including his or her own family, and in the process finds herself increasingly alone.

This is not to say, however, that marital and family relationships are to be discarded. Variations on the therapeutic ethos do make it possible to extend the circle of concern from the atomistic self to the private sphere that includes one's spouse and children. Consider, for example, this passage from a recent text on marriage:

> More than any other human institution, marriage is the vehicle for transmitting our values to future generations. Ultimately it is our loving connections that give life meaning. Through intimate relationships we enlarge our vision of life and diminish our preoccupation with self. We are at our most considerate, our most loving, our most selfless within the orbit of a good family. Only within a satisfying marriage can a man and woman create the emotional intimacy and moral vision that they alone can bequeath to their children.[52]

Does this idyllic picture seem more hopeful than the passages cited earlier? At first the text appears to have a broader moral vision: it speaks against self-preoccupation and for the responsibility of teaching values to our children. So far, so good. Notice, however, the limited portrayal of values. Love and intimacy themselves seem to be the meaning of life. This transcends the individual, to be sure, but apparently not the boundary of the family: consideration and selflessness are expressed primarily within the family "orbit." And why is it that only the happy married couple can bequeath values and moral vision to the next generation? This is once again the modern vision of the family as haven, with a therapeutic moral twist.

In all of this we must be careful not to simplistically cast the profession of psychotherapy into the causal role. The therapeutic professions do not create the values of modern individualism; rather they refine and refract them, providing new languages for their expression. The culture of therapy is founded on the modern assumption that life difficulties are not simply the result of fate or inherited status but problems to be solved by technical means. Psychology, as the science of human behavior, has sought to identify the causative factors, and psychotherapy has attempted to offer the technologies of relief. There has always been an uncertain relationship between the two, however, for the latter is far more subject to the pull of the marketplace. It is this that professionals disdain as the trivialization of their discipline into "pop psychology" and self-help.

Indeed, some therapists fear that the current trend of subsuming psychotherapy services under the auspices of managed-care companies may be a disastrous capitulation to the culture of the marketplace. Mary Sykes Wylie, for example, writes that while yesterday's therapy clients were like "supplicants at the font of therapeutic wisdom," today's clients in a managed-care environment are "skeptical shoppers scrutinizing the undoubtedly fake Rolexes of a street vendor."[53] In a modern age it is still possible to believe in the unique authority of therapeutic narratives, authenticated by the therapist's presumed expertise. In a more post-modern age such authority can be granted only by a willing consumer. Managed-care corporations, for their part, are less interested in vague pronouncements of therapeutic outcomes than in concrete measures of customer satisfaction, placing even more power in the hands of the individual consumer. "Has the day finally arrived," Wylie wonders, "when consumers rule the therapy marketplace as well?"[54] Neither therapists nor managed-care companies nor consumers, however, are simple villains in this drama. All share alike in the modern values that apply technical rationality to the management of life, and all submit in some way to the logic of the all-consuming marketplace.

Living Where the Horizons Meet

The purpose of this chapter has been to suggest the contours of three modern habits of the heart that shape our understanding of who we are and how we should live. I do not claim, of course, that these moral horizons can comprehensively explain all of American culture. I hope, however, that the discussion leads us to consider more carefully whether our very own assumptions are part of whatever moral crisis is at hand. Each of us as individuals, and in our families and churches, must examine the extent to which the three horizons set limits to our moral vision. We are as many and as varied as snowflakes, and the results of our reflections will no doubt be as diverse. But then and only then will we be able to see more clearly what virtues the church is called to embody in the present age. More will be said of this in the latter part of the book.

The horizons, of course, do not describe discrete moral domains. They overlap and interpenetrate, and they bias our ethical sensibilities in different ways. Depending on the influence of tacit assumptions in each domain, we will be more or less committed to a form of modern individualism that may interfere with the articulation and realization of our more consciously acknowledged values. It is intrinsic to the postmodern condition that we may continue to hold competing sets of values while lacking a more comprehensive and socially reinforced story to make coherent sense of them. Furthermore, the hyperindividualism of our age continues to erode the community contexts that would nourish such metanarratives. Rasmussen puts the moral problem of the age this way:

> We stand center stage at a curious modern-postmodern moment when we must respond to unprecedented moral demands—both basic character formation and a bewildering array of social problems—just when the moral codes and the communities that put flesh on them are exceptionally weak.[55]

The question is whether such communities of moral formation are truly necessary or even capable of reconstruction. The modern individual is self-made, choosing her own destiny. Armed with legal rights to ward off those who would interfere with her project, she steps forth confidently into a limitless world of consumer possibilities, manufacturing her self-chosen lifestyle. Is this to be the ideal for all who wish to live in the reality of the present? Charles Sykes submits that in the end, the modern/postmodern ideal becomes a source of despair rather than hope. Reflecting on the roots of the malaise that gives rise to a culture of victimhood, he writes:

> By expanding without limit the definitions of human possibility, the new culture guarantees not fulfillment but a nagging sense of falling short, of not living up to one's potential. By declaring that all manner of joy is indeed attainable, the culture manufactures a perpetual sense of grievance as the new techniques fail to fully compensate for the loss of the discarded values.[56]

Similarly, for Charles Taylor true authenticity cannot be attained through narrowly defined notions of autonomy nor narcissistic emphases on fulfillment. He argues that the very notion of self-determining freedom is an illusory source of meaning, and its pursuit a self-defeating occupation:

> In a flattened world, where the horizons of meaning become fainter, the ideal of self-determining freedom comes to exercise a more powerful attraction. It seems that significance can be conferred by choice, by making my life an exercise in freedom, even when all other sources fail. . . . This sets up a vicious circle that heads us towards a point where our major remaining value is choice itself.[57]

Here Taylor suggests that the moral horizons I have sketched in this chapter take on greater significance when the grander stories are in question. But if these writers are correct, then the individual cannot be the source of her own significance. Christians implicitly know this. Even so, the ways in which we assert our values frequently betray the fact that we are more the children of modernity than we care to realize. We may consciously shun the more egregious manifestations of individualism. In subtler ways, however, we still retain the related modern ideals. The answers we give on an opinion survey may demonstrate what we consciously value, but how we speak at length about values reveals more thoroughly the moral horizons of our vision. What modernistic horizons influence how Christians think about family values? We will explore this question next, by examining how Christians speak about divorce.

Five

UNTIL CULTURE
DO US PART?

. . . .

Marriage has become a context for expressive individualism. . . .
The sphere of individual decision within the family is growing. . . .
One can leave a marriage one doesn't like.
Divorce as a solution to an unhappy marriage, even with young children,
is far more acceptable today than ever before.
ROBERT BELLAH ET AL., *Habits of the Heart*[1]

Every thirteen seconds, someone gets divorced.
Each year, in the United States alone, over one million families experience divorce.
Each year, for every two couples that get married, one couple gets divorced.
Not one of these couples likes getting divorced. They agonize over it,
usually for years, and say it has been the most difficult time of their lives. . . .
It is an extraordinarily painful experience that invades one's whole life space.
CONSTANCE AHRONS, *The Good Divorce*[2]

O f all the myriad social issues that we bring together under the banner of family values, divorce is probably the most visible. As we have seen in chapter one, Christians participating in the Religion and Values Project overwhelmingly agree that America is facing a crisis of family values and cite divorce as a marker of this crisis more frequently than any other issue. Related matters, such as single parenthood and father absence, were also common themes. The high visibility of divorce makes it a good test case for a closer examination of the roots beneath our family values.

The contemporary divorce literature is a good example of the two opposing approaches to family values represented in our culture. On the one hand are those who write of a "divorce culture," an alternative set of values, promoted by the media, that emphasizes individual freedom over family responsibility. These authors call for a revolution in values that would embody a renewed commitment to the two-parent family norm and in some cases advocate social policies that would make divorce more difficult to obtain.[3] On the other hand are those who urge what they consider to be a more compassionate and realistic approach. They give greater weight to the economic and other social factors underlying the prevalence of divorce. While these writers do not glamorize divorce, they argue that divorce is here to stay. Their primary concern is the well-being of divorced families and their children, and insist that it is our cherished social myths about the family that prevent us from developing more divorce-friendly policies.[4]

There is something valid in each of the perspectives. We cannot ignore the values issues embedded in contemporary debates about divorce. But we must also be careful not to frame these issues in ways that either blind us to our own complicity or deter us from expressing compassion. We live in a culture of competing ideals. When it comes to divorce, Christians are not of one voice. Indeed even individual Christians may speak with multiple voices, representing the diverse moral languages we have learned from our culture. How do these different voices and languages express themselves when Christians speak of divorce? This chapter begins by examining the idea of a divorce "culture," as preliminary to exploring the moral themes manifested in the RVP data on what Christians believe about divorce.

Are We Living in a Culture of Divorce?

As media critic Michael Medved has argued, the entertainment industry continues to churn out depictions of destructive and bizarre family situations, on the premise that "happy marriages don't sell," despite box-office evidence to the contrary.[5] Even more significant than such marginal images, though, are the more successful films with which we resonate emotionally. In 1993 Americans flocked to see *Mrs. Doubtfire*, a comedy in which Robin Williams portrays Daniel Hillard, a fun-loving father who deeply loves his children. His wife, Miranda, however, views him as irresponsible: he seems unable to hold down a steady job, and he conspires with the children to violate Mom's household rules. Fed up with his antics, she eventually seeks a divorce. When Miranda limits his visitation rights, a desperate Daniel dons makeup and dress to become Mrs. Doubtfire, whom Miranda unsuspectingly hires as the children's new nanny. Complications of leading such a double life naturally ensue, and it is Daniel's frenzied attempts to keep the ruse a secret that drive the plot. On a more serious level, however, *Mrs. Doubtfire* may be interpreted as "a movie with a mission: to affirm the possibility of better divorce."[6] In the end the divorce transforms both Daniel and Miranda into better parents and better people. The ultimate message is that what really matters is not whether parents live together in a single household but whether they love their children. This is an example of what Barbara Dafoe Whitehead has called the "Love Family" ideology, in which what truly matters "is not what a family looks like on the outside, but how it feels on the inside."[7]

David Blankenhorn, in his book *Fatherless America,* argues that the very popularity of the movie is itself evidence of the "steady displacement of a marriage culture by a divorce culture." He writes:

> In a marriage culture, the happy ending is marriage. Boy meets girl, boy gets girl, boy and girl triumph over adversity—this was the classic Hollywood formula. But the happy ending today is more likely to be the good divorce. Boy and girl grow up by growing apart. . . . Divorce becomes a metaphor for adult rebirth and renewal. This theme is important in America. . . . The vision of the good divorce—a vision of personal freedom—captures much of the essence of the American character.[8]

Blankenhorn's major concern is fatherlessness rather than divorce per se. He contends that fatherhood is a social creation, designed to channel competitive male impulses in a constructive direction, namely the care of the next generation. But if marriage fragments, can fatherhood be far behind? Judith Wallerstein argues that once fathers leave the commitment of marriage, they are far less likely to maintain their ties to their children, with long-term consequences to the children's emotional well-being.[9] For our present purposes the question at hand is whether Blankenhorn's diagnosis is correct: are we transitioning into a culture of divorce?

Wallerstein's work was an important basis for Barbara Dafoe White-head's controversial *Atlantic Monthly* piece "Dan Quayle Was Right." More recently Whitehead has written *The Divorce Culture*, in which she more fully charts the historical development to which Blankenhorn alludes. Whitehead observes that from its inception American culture has promoted values that contained the seeds of a divorce culture. The same voluntarism that made marriage a freely entered union would eventually also make it freely left. The intrusion of market logic into all areas of institutional life would create a consumerlike attitude toward the marital institution as well. But prior to the 1960s the growing divorce rate, though it had stimulated public outcry in every era, was still largely contained by a moral tradition that valued institutional marriage in its own right. Andrew Cherlin writes that as more companionate ideals of marriage replaced older images of an economic partnership, the United States entered into an "era of divorce tolerance," in which courts were more sympathetic to the plight of maltreated women.[10] Divorce was to be accepted as a modern fact of life, but one still under the aegis of the institution of marriage. The crucial shift came in the mid-1960s to the early 1970s. As suggested by the quote from Bellah in the epigraph to this chapter, divorce came to be understood more and more in the terms of expressive individualism. This change in understanding was concretely embodied in the advent of no-fault divorce in California in 1970. Cherlin states:

> Coming several years after rising divorce rates had begun to clog the courts, no-fault divorce was hailed as the way to bring the law into line with changes in societal attitudes toward divorce. It reflected the belief that a person should not be forced to continue in a marriage that she or he found to be personally unacceptable. Such an individualistic view of the marriage bond would have outraged the American colonists. . . . Divorce had changed from a way for wealthy men to protect their property from heirs fathered by other men to a way for the average person to improve her or his own sense of well-being. In the most liberal no-fault states and nations, it had become something close to an individual right.[11]

Under the ethic of expressive individualism, in which one's first obligation is to oneself, divorce became a matter of the individual's right to fulfillment, a right that could not be easily reconciled with the claim of others upon the self. The legal and ideological trend, White-head observes, has been toward further deregulation, where no one can trump the individual's free exercise of choice.[12] Beneath this trend Whitehead discerns the narrative of capitalism, recast in therapeutic terms, whereby the moral good is culturally redefined as the maximi-zation of "psychological capital."[13]

More precisely, then, the "culture of divorce" turns out to be but one manifestation of the values examined in the preceding chapter: the ideals of American individualism, swathed in the interpenetrating languages of rights, consumerism and therapeutic ideology. Why is this important? Because even those who haven't been divorced can hardly claim to be unaffected by these pervasive values. Certainly there are people who divorce for selfish reasons and who take their familial commitments far too lightly. For each one of these individuals, however, there are many more who share values very similar to our own, who divorce with deep regret and, often, an accompanying sense of failure.

Nor is it the case that the consequences of divorce are universally and irredeemably negative. Constance Ahrons, in her book *The Good Divorce*, argues against the unthinking prejudice that stigmatizes di-vorced families, while candidly expressing the doubts and fears that attended her own divorce. In her conclusion she writes of her lingering concern over the impact of the divorce on her children:

> You see, no matter how expert one is or how hard one tries to achieve a good divorce, even if one is confident that one has, finally, achieved one, there remains some fear—fear that one's choices, no matter how reasoned and correct, have adversely affected the children.[14]

Her daughter, however, sent her a copy of an essay she had written in the process of applying to graduate school. The application required that she write about the people and events that had shaped her identity, and the daughter chose to focus on the experience of being from a divorced family. Her essay concludes with the following paragraph:

> My parents' divorce and the evolution of my family since then have had an amazing impact on my life. There have been difficult times, but overall, I have gained from the divorce. Though I would not wish it on anyone, and I hope never to experience it personally, my parents' divorce has afforded me many wonderful opportunities

which I could not have otherwise experienced. My close family ties form the foundation that has allowed me to become who, and what, I am.[15]

This is not, to use Blankenhorn's language, "a hymn dedicated to the promise of better divorce."[16] It is a retrospective appraisal of a childhood that contains not only hurt but also healing and integration.

Whitehead and Blankenhorn are perfectly correct in calling us to reassess the values manifested in current attitudes toward divorce. But we should not let the notion of a divorce culture lead us to picture ourselves as a nation of purely egocentric individuals who would rather leave than make personal sacrifices for our families. As we shall see, Americans in general, and Christians in particular, still value the ideal of a lifelong marital commitment. The question is whether or not, given the competing values that we hold, we are capable of either coherently articulating the reasons for that commitment or living it out.

A Culture of Permanence

The familiar words of the wedding vow, "till death do us part," express the ideal of marriage as a lifelong commitment, or marital permanence. This ideal is still valued by a majority of Americans. A 1992 study by George Barna interviewed more than one thousand American adults of all ages regarding their beliefs about marriage. Respondents stated whether they agreed or disagreed with several statements presented to them. Three of the items indicate that a norm of marital permanence still exists in our culture. First, a full 79 percent of the respondents agreed that "God intended for people to get married and stay in that relationship for life." Second, and conversely, 74 percent *disagreed* with the statement "Marriage should not automatically be thought of as a permanent arrangement between two people." Not even the word *automatically* seemed to deter these respondents from affirming the permanence of the marital relationship. Nor do people appear to believe, third, that divorce is inevitable; 77 percent disagreed that "people getting married these days should expect that at some point their marriage is probably going to end in divorce."[17] If there is a rising culture of divorce, such data would suggest that there is also a strong remnant of a culture of permanence.

Christians, as a group, hold even more strongly to the ideal of a lifelong partnership. The RVP included two relevant items, one of which measured marital permanence as a *belief* and the other as a *personal value*. The first item, measuring permanence as a belief, was one of several value statements pertaining to family relationships. Respondents rated their agreement with each statement, using a six-point scale that varied from "strongly disagree" at one end to "strongly agree" at the other. One of the statements read simply, "Marriage is for life." The sample was in clear support of this ideal. With a score of 6 representing "strongly agree," the average response was 5.561; almost 93 percent of respondents checked either "agree" or "strongly agree." This response was not influenced by either the participant's level of education or gender. While married Christians gave slightly higher ratings overall than did those who were divorced or separated, the latter still averaged 5.37 on a scale of 6.[18]

The second item, which measured permanence as a value, was presented as one of the twenty-eight family values identified by Mark Mellman and his colleagues, as discussed in the first chapter of this book.[19] Mellman's list of values was presented in random order, and respondents were requested to rate how important each value was to them personally. Note that this is a different approach from the earlier survey, in which respondents merely agreed or disagreed with an item without indicating the personal significance of the statement itself. The value ratings were performed on a four-point scale, running from "not very important" at the low end to "somewhat important," "very important," and finally, "absolutely essential."[20] One of the items, "being married to the same person for life," was used as an indicator of marital permanence as a personal value. Again, the RVP sample strongly supported this value. With a score of 4 representing "absolutely essential," the average was 3.568, with more than 93 percent of the respondents checking either "very important" or "absolutely essential." The latter was by far the most common response, given by nearly two-thirds of the group. The response on this item was also unaffected by participants' gender or level of education. Again, married participants tended to rate this value more highly than their divorced or separated counterparts, but the average for the latter was still 3.16, meaning that the value of lifelong marriage was still "very important" to them personally.[21] Whether measured as a belief or a personal value, then, Christians hold to the ideal of marital permanence even more earnestly than the general population. Moreover this ideal appears to retain its importance regardless of a respondent's gender, education or marital status.

Can we go further? The arguments for a divorce culture suggest that the values of expressive individualism are associated with an ideology that supports divorce. Can it be demonstrated statistically that there is a relationship between values related to rights, freedom of choice or therapeutic self-fulfillment, and a belief in the validity of divorce? This question is addressed in the next section. In this section, however, a similar question may be put to the matter of marital permanence. What values, beliefs and behaviors are associated with this ideal? The answer to this question can be approached by examining the statistical relationship between our two marital permanence items and other measures used in the RVP. In particular, four types of items are used for this analysis.

Three of the four represent different ways of measuring values. The first we have already seen: participants were presented with Mellman's list of *family values* and asked to rate each on a four-point scale of personal importance. The second approach uses the same four-point scale, from "not very important" to "absolutely essential," but presents a different list of items, which we will call *self-worth factors*. The items were taken from sociologist Robert Wuthnow's Economic Values Survey.[22] Wuthnow asked interviewees, "How important is each of the following to your basic sense of worth as a person?" and presented them with a diverse list of thirteen items, including, for example, "your family," "your relation to God," "making a lot of money" and "living a comfortable life."

The third measure of values also used a method borrowed from Wuthnow but adapted for the RVP. Wuthnow asked interviewees to imagine that they had a "tough decision to make at work." He presented them with seven factors that could influence the decision, such as "what you thought was morally right" and "whether you would feel good about it."[23] Adapting Wuthnow's list for a nonwork context, an expanded set of fourteen factors was created for the RVP, including items such as "the Bible," "the teachings of your church" and "what your parents would have done." Participants were asked to rate how important each of the factors was to them in making life decisions, using a five-point scale from "not very important" to "very important." Thus we will call these items *decision factors* and explore their relationship to marital permanence.

The fourth and final item type is a straightforward measure of religious *behavior.* Participants were asked how frequently they prayed, read the Bible and attended religious services.

The method, in summary, is to use the two measures of marital permanence as *belief* and as personal *value,* and examine their relationship to various items classified under the four item types of *family values, self-worth factors, decision factors* and *religious behavior.* The intention here is not to focus on each and every finding but to look for patterns of response that might indicate the contours of a "culture" of permanence, as opposed to a culture of divorce. So as not to clutter the text with numbers, the actual statistical results may be found in appendix A.[24] Let us therefore ask the question again: what values or behaviors are associated with the ideal of marital permanence? For the purposes of the present discussion, two general conclusions will suffice.

The first conclusion is that *religion plays a positive role.* This can be demonstrated in at least two ways. First, religious behavior is associated with the notion of permanence. The more Christians pray, read their Bibles and attend church, the more they believe in the ideal. The connection between religious behavior and permanence expressed as a personal value is somewhat weaker, but still present. Second, other markers of religious devotion are similarly related. The more these Christians relied on the Bible as a factor in making daily life decisions, the more they supported lifelong marriage; this decision factor ranked first with regard to permanence as a belief and fifth with regard to permanence as a value, though the latter relationship was actually somewhat stronger. Other decision factors, such as obedience to God and the teachings of one's church, played similar roles, as did the self-worth factor of "your relationship to God." Together these findings suggest a religious dimension to the cultural ideal of marital permanence.

The second general conclusion, related to the first, is that *marital permanence is an other-directed ideal.*[25] Many measures of a more individualistic self-directedness were included in the RVP, such as the self-worth factors of "taking care of yourself" and "being able to do what you want to do" or the decision factors of "personal needs" and "personal rights." These items and others like them show no relation to either measure of marital permanence. This other-directedness shows different facets, depending on whether one is looking at permanence as a belief or as a personal value. On the one hand, permanence viewed as a value reveals an *interpersonal-familial* orientation. The three items that show the strongest relationship to the value of "being married to the same person for life" are the family values of "having a happy marriage," "having good relationships with your extended family" and simply "being married." The interpersonal orientation is further suggested by items that are uniquely related to permanence as a value but not as a belief: the family value items "having good relationships with your extended family," "respecting one's children," "being able to provide emotional support for your family" and "being able to communicate your feelings to your family," as well as the self-worth factor "helping people in need."

On the other hand, permanence as a belief seems to be associated with a more *transcendent* aspect of other-directedness. The items most closely related to the belief that "marriage is for life" point to realities that transcend the interpersonal realm. These values are, in order, reliance on the Bible in making life decisions, the value of "following a strict moral code," the value of "having faith in God" and the criterion of obedience to God as a decision factor. This discussion, of course, should not be taken to imply an absolute distinction between permanence as a belief and permanence as a value. Rather, one might think of other-directedness as having two dimensions, with the transcendent representing the vertical and the interpersonal-familial representing the horizontal. Both dimensions are present in each of the measures of permanence, but permanence as belief can be understood as emphasizing the vertical, while permanence as value emphasizes the horizontal.

As a cultural ideal, then, marital permanence does not stand in isolation. In the minds of these Christians at least, it is closely associated with a broad cluster of values that emphasize religious devotion, moral uprightness and the importance of family relationships. Permanence has a subjective, psychological dimension: "having a *happy* marriage," for example, is more closely related to the ideal than the more institutional value of simply "being married." Nevertheless, these findings indicate that a vital moral tradition still exists, one that is not yet fully in the grip of a postmodern hyperindividualism.

But even if marital permanence is not an individualistic ideal, neither is it a specifically *anti*-individualistic one. The self-oriented measures of the RVP were not *negatively* related to marital permanence; they simply showed no relationship at all. This means that the extent to which one holds self-directed values has no bearing on whether one also believes in the permanence of the marriage relationship. Can the same be said with regard to divorce?

The Freedom to Divorce as a Value

As Whitehead observes, the cultural ideal of marital permanence may be waning in the face of a divorce culture.[26] Even if it can be argued that a culture of permanence still exists, a culture of divorce may coexist with it. As we saw earlier, Barna's research shows that most Americans still believe that marriage should be a lifelong commitment. But there is another, competing value that Americans also hold. When survey participants were presented with the statement "Marriage should be used by people to help them cope with life more effectively, but it should not limit a person's activities or opportunities in any way," Barna found that 68 percent, or over two-thirds, agreed.[27] Here marriage is defined in terms of its benefits to the individual. Marriage is for life, it seems, unless something better comes along.

Do Christians support the ideal of an individual's freedom to seek a divorce? RVP participants were presented with the statement "A couple should be able to get a divorce if they want one" and asked to rate their agreement on a six-point scale. The response to this statement was far more ambivalent than for the ideal of marital permanence. As we saw earlier, over 92 percent of the sample clearly agreed with the statement that "marriage is for life." It is reasonable to expect that a similar percentage would clearly *disagree* that a couple should have the freedom to divorce, but in fact only 40 percent of the sample actually did so. Again, the average level of agreement on marital permanence was over 5.5 on a scale of 6. The average level of agreement, however, on the divorce item was just slightly over 3, barely tipping the scale toward disagreement. Furthermore, the divorce item reflects values that span demographic categories. As with the permanence ideal, neither gender nor level of education affected agreement ratings on divorce. Unlike permanence, however, the divorce item was not influenced by the respondent's marital status. Married Christians were neither more nor less likely to support the freedom to divorce than their divorced or separated colleagues. Christians are neither enthusiastic about divorce nor strictly set against it.

Can a statistical profile be drawn of the values associated with a culture of divorce? A second set of analyses, similar to those described in the preceding section, was performed to answer this question. How are religious behavior, family values, self-worth factors and decision factors related to the ideal of the freedom to divorce? The profile is not simply a mirror image of the culture of permanence. The permanence ideal, on the one hand, was positively associated with both religious and other-directed values. The culture of divorce, on the other hand, is characterized by an equal number of positive *and* negative associations. The full statistical data are found in appendix B; the results are summarized in the following paragraphs. Three broad observations are relevant.

First, an examination of the negative relationships suggests an oppositional definition of the divorce culture: its existence is defined in contradistinction to the traditional values represented by the culture of permanence. The response on the divorce item was negatively correlated with seventeen values that were all associated with marital permanence. Not surprisingly, respondents who agreed that couples should be able to choose divorce were less likely to personally value being married to the same person for life. But why should the same negative relationship extend to nearly all the items associated with permanence? In terms of variables of religion and transcendence, Christians who support the freedom to divorce are less likely to read the Bible, attend religious services or pray; they are less likely to view adherence to Scripture or obedience to God as important factors in making life decisions; their faith in and relationship to God are not as highly valued; and following moral standards is less important to their sense of self. On the political family values front, they are less likely to be against abortion or for school prayer. They also place less value on respect for authority or their parents, having a happy marriage or even just being married.

Second, however, another set of seventeen positive correlations helps to define what the culture of divorce *is* rather than what it is not. Here the moral horizons described in chapter four predominate; these values are profoundly individualistic, reflecting the images of the independent bearer of rights, the materially minded consumer and the therapeutic self in search of fulfillment. Christians who agreed more strongly that couples should have the right to divorce seemed to do so from a more general perspective of individual freedom. Three of the four values most closely related to agreement on the divorce item were "being able to do what you want to do," "being independent" and an emphasis on personal rights as a decision factor. The values of the self-interested consumer in the marketplace also loomed large: "being successful," "making a lot of money," "what would benefit you the most," "being financially secure" and "earning a good living" were all positively associated with the divorce ideal. Other values, such as basing one's decisions on "whether you would feel good about it" or "your personal needs," represent the triumph of the therapeutic, as does the value of "paying attention to your feelings." Still other values seemed to blend market and therapeutic ideals, as in "living a comfortable life" and "having nice things." The values positively associated with the divorce ideal, in short, are strikingly self-oriented.

We may also briefly observe, third, that the negative definition is somewhat more salient than the positive; the negative relationships are stronger in nearly every case. Culturally this suggests that if a postmodern divorce culture does in fact exist, it is a little more *post-* than *modern*. In other words, its identity may be more coherently defined by opposition to the values of its predecessor culture than by the mélange of exaggerated individual values it seeks to embody.

It is important not to interpret this statistical excursus as an argument for the moral rightness or wrongness of either the culture of permanence or the culture of divorce. The point of this section and the preceding one has been to give at least some empirical justification for speaking in terms of two cultures by showing that distinct sets of values are associated with each. An ideal of lifelong marital union continues to exist in our culture, bolstered by a set of religious and ethical ideals that are other-directed in nature. The culture of divorce blends the moral ideals of individual freedom and fulfillment in an expanding market. Its compass is self-directed. The oppositional character of the divorce culture makes it unlikely that its adherents will strongly hold values associated with the culture of permanence. The reverse, however, is not necessarily the case. Those who believe in lifelong marriage may nevertheless hold self-oriented values, even if they do not fully support the notion of divorce as an individual right. What this means, in practice, is that even though Christians overwhelmingly favor a religiously shaded ideal of permanent matrimony, they may also speak the language of another culture, the divorce culture.

A Conflict of Cultures

What we have is a conflict between cultural ideals. In chapter four we saw how a group of university students discussing divorce could not reconcile their values of parental responsibility, on the one hand, and the individual freedom of the spouses, on the other. A similar ambivalence is found in both Barna's study and the RVP. Over three-fourths of Barna's sample held to an ideal of marital permanence, but over two-thirds of the same group did not believe that marriage should impose any limits on an individual's activities or opportunities. For the Christians in the RVP study, lifelong marriage was an almost universal ideal. Yet only 40 percent of the respondents clearly disagreed with the statement that a couple should be able to divorce if they so choose. It would seem that marital permanence remains an important ideal, but the number of acceptable barriers to permanence have increased. Moreover, as divorce becomes more and more common, the languages and moral perspectives used to legitimate it also become more widely disseminated, so that it becomes harder to consistently articulate why people should remain married in the first place.

This disarray in our moral landscape is illustrated in the interviews with Christians conducted for the RVP. Approximately midway through each interview, participants were asked to respond to the statement "Christians shouldn't divorce." The question was one of many designed to elicit the moral horizons implied by how Christians speak about family relationships. Some responded with general agreement, while others reacted almost automatically to the restrictiveness of the implied rule. Some participants conversed in the language of permanence, others voiced the culture of divorce, and most spoke from an amalgamation of the two. The following excerpts demonstrate the wide range of perspectives, from those whose responses bore few if any marks of faith, to those whose use of Christian language was subject to other moral horizons, to those whose vision was dominated by the Christian narrative. The handful of individuals quoted here, of course, cannot be taken as statistically representative of Christians as a whole; it is hoped only that their remarks illustrate concretely the problem of conflicting cultures in the church.

Consider, then, the comments made by Sharon, who has been a Christian all her long life.[28] Not long ago she celebrated her golden wedding anniversary, a tribute to marital permanence. Confronted with the statement that "Christians shouldn't divorce," however, she readily demurred "No, that's a blanket statement. . . . There might be grounds for divorce." Asked to explain what these grounds might be, she replied: "Well, cruelty or mistreatment of one by the other, either for alcohol or drugs. . . . You can't live with that." She appeared to recognize that these might be marginal cases and offered that Christians who know each other well enough before they marry would have little to fear in this area. When the interviewer asked if there were any conditions in which she would personally consider divorce, Sharon gave a fascinating answer:

> Oh, if my husband had found another woman that he liked better when he was away from me, I suppose that I would have withdrawn from the marriage. Otherwise, I can't think of anything. I can't imagine finding someone else myself, that would be the only [reason], or if he could not support me, or wasn't interested any longer in having children or any of those things. Some men find children a nuisance, a worry and a bother. And I would imagine sometimes wives would have to leave.

Her original reasons for why one might seek divorce were common to many other respondents: cruelty, drug or alcohol abuse or adultery. The finality of adultery is itself striking: she simply states that she would probably have "withdrawn" from the relationship and gives no hint as to whether she might work to preserve it instead. She then suggests that she might have divorced her husband if he could not "support"

never say "never" strategically?

her or had not wanted to be bothered with children. Is this on the same order as abuse or adultery? For Sharon, who has maintained both her faith and her marriage for over half a century, the barriers to divorce seem low indeed.

At the other end of the age spectrum we find Arlene, a vibrant youth pastor who was born into a Christian family. Unlike Sharon, she not only agrees that Christians shouldn't divorce but goes even further: "I don't think anybody should divorce." Also unlike Sharon, whose response was completely devoid of any references to specifically Christian perspectives, Arlene freely uses the concept of sin in her response: "I think when Jesus talks about not divorcing, and it being a sin, . . . I look at sin as going against what's best for us and who we're created to be." First, we should recognize that Jesus does not directly label divorce as a sin. In the Gospel of Matthew, for example, the Lord's concern is less with divorce than with the hardness of heart that makes legal custom more important than recognizing God's handiwork in the "one-flesh" relationship of marriage. The specific sin is thus the adultery that almost inevitably follows the sundering of the union (Mt 5:31-32; 19:3-9).

Second, and more significant for our purposes, note how Arlene understands sin itself; it is "going against what's best for us and who we're created to be." Sin ceases to be a transgression against a holy God and becomes instead a transgression against the self, against human potentiality. The triumph of the therapeutic is confirmed as she continues:

> I don't think of it as being a punitive thing; so the reason I think Christians, or anyone, should not divorce is not about because you've sinned but because you're hurting yourself. I think the hurt comes about because it's a violation of the intimacy and commitment to one another that we're able to experience in the relationship. [Divorce] is just very damaging to each other because there is no longer a trust, and there is no longer the security, and that just continues to affect others—it cycles to affect the children, the other relationships they are in. It's just really damaging. I don't think of divorce as being right or wrong, it's just a detriment to the person.

Note here the mixed messages regarding the role and nature of sin. Arlene has already redefined sin in therapeutic terms but then proceeds to dispense with the language of sin altogether; the notion that "you've sinned" is replaced by "you're hurting yourself." In the end the more public moral categories of right and wrong do not even apply.

There is good in what Arlene says: divorce is painful, and it can have detrimental consequences for others beyond just the individuals involved. But the images of broken intimacy, trust and security suggest a romanticized modern ideal of marriage as emotional companionship. She implicitly portrays the marriage relationship as the repository of human hopes and dreams of fulfillment and domesticates the transcendent language of sin to fit this ideal. Ultimately, then, for this youth minister it is the horizon of the therapeutic that governs her vision.

The therapeutic also speaks strongly through Morris, a retired man who has difficulty pinning down how long he has been a Christian. Morris rejects the idea that there should be a specific rule for divorce that applies to Christians: "I don't think it has to do with whether you're a Christian or a Muslim or any other religion whether you divorce or not." His perspective is built, in part, on his own experiences in counseling with his pastor, "who says the Bible allows divorce." Morris takes a pragmatic view:

> I think you have a divorce if you find that you can't solve your problems. A lot of times you find that you can't solve your problems, but that's because you don't know how to, and you could solve your problems by reading *Men Are from Mars, Women Are from Venus* [a self-help bestseller by John Gray about gender differences in communication], or going to a counselor, or going to a marriage weekend, or all kinds of things that can help you solve your problems, but some people don't solve them that way.

The key phrase here, obviously, is "solve your problems," repeated almost as a therapeutic mantra. Couples do, of course, have difficulties, but the question is whether or not these should be understood automatically as problems to be solved by therapeutic means. Morris suggests that couples could learn to resolve their difficulties if they would read self-help books, see a therapist or attend an enrichment weekend. But he is not out to proselytize converts to a therapeutic gospel. He flatly recognizes that some people don't choose to use therapeutic solutions, and for them divorce should be an option. Divorce, moreover, may be an instrument with which people fine-tune their lives. He continues:

> I see so many examples of people whose first marriages were terrible, [but] the second marriage, [or] sometimes the third, gives a permanent life situation, where they have been able to make better judgments as to their spouse, and they are more mature people. So I think it would be a crime to stick with the first bad marriage and lose the opportunity to have a real lifelong marriage.

Here, the word *crime* seems to function for Morris in much the same way as did the word *sin* for Arlene: the crime is not against God or society but against the self and its opportunities for happiness. He elaborates on the notion of correcting the consequences of poor judgment:

> People make mistakes in their first choices very frequently, because they are very young when they make those choices, or they have other reasons that are a necessity, so I think divorce is an important part of getting the right marriages. It can obviously be abused.

This is a telling phrase: *Divorce is an important part of getting the right marriages.* It is couched in a context that everyone would understand: people do indeed make mistakes, and we would like to believe that the mistakes can be corrected as painlessly as possible. This is not to say that Morris would not recognize, as does Arlene, the pain involved in the process. But the rendering of divorce as a tool makes it difficult to even raise the question whether the decision to divorce might itself be a mistake. This is passed over in favor of the goal: who wouldn't want the "right" marriage? Morris seems to recognize that there are moral limits to his perspective, since it "can obviously be abused." Asked by the interviewer if there are any reasons for keeping a marriage together, he first vaguely agrees, then falls rapidly back into his pragmatic and therapeutic stance:

> If there is any reason to marry in the first place, then of course there's still a good reason to keep it together, unless it's not working—unless all the things I've said don't work and you can't solve it, then you made a mistake. I mean, people make mistakes all the time. So if you have made a mistake and you realize you've made a mistake, then it's better to get out of there than to live with your mistake forever. That's the way we learn—is by mistakes a lot of times.

If you can't solve your problems, it is simply evidence that you made a mistake, an error of judgment to which we are all prone. Here we find no biblical or Christian horizon: the only moral justification of his instrumental view of divorce is the truism that we learn by our mistakes.

But there appears to be another horizon operating in the remote distance: the horizon of the market, where relationships begin to be thought of as commodities and the customer is always right. The relentless logic of consumer choice, here applied to divorce, goes something like this: If you have a problem, try to fix it; if you can't fix it, there must be some mistake; if there is a mistake, get a new one. I am reminded of the new carpet we recently had installed in our living room. The carpet came with an incredible guarantee: if for any reason we were not satisfied with the carpet within fifteen days, the company would replace it for free. If we had decided on a whim, for example, that we simply didn't like the color, the installers would have torn out the carpet and replaced it with a different color at no charge to us. This is obviously of much greater consequence, say, than returning a shirt to the store, but the logic is the same: if you have made a mistake, then you shouldn't have to "live with your mistake forever." Applied to divorce, marriage comes with a guarantee of satisfaction.

A similar view is expressed by Stan, a pastor in his forties who came to Christ in his teenage years. Presented with the statement that "Christians shouldn't divorce," Stan categorically replies, "That's not true." He explains:

> I think that there are certain situations where Christians should divorce because they have made a bad choice. The worst case I think is for two people, who for whatever reason aren't healthy or not good for each other, not because they intend to, but who by virtue of their own personality, or temperament, or other past experiences bring out the worst in each other. It's like they touch a hot button. I have been working through this with a couple from church. It's a sad situation, but they should have never gotten married! Never. They took one of those analyses, and their chance of success in marriage was less than one percent. And they got married.

The languages of both choice and therapy dominate the pastor's narrative. In response to a further question from the interviewer, Stan confirms that he is referring to a premarital inventory that the couple took but chose to ignore. He continues:

> But they were under the myth that "Hey, we're Christians, God
> brought us together." /. . What I think is perhaps a supreme irony
> in our Christian culture is that so many Christians spend big bucks
> for the wedding, and spend hardly squat in preparing for the
> marriage: premarital counseling, doing whatever it takes to work
> through it. That, to me, is the real sin. So, in terms of that question,
> some Christians should get divorced, and also should get some help
> working through some of the issues that either they brought with
> them, or that the marriage helped to create, before they even
> consider remarrying.

I agree with Stan that the work of preparing for the marriage commitment is easily overlooked in favor of the splashy wedding ritual. I also
recognize the value of premarital counseling and psychological inven-
tories and agree that the results of these should not be neglected. But
the "supreme irony" here is not simply, as Stan would have it, in the
fact that people expend more money and effort on the wedding than
on premarital counseling. Rather, the irony is that it is the couple who
use Christian language, however imperfectly, and their pastor who
substitutes the therapeutic narrative for the "myth." Granted, young
couples do marry against all wisdom, therapeutic or otherwise, and
they may use Christian language to sanctify their heedlessness. But by
what moral logic does the pastor then try to counsel them? Should
Pastor Stan discard the myth or attempt to redeem it?

Note also the use of the word *sin*. It was Arlene, also in the ministry,
who used the term in a previous example. For her, sin was a transgression against the self. For Stan, however, the sin seems to be against a
form of wisdom, framed in the language of therapeutic rationality. The
role of counseling is taken for granted and forms the horizon within
which sin is to be understood. As an aside, consider in this regard the
words of Kelly, a young woman who, unlike Stan, agrees that Christians
shouldn't divorce: "I agree with that statement, and I don't think there
needs to be an 'except when.' Because I think that we shouldn't divorce,
I think that we should get counseling." She laughs and then continues
more seriously, holding to the rule against divorce even in the face of
physical abuse: "So, if your husband beats you, then I think that you
shouldn't bail, but you should pursue counseling. But of course, most

people do that, and nothing happens—but anyway, no, I think
Christians shouldn't divorce." What is remarkable about her statement
is the way the role of counseling is taken as almost axiomatic, despite
her personal opinion that, at least in some cases, it does little good.
Both Kelly and Stan frame their responses within a therapeutic
horizon. For Kelly therapy comes after marriage as the only alternative
to divorce. For Stan counseling is the prerequisite to marriage and takes
on moral force in its own right. Remember that the original question
was to respond to the statement "Christians shouldn't divorce," not
"Christians should seek counseling before they get married." Stan's
response veers immediately away from divorce and reframes the moral
issue as a matter of premarital preparation. It is the lack of preparation
that is the "real sin," and this said, divorce is reintroduced almost as a
natural consequence, not a moral issue in its own right. If any work is
to be done after the divorce, it is to correct the earlier mistake; for
heaven's sake, the pastor seems to say, don't get married again until
you get some counseling first.

To be fair, Stan does recognize a higher ideal, as the following
statement demonstrates:

Jesus' call to us, I think, is that it's ideal that you don't get divorced.
My wife and I, while we've had our rough moments, I don't think
that we have ever felt like divorce was an option. That is a call that
I embrace—I preach and teach that. But it can't be used legalistically;
Jesus didn't say it that way.

For his own part Stan attempts to embody something more than
therapeutic rationality. The language of *call* is a transcendent one; it
points to a moral reference point that cannot be reduced to the internal
workings of the self. He teaches and preaches that call and personally
embraces it in such a way that it has seen his own marriage through
troubled times. But the notion of a transcendent call also raises the
specter of legalism, that well-worn label that can be indiscriminately
applied to virtually any moral principle that limits human freedom. An
unthinking and narrow kind of legalism does, of course, exist, but in
our day people are equally as likely to personalize their moral values
in such a way that they cannot publicly articulate why anyone else
should be guided by them. In this way Pastor Stan's views on divorce
thus present us with a basic dilemma. He espouses, albeit nebulously,

a transcendent marital ethic, which he conceives in Christian terms as a call. But how does he relay that call to others, specifically to those who may have "made a bad choice" in marital partners? The accusation that a transcendent demand may be legalistic tends to eviscerate the very notion of call. Indeed the almost knee-jerk concern about legalism implies that Stan recognizes, and to some extent holds, a privatistic view of morality for which therapeutic language is more politically correct.

Jenni, a "thirty-something" woman who works in a hospital, has been a Christian for as long as she can remember. She generally agrees that Christians should shun divorce ("I think on the whole that's probably true") but allows that there are exceptions.

> I think that some Christians have used and abused the opportunity to get out of marriages that are difficult, and I think it is a lot easier to go it on your own after a while than to keep on keeping on. But I think that there are situations, and the Bible has allowed for them, that are appropriate for divorce. I think there are situations that . . . if you don't have two who are committed to making it work, it isn't going to work. I think separation is a really appropriate option, and giving some time for things to work through. But I would not feel comfortable with saying all Christians should not get divorced.

The interviewer pressed her to specify in which situations divorce might be justified, and Jenni responded:

> I think certainly physical abuse, safety, emotional abuse, sexual abuse. I know I could not stay in a marriage if I had a partner sexually molesting my children. I would have to absolutely distance myself. There is no way to come back and trust that person and respect them in the same way and have that same level of intimacy when such a violation has taken place. I think safety always has to be the number one factor.

Other interviewees cited similar reasons. Without attacking the validity of her statement, we should observe that it could easily have come from the lips of a therapist. She states that there are situations in which divorce is appropriate for Christians and that the Bible allows for these. In what way, however, does the Bible address such issues as personal safety, emotional abuse and the sexual molestation of children? Jenni recognizes that there are biblical grounds for not turning Jesus' teaching into a new and absolute law. But this seems to serve as a general justification for beliefs that are held on extrabiblical grounds.

She is not alone in this. It is quite common for Christians to cite the Bible as authorizing a variety of beliefs, while being unable to specify exactly where and how the Bible says what they think it does. One of the interviewees, a pastor in his sixties, distinguished himself by actually citing the text where Jesus taught about divorce; unfortunately he cited the *wrong* text, pointing to Mark 7 instead of Mark 10. But to her credit, Jenni attempts to articulate a broader vision that goes beyond anything said thus far by the others. In response to the interviewer's question as to why Christians should keep a marriage together, she explains:

I really think God calls us to stick it out. I really believe that God calls us to do the impossible sometimes, and to show our children those situations in which we overcome extreme anger, extreme hurt—that God calls us to turn to him and wait on his miracles, and that no situation is hopeless. So, I think, there are a lot of situations that warrant sticking it out. You know, even just pure personality conflicts over a period of time can be wearing, but I think when we don't just rely on our own power, we're delivered from it.

This is a deeper notion of call than the one used by Pastor Stan. The transcendence of a call from God is a source of hope, one that sustains us through both anger and pain. Moreover, Jenni adds two other dimensions that reinforce this call. The first is the other-directed idea that perseverance is a witness to the next generation. To her this is itself justification for bearing the personal discomfort that Sharon and Morris are so ready to reject. Second, she implies what many Christians believe but find difficulty vocalizing within a therapeutic horizon: that God provides the power to persevere through the gift of his Spirit. Thus while Jenni may falter in articulating the biblical details, her response to the question of divorce exhibits the most specifically Christian horizon thus far.

Finally, consider the response of Lili, a schoolteacher in her late twenties who has been a Christian since her midteen years. The horizon of Jenni's faith, discussed previously, showed itself most explicitly and consistently in her vision of how Christians handle marital difficulties. For Lili, however, the Christian narrative defines the very nature of marriage itself. Instead of directly responding to the question about divorce, she states what for her is the more fundamental norm of permanence: if two Christians marry, then "they should be together forever to exemplify the model that Christ has, that Christ loves his church forever and is not just there for whenever it's easy, to emulate that model of committing everything." Marital commitment, to Lili, is a sign of Christ's continual giving of himself to the church. Of all the respondents cited here, she is the only one to mention the church; to this point the views expressed by these Christians have largely taken for granted that marriage and divorce are private affairs. The ecclesial emphasis, moreover, has practical consequences for how couples deal with marital difficulties. She continues:

> And if they are having some problems with that then I think the Christian community around them should take a role. Maybe their friends haven't been praying for them as much. Maybe the couple should go to a group of up to four other couples where they can share that they all have the same problems and disappointments, and how they dealt with them. The whole group is committed to everyone staying together, because it's God's command.

There is a clear communal stake in marriage, which translates into a more group-oriented, as opposed to privatistic, approach. The story of Jesus forms the moral horizon that dominates how Lili understands marriage. Asked to give her reasons why Christians with problems in their marriages should keep their relationships together, she replies:

> We're part of that model that Christ has love for us. What if Christ just said, "Forget it, you guys are too horrible. I don't want to commit to my side of the bargain with you guys"? Of course, we're always on the erring side, we're always the unfaithful ones . . . so you can see that Christ's love is that unconditional, undying love—it's so amazing that he would do that for us. . . . It's the same thing that we, with Christ's power, can aspire to. . . . Even though the other person might be really not doing their part anymore, then we have that power to do [our part]. Since we know about that kind of love, [that] God has given to us personally, then we in turn almost have that obligation or [desire] to do the same thing for someone else—to be gracious, to continue to love—even though maybe for both of them the interest is gone, or there's so much hurt.

Lili implies a notion of sin, though she doesn't use the word. But she does not understand sin as a crime against the self or the rejection of therapeutic rationality. Sin is rather our unfaithfulness to a God who offers us an "undying love" in response. Lili does not regard unconditional commitment as a rule but as an aspiration, whose moral force lies in the response of gratitude. Knowing the love of a gracious God, we in turn show ourselves to be disciples of that God by showing love to one another, even to a spouse to whom we may no longer wish to remain married. This in turn is made possible by participation in a community that understands itself as standing under that divine love, a community that is as committed to its own unity as it is to the unity of marriage.

If these interviews are any indication, Christians differ greatly from each other in terms of how they articulate their faith. In all fairness we should recognize that if each respondent was pressed to articulate his or her views more thoroughly and given more time to do so, it is quite possible that either broader or more nuanced positions might emerge. But in ordinary conversation, which is the form of social intercourse that most of us actually engage in on a regular basis, we are more likely to rely on first responses. Without the commitment to sustain and deepen the dialogue, such responses may well constitute the whole of the conversation, and hence a good part of the moral horizon thus created in the repeated interchanges of a community. It is also important to remember that the statement to which they responded was "Christians shouldn't divorce," not "People shouldn't divorce." The moral horizons elicited should have been particular to the church. As we have seen, however, the interviewees frequently resorted to language that was much more reminiscent of the culture of divorce than of the Christian faith. Theological notions such as sin were redefined by the rhetoric of self-oriented moral viewpoints, and specific biblical warrants for their beliefs were largely absent, even among the pastors. Nevertheless, some of the responses, especially Lili's, indicate that a specifically Christian horizon is still discernible within the church.

Luke Timothy Johnson reminds us of the church's responsibility to align both its behavior and its ethics, regarding issues such as divorce, with scriptural norms:

Taking the texts seriously means that in our ecclesial—as well as personal—decisions we are willing to take our stand over against as well as under the text. Do we allow divorce in our community despite Jesus' clear condemnation of divorce? Then we do not live in accord with this text. To be faithful to the Scripture, we cannot suppress its reading; we must be able to say *why* we do not live in accord with its clear directive. This means that we must find *authorization* for our position somewhere else in these writings.[29] Other perspectives may, of course, be relevant. In any particular instance of marital strife we may need to consider the rights of the individuals involved, the therapeutic aspects of the case or even the economic implications. A specifically Christian response, however, is neither controlled nor justified by these horizons. Nor is the church merely the guardian of biblical texts that have been fashioned into ironclad rules of conduct. The church is a moral community, where the ecclesial and personal spheres interpenetrate. That community practices discernment, and that discernment is bounded by the moral horizon of the biblical text.

I hope that my divorced sisters and brothers do not understand me to be pointing a finger of condemnation at them. I do believe that the New Testament clearly teaches against divorce; but it also speaks against gossip and disrespect for one's parents, and I suspect that far fewer of us would escape from these charges. My intention is not to castigate but to illustrate—to use Christian attitudes toward divorce as a test case for the cultural analysis of the preceding chapters. The church lives at the intersection of cultures, a culture of divorce and a culture of permanence, and Christians speak conflicting languages when trying to articulate what they believe. Divorce is only one prominent issue; the same could potentially be said about any other matter that may be gathered under the rubric of family values. In this way we are all implicated to a greater or lesser degree. The question is not simply whether divorce is right or wrong, whether it is to be lauded, tolerated or damned. The church's task is not to draw up an eternal list of family do's and don'ts and then congratulate itself for being a champion of family values. Rather, the questions that the church should be asking are put thus by Richard Hays:

> What must we say to bear witness against shallow and false understandings of marriage in our culture, just as Jesus and Paul bore witness against shallow and false understandings of marriage in

theirs? What must we say and do to form our communities so that they bear witness to God's creative intent for the permanent one-flesh union of man and woman in Christ? When these become the framing questions for our normative discourse, we will find creative ways to make the New Testament's witness against divorce speak to our time, just as the New Testament writers found creative ways to make Jesus' teaching against divorce speak to theirs.[30]

The normative question, in other words, is not what family values we should hold but what kind of a church we should be in order to witness to the truth of the gospel. The church's participation in cultural debates about family values cannot take precedence over this far more fundamental matter. We must learn to discern the extent to which cultural narratives captivate our moral vision, and determine to engage in the reconstructive work of ordering our language and behavior to the horizon of the biblical narrative. The language of family values has become too politicized to be serviceable in this regard; I submit that what the church needs instead is to revitalize the language of Christian virtue. This is the burden of part two of this book.

Part II

CHRISTIAN VIRTUE

· ·

SIX

FROM VALUES
TO VIRTUE

....

Instead of talking about "family values," everybody would be better off
talking about the virtues that a decent family tries to inculcate.
JAMES Q. WILSON[1]

The kind of character necessary to sustain the kind of family
Christians care about involves more substantive convictions than the family
itself can provide. Put simply, if we have not first learned what it means to be faithful
to self and other in the church, then we have precious little chance of learning it
through marriage and the family. Marriage and family may help reinforce,
or even awaken us to, what we have learned in the church;
but it cannot be the source of the fidelity necessary for either marriage or family.
STANLEY HAUERWAS[2]

Observers of our culture, across the political and ideological spectrum, generally agree that there are serious problems confronting the contemporary American family. The disagreement is in what constitutes a problem and what is to be done about it. In actuality the family values debate is at least two debates, one about the state of the family and one about the role of values. As David Blankenhorn writes, for example, for over two decades "policy makers and other opinion leaders in the United States have been engaged in a vigorous and often politically divisive debate over 'the family' and 'family values.' " He proceeds to assert confidently that the "old debate is over because one side won. . . . Child well-being is declining. The family is weakening.

Case closed."³ His conclusion is that the empirical evidence overwhelmingly points to a diagnosis of family decline rather than merely change. If we assume, with Blankenhorn, that the evidence is indeed this unambiguous, we might agree that the debate about the family is over. But what about the debate over values? If the issue regarding the state of the American family is decided, are the questions of values resolved as well? Not likely. Even if all scholars and policymakers were to agree, for example, that child well-being is the primary indicator *and* that American children are worse off now than they were a decade ago, this does not mean that they would agree on the causes and solutions. In the current political climate any proposed solution is still likely to be perceived as promoting the values of a particular special interest or political agenda.

The values debate, in other words, is still alive. We have seen that nearly all the Christians surveyed for this book believe, to a greater or lesser extent, that America is in the grips of a crisis of family values. Similarly, a 1994 *Newsweek* poll revealed that 76 percent of the American public agree with the statement that "the United States is in a moral and spiritual decline."⁴ If the debate now seems less prominent than in the recent past, it is probably because people have begun to tire of it. Our values may be strongly and passionately held, but we soon run headlong into others who are equally passionate about opposing values. What then? As others have noted, it is not true that there are no common values that Americans share. Stephen Carter, for example, calls this notion "dangerous nonsense" and asserts that "on the basics, our agreement is broad."⁵ But the hyperindividualism of our times makes it more and more difficult to establish a common and morally binding framework within which to proceed with the discussion. In practice we generally opt for one of two choices: to become increasingly strident in our opposition or to withdraw into the mutually tolerant silence of relativism.

In the end, to frame our current difficulty as a problem of values is counterproductive. This is because the modern language of values already presupposes that values are relative and suspects that any tradition that possesses the capacity to bind us morally is only a thinly disguised manifestation of some particular group's desire to dominate. Friedrich Nietzsche is paradigmatic of this understanding of values. Gertrude Himmelfarb comments on how a Nietzschean interpretation of values came to replace the older and more stable notion of Victorian virtue:

It was in the 1880s that Friedrich Nietzsche began to speak of "values" in its present sense—not as a verb, meaning to value or esteem something; nor as a singular noun, meaning the measure of a thing . . . but in the plural, connoting the moral beliefs of a society. . . . His "transvaluation of values" was to be the final, ultimate revolution, a revolution against both the classical virtues and the Judaic-Christian ones. The "death of God" would mean the death of morality and the death of truth—above all, the truth of any morality. There would be no good and evil, no virtue and vice. There would be only "values."[6]
At our point in history we take for granted the relativism of values and suspect that any who attempt to enforce their values on others are infringing on individual freedom. As Alasdair MacIntyre notes, Nietzsche discards the Enlightenment attempt to ground morality on an objective and rational basis as an illusion. But rather than discredit the notion of an autonomous moral subject, he advocates that we "let will replace reason and . . . make ourselves into autonomous moral subjects by some gigantic and heroic act of the will." Morality, finally, becomes nothing but an exercise of naked will: "if there is nothing to morality but expressions of will, my morality can only be what my will creates."[7]

Here we see the stark moral isolation of the modern individual. But philosopher Charles Taylor rejects this kind of moral solipsism as incoherent. What make self-choice possible as a moral ideal are "horizons of significance" that define some choices as weightier than others. If all choices are equal, then choice itself becomes trivial. As Taylor puts it, "Following Nietzsche, I am indeed a truly great philosopher if I remake the table of values. But this means redefining values concerning important questions, not redesigning the menu at McDonald's."[8] The significance and meaning of a human life cannot be defined solely by internal standards or willful self-determination. Authentic identity is defined against the backdrop of the transcendent. Again to quote Taylor, "To shut out demands emanating from beyond the self is precisely to suppress the conditions of significance, and hence to court trivialization."[9]

The Paradox of Values Language

Taylor points the way toward recognizing a paradox embedded in the language of family values itself. On the one hand, as the preceding discussion would suggest, values language is a poor basis for articulating a truly transcendent dimension of human identity. Our modern understanding of values, typified by Nietzsche, is too susceptible to the divisive pulls of self-interest and moral autonomy. On the other hand, the very notion of family values aspires to something higher. It attempts to identify something of significance that transcends the individual self. To use again Gillis's distinction, the families we live *by* embody ideals that make the families we live *with* seem pale and insubstantial by comparison. Anne Borrowdale makes a similar suggestion:

> Most of us see the family as larger than life, symbolic of something important, regardless of whether we love or hate our own kin, and the term "family values" represents all of that. Anything that seems to threaten family life threatens the possibility of love, security, and happiness in general, so it is hard to be entirely objective about it.[10]

More specifically sociologist James Davison Hunter argues that the debate over family values is a debate over our national identity: "If the symbolic significance of the family is that it is a microcosm of the larger society . . . then the task of defining what the American family is becomes integral to the very task of defining America itself."[11] Either way, *family* becomes a codeword for transcendent ideals, the horizon of our significance.

The more we debate family values, the more deeply we become entangled in this modernist paradox. How can we speak consistently and meaningfully of transcendent horizons of significance using moral language that spurns transcendence? Can the language of values be rehabilitated? Is there another option? Here we must consider both postmodern and premodern perspectives.

In some ways, as we have seen, postmodernism represents an exaggeration of the individualistic ideologies that Taylor disparages. But it may also be viewed more positively, as an opportunity to seriously engage our modernist presumptions. Diogenes Allen, for example, interprets postmodernism as the breakdown of modern secularism, which sought to explain anything and everything by rational principles without recourse to religious language and concepts. The modern project, believing that knowledge was inherently good and progress inevitable, sought to found both morality and society on the dictates of enlightened reason. For Allen the erosion of this secular faith leaves an open door, which Christians may use as an opportunity to assert the intellectual viability of their faith.[12]

Certainly scholars other than Allen are stepping through the door. This is particularly important, for example, in fields like psychotherapy, which has played such a vital role in both expressing and shaping emergent American values. Therapists, long steeped in the professional myth of moral neutrality, have begun to acknowledge the frankly moral nature of their craft. Two examples of this literature are given in the following paragraphs. Together they represent heuristically the possibilities for overcoming the values paradox, using both postmodern and premodern perspectives.

Robert Fancher represents the more postmodern option. He locates the practice of therapy solidly within the larger cultural myth of self-determination: "It is partly our illusory faith that we can master our fate, and that mental health care can help us do it, that makes the United States far and away the most therapized country on Earth."[13] Through a penetrating examination of the fields of psychoanalysis, behaviorism, cognitive therapy and biological psychiatry, Fancher presses the thesis that each field represents what he calls a "culture of healing." They are ideologies, each centered on a core of values. Clinicians are trained to see the world through the values and meanings of their respective therapeutic cultures, and they in turn "enculturate" their clients. Fancher insists that the role of empirical science here is ambiguous. As Thomas Kuhn has argued in another vein, a particular community of professionals may continue to promote their theories even in the face of evidence to the contrary.[14] This is not to say that Fancher disparages the practice of therapy. His argument is rather that we should understand honestly what a therapist actually does, and on what grounds. Therapy is a dialogue between a person in distress and a clinician, who functions as an "emissary" of a particular therapeutic culture.[15] It is a modern conceit that our practices can be fully founded on a bedrock of scientific evidence. Fancher calls for a more candid recognition of the lack of such a foundation for therapy and the value-laden nature of the enterprise itself: "The problem with cultures of healing is not that they are cultures. The problem is both that they do not know they are cultures and that they claim to be more than cultures."[16]

While Fancher acknowledges the intrinsically moral nature of therapy as enculturation, he does not hold that the values of these cultures are created out of thin air. They are, in essence, limited embodiments

that's all

of the values of modernism. William Doherty makes a similar point, albeit from a different line of argument. Fancher's analysis presents the various cultures of healing as intentionally replicating their values; Doherty sees therapists reinforcing cultural values by default because of their *lack* of intentionality on moral issues. He laments that therapists who confront moral issues today seem to suffer a form of postmodern paralysis. The psychotherapy profession "lacks a conscious moral tradition," leaving cultural ideals to fill the vacuum. He writes: "If you don't have a coherent framework of moral beliefs, you inevitably fall back on good old-fashioned American individualism—which is, in fact, a far more influential cultural legacy than either Mom or apple pie."[17]

Doherty argues that therapists have by default adopted the modernist emphasis on individual self-interest over responsibility to others. He calls for the reconceptualization of therapy as an intrinsically moral practice. Moral issues such as commitment and truthfulness in relationships, Doherty argues, have always been present during the therapy hour. Therapists, however, typically have not been trained to address such issues with openness and respect. Thus he specifically urges "the cultivation in therapists of the virtues and skills needed to be moral consultants to their clients in a pluralistic and morally opaque world."[18] This radical suggestion, from a well-respected therapist, calls for yet a further step. Not only are therapists to be moral consultants, but such a role requires that therapists be "part of a moral community of colleagues who are struggling with the same issues and part of a broader moral community of diverse individuals and groups."[19]

What can we glean from these two points of view? From a postmodern standpoint, Fancher's critique attempts to deconstruct the modernist pretensions of psychotherapy. (Therapy is not the objective application of technologies of healing but the process of enculturating clients into a world of values, which may or may not provide new and helpful options for clients dealing with specific problems.) Fancher's contribution provides us with a model for reevaluating our entrenched and largely unrecognized modern beliefs.

But where can we go from there? Is it all once again simply a matter of competing values, of choosing from among alternative cultures?

Doherty reaches into the more premodern language of virtue and the associated notion of communities of moral formation. His is a more transcendent approach than Fancher's and may therefore represent a more constructive alternative. But here, too, we should be careful to recognize the limitations. The therapist is a moral consultant, not a priest. The problem with modernism is not, *contra* Fancher, that it disguises the values of the *therapist's* professional culture behind a cloak of science. Rather, the problem is that modernism explicitly excludes moral issues from the scope of therapeutic concern. Thus the morally sensitive practitioner must have the courage to identify the client's moral issues and bring them to light in the therapeutic dialogue.

It is significant that Doherty tends to apply the language of virtue explicitly to the professional and personal development of therapists, but in a much less central way when speaking of the moral responsibilities of clients. He defines virtue as the "predisposition to do what is good or right" and recognizes that virtue is "always defined and practiced within a cultural, religious, or professional tradition."[20] He notes the recent interest in virtue-centered approaches among ethicists, in contrast to the more rule-oriented approach that currently dominates psychotherapy ethics. The problem with virtue ethics, Doherty observes, is "the tendency to create laundry lists of desirable human qualities."[21] His solution is to create a more specific list of virtues that would define the essence of being a good therapist. As we have already seen, such virtues are encouraged by participation in a community of like-minded professionals; to this end he proposes the creation of "network forums" for the discussion of moral concerns that are not addressed elsewhere.[22]

This is helpful, as far as it goes. But the restriction of virtue language to the professional world of the therapist creates an interesting moral split. Although he does not fully articulate it, Doherty seems to suggest that the professional network forums play the role of communities of moral formation, helping therapists to develop and apply their ethical sensibilities. When discussing the client's relationship to her community, however, the moral issues resolve into a matter of reciprocal obligations— either the community's responsibility to its members or vice versa. This is an important insight, but why is there so little here that parallels the discussion of the moral horizons of the professional therapist? Does or should the client have relationships to communities of moral formation? Granted, to address such questions would take Doherty well beyond the scope of his book. But the point here is that Doherty's captivity to a therapeutic framework limits his discussion of virtue. The paradigm of the consulting role ultimately yields two different moral visions: the therapist is the one who engages in self-transcendent dialogue with others who shape her moral horizons, but the client is the heroic individual who must learn to face up to his own moral standards.

Psychotherapy, as we have seen, is a major force in molding our ideals about self and family. These two authors show us that there are pivotal changes afoot in this cultural institution, a revisioning of therapy as an essentially moral endeavor. The centrality of values and ethics comes clearly to the fore. Although they offer tantalizing direction pointers, Fancher and Doherty do not finally escape the values paradox. We are left with multiple cultures of healing, content to acknowledge their speculative roots. Clients who encounter these professional cultures will be challenged to admit their own moral responsibilities in relationships. But this is empowerment, not discipleship; the therapist is a consultant who helps clients to enact their highest moral ideals but shies away from specifying morals in any way that may be deemed coercive. Clients, once again, are left to their own moral horizons. Where is the voice of transcendence?

Again, if these accounts are incomplete, it is because the horizon of psychotherapy limits their scope. Neither Fancher nor Doherty can be faulted for writing within their own professional domain. Still, it is encouraging to note such trends in so formative a cultural institution. The positive side of the postmodern critique is that it creates space for the resurgence of premodern themes. But does virtue language provide a way out of the values paradox? More particularly, how might a virtue ethics rehabilitate or redirect our concern for family values?

The Saltiness of Virtue

As noted in the preface, the debates over family values in recent years have given rise to a new buzzword: *virtue.* Former secretary of education William Bennett's *The Book of Virtues,* a compendium of story and verse, was a massive bestseller and has spawned a cottage industry of books and other media on virtue and character. The endless quarrels over values, it seems, have left Americans with a hunger for something more universal, and into this yawning gap the virtue industry has leaped. Consider the virtues cataloged in Bennett's volume: self-disci-

pline, compassion, responsibility, friendship, work, courage, perseverance, honesty, loyalty and faith. We may disagree as to whether
marriage should be a lifelong commitment, but who wouldn't agree
that perseverance is a desirable trait? We might argue about how
accessible divorce should be, but wouldn't we all insist that the parties
involved show some responsibility? Wouldn't we all aspire to be more
compassionate, courageous, honest and loyal? Virtue language suggests
that relativism is not the last word; beyond our disagreement lies a more
fundamental core of agreement on what constitutes good character.

The burgeoning popularity of virtue rhetoric made the cover of
Newsweek magazine in 1994.[23] Among the so-called virtuecrats cited in
Howard Fineman's cover story were Bill and Hillary Rodham Clinton,
Republican speechwriter Peggy Noonan, law professor Stephen Carter
and, of course, Bill Bennett. While everyone in this diverse group shares
a common interest in rebuilding American character, they disagree over
the exact role that government and religion should play. Some, like Bennett
and the Clintons, support the idea of character education in the public
schools. Bennett himself appears ambivalent about the role of religion in
this kind of moral training, saying, "You can be a virtuous person without
faith in God. I think. I mean I know some people."[24] Others, like Noonan,
are dubious about the involvement of government and point instead to
the morally constructive role of religiously motivated voluntarism.[25]

How substantive is this new virtue rhetoric? Much of it appears to
be merely grafted onto prevailing cultural assumptions without being
allowed to challenge those assumptions at their root. Hauerwas, for
example, expresses skepticism about the "neoconservative" use of
virtue language:

> They want society to recover "traditional values," which they rather
> uncritically identify with virtues, yet they adhere to an ideology that
> undercuts the very values to which they adhere. That is, they want
> a society that makes freedom of the individual the supreme value,
> but then they are upset when some use that freedom to buy
> pornography, and then they fall back into sermonizing about
> "freedom without responsibility."[26]

In other words, even though the rhetoric of virtue may at first seem to
point to something more enduring than values, merely substituting the
language of virtue will not provide an escape from the values paradox.

A true virtue ethic must be allowed to challenge cultural preconceptions, or further paradoxes may result.

Consider, for example, Bennett's teaching on self-discipline, which he interestingly places first in his list of ten virtues to be addressed in his volume. In the introduction to the book, he rightly emphasizes the role of stories in providing each new generation with moral "anchors" and "reference points." Teaching through moral stories, he writes, is a communal act, "an act of renewal. We welcome children to a common world, a world of shared ideals, to the community of moral persons."[27] Contrast this, however, to his description of the virtue of self-discipline: "In self-discipline one makes a 'disciple' of oneself. One is one's own teacher, trainer, coach, and 'disciplinarian.' It is an odd sort of relationship, paradoxical in its own way, and many of us don't handle it very well."[28] If this is virtue, what has happened to the "community of moral persons"? I submit that the paradox that Bennett notes is not merely the self-reflexiveness of being one's own disciple, even though there are philosophical questions about the nature of selfhood that could be addressed here. The more central paradox, for our understanding of virtue, regards the question of what kind of community can have the moral autonomy of the individual as a core "shared ideal." A group of individuals who are governed only by their own moral principles is not in any proper sense a moral community. It is closer to what Bellah calls a "lifestyle enclave," a loose association of people held together only by their common lifestyle preferences.[29]

One might see in Bennett's virtue of self-discipline the ghost of the Protestant work ethic that was so crucial to the rise of American capitalism. It seems a somewhat tepid substitute, say, for the older notion of the cardinal virtue of temperance. But discipline does involve discipleship, and how we understand discipleship is key. To Christians, Bennett's notion of being one's own disciple should at least seem peculiar. In the biblical story the disciples were a ragtag community held together only by their common devotion to the Lord and his teaching. More often than not, the Gospels portray them as obtuse, stubbornly clinging to their narrow preconceptions. They are only scarcely more able to discern the presence of God's kingdom than the bustling crowds. Even after the resurrection, they are stunned, confused and afraid, unable to see clearly the miracle of God unfolding before their eyes. But it is precisely this motley group that is the foundation of the church of which we are now members. Their place in history is not given by their great moral stature as individuals or for their ability to actualize the human potential that had always lain dormant within. Nor is the essence of their discipleship that they had the right "values," at least as we typically understand them. As Jesus taught, their greatness lay in their weakness. Their destiny, and ours, is found only in submission to the transcendent call of God's kingdom. This call establishes a community, the church, which, through its life, witnesses to the present reality of God's reign among humans.

But as was suggested in earlier chapters, we might well raise the question as to how fully the church embodies this discipleship. As we saw earlier in our exploration of family values, there is good reason to believe that the church is as much a subculture as it is an alternative culture. The church is a disciple, in other words, not only of our Lord but of the larger social world it inhabits. Christians trying to articulate what they believe about divorce, for example, are more likely to employ the language of therapy than that of Scripture. Even where biblical references appear, they may be subsumed under the more authoritative ideals of self-fulfillment and freedom of choice. Thus while seeking to concretely incarnate its faith, the church also demonstrates, through its language and actions, values that owe more to cultural ideals than to a communal engagement with Scripture. This includes the notion of the family as a "haven" from the outside world and the veneration of the family as a private domain of affection and spirituality. It includes the ways in which the image of the rights-bearing individual, set free in the consumer marketplace, pervades our discourse. And it includes the manifold incursions of the therapeutic into how we understand our obligations to self and other.

This is not to say that such dual discipleship can or should be avoided entirely. We are social beings. Because of this we will always to some extent reflect the manners, customs and beliefs of the cultures and families into which we were born. Moreover, the church is not called to separate itself from culture but to transform it from within by embodying the presence of God's kingdom. As Jesus taught, the church is like the yeast that leavens the dough (Mt 13:33) and the salt that seasons the food (Mt 5:13). The church is to penetrate, not separate.

It is significant that Jesus uses the metaphor of the church as salt immediately following the Beatitudes. There, at the opening of the Sermon on the Mount, Jesus describes in rich and surprising adjectives the character of true disciples of the kingdom. He pronounces them blessed, a word whose meaning far surpasses our typically insipid notions of personal happiness. He then declares them to be the salt of the earth, that which gives both flavor and zest to life and preserves from decay. It is precisely in the demonstration of the character qualities described in the Beatitudes, in other words, that the church functions as salt.[30] Thus the issue is not whether we are or should be disciples of two realms. Here we should recognize our dual status both as an unavoidable fact of our humanity and as a necessary precondition for relevant witness. The real issue, if you will, is the saltiness of church. What happens when the salt has lost its savor? A society in moral decay needs salt; it needs the church to be the church. But when the church becomes so thoroughly immersed in the values of modernity that the distinctive marks of Christian character are lost to sight, the salt has become useless.

This is the importance of true Christian virtue as over against family values. In a pluralistic, hyperindividualistic and postmodern society, a declaration of family values, even when backed by proposed legislative sanctions, is an insufficient basis for cultural transformation. The language of values itself is already too thoroughly modernist in its presuppositions. The continued use of values language shapes our understanding in subtle ways, conforming our discourse and even our perceptions to secular norms. When this happens, Christians may begin to interpret their identity and distinctiveness more and more in terms of the values that they hold. The church is the church, one might suppose, by making a public stand against abortion. A local congregation may well do so, but this is not what makes it the church, the representation of God's reign.

The nature and quality of the stance that a congregation takes on any public issue grows organically from the type of community that it actually is. A congregation whose life together is saturated by grace, forbearance and sacrificial love will have a public witness that demonstrates those qualities. A congregation where values discourse reigns, however, is probably characterized by a moral and spiritual individualism, where the center of its identity as a group comes more from professing the same values than living under the same story. In a world dominated by values discourse, it becomes possible to believe that who we are as a church is given simply by what we profess and not how we live. Which is more constitutive of the kingdom: debating the morality of abortion or deciding how best to extend God's love to unwanted infants? Which speaks more to the truth of the gospel: taking a vociferous stand against physician-assisted suicide or learning to care for the infirm and dying within our midst? Again, there is nothing intrinsically wrong with either moral debate or political activism, provided both actually grow out of the life of a local community of believers. It is a matter of putting cart and horse in proper order. The community that lives intentionally as the presence of the kingdom of God may come to particular conclusions regarding values and act upon these conclusions. But values, even those considered the "right" values, are an inadequate starting point where true community is the goal.

What then? Do we turn away from the language of values and embrace virtue instead? Yes, but we must keep in mind that even the language of virtue is of little use if it is only used as a code for traditional values. The problem, moreover, is not that the values themselves are "traditional" but that they are presented as a disconnected laundry list of desirable human qualities. Bennett's eclectic collection of stories, for example, is richly diverse, providing a good deal of raw material for moral reflection. But without an organizing center, such an eclecticism makes the book useful only as a sourcebook for individual readers, who may pick and choose from among the tales as consumers of moral insight. Without a unifying narrative, an authoritative story that grounds the various virtues presented, such a collection cannot possibly draw together diverse individuals into a community of moral formation. This may not be a problem for a culture that seeks only to develop morally heroic individuals, but it is entirely inadequate for a church that seeks to fulfill its commission to be the salt of the earth. A world sliding into postmodernism and in search of transcendence cannot finally find it in individuals who live by their own self-made convictions, however praiseworthy those convictions may seem. It finds it rather in communities that by their lives together demonstrate their commitment to horizons of significance beyond the individual self.

But we must consider a potential objection before we turn to discuss the nature of true virtue. Wouldn't the preceding suggest that any transcendent horizon would do? Doesn't this amount to a generic endorsement of any religion or other tradition, provided it was oriented toward the transcendent and practiced consistently? Doesn't this undercut the uniqueness of the Christian faith? In principle, nothing said thus far would argue conclusively that the Christian story is the only horizon of meaning on which truly transformative communities could be based. Doesn't this reduce Christianity to the status of just another option in the religion marketplace?

There are three responses to this. First, we must come to grips with the possibility that to someone who stands outside the faith, that is all Christianity is anyway. The Christian story no longer holds the privileged place that it once did in our history and culture. As some have observed, for example, the role of faith has been virtually erased from the way that the American story is taught to the next generation in our public schools. The practical reality is that no amount of hand-wringing or politicking is going to restore Christianity to its former status in cultural memory.

Second, this book is not intended as an apologia for the Christian faith. Indeed I suspect that too often the apologetic intent to offer a reasoned defense of Christianity has effectively given modern rational ideals precedence over the moral imperative of actually living out the biblical story.[31] The historically and philosophically informed defense of the faith is a valid calling, especially, as discussed earlier in reference to Diogenes Allen, in a postmodern era when such a defense can be heard with renewed openness. But this is a calling for those who have been gifted by God for the task, and even then such gifts are to be exercised within the context of their contribution to the life of the community. To put the matter differently, while it may be the task of some in the body of Christ to demonstrate the reasonableness of the faith, it is the task of all to live it.

Finally, the uniqueness of the Christian faith arises from the particularity of its narrative. The one Creator-God chose a specific people for his own, to be the bearers of his name. To this people he came as God incarnate, the one man Jesus. Through the work of this man, historically bounded in time and space, God accomplished the salvation of all and established again a people who would bear his name. To them also he gave his Spirit, that they might truly live as his representatives in this world until the time when he once again comes to claim his own. The truth of this revealed story is not demonstrated by reasoned argument or archaeological evidence, as important a role as these might play. Ultimately it is the existence of the community that calls on the name of Jesus and lives faithfully by his example that shows the truth of the story. If, therefore, we are concerned to defend the truth and uniqueness of the Christian story, should not our first priority be to live truthfully?

The Nature of Christian Virtue

Having come thus far, it is time to delineate the meaning of *Christian virtue* more explicitly. I approach the task with some reluctance, not presuming to improve on what has already been done by my betters in philosophy, ethics and theology, and from whose writings I have still far more to learn.[32] Part of the difficulty of the task, as Hauerwas writes, is that "there has been no satisfactory, unambiguous moral definition of the virtues."[33] He begins his general discussion of virtue by noting that for the ancient Greeks, the term referred to a combination of both excellence and power, related to a thing's capability to fulfill its proper function. A knife is virtuous if it cuts well and smoothly, and its power to achieve this excellence is related to its sharpness and the temper of its blade. But whereas the excellence proper to a knife is easily identified, it is not so with human beings. The idea of specifically human virtue founders on the difficult question of what constitutes the proper understanding of human nature.

Still, we are apt to associate the notion of virtue with character, or simply with "the kind of person one is."[34] Gilbert Meilaender suggests that character is only one understanding of virtue. Some have understood virtue as the disposition to act rightly. On this account, for example, the virtue of honesty is the predisposition to act and speak truthfully and not merely the act of making true statements. Others think of the virtues as skills that "suit us for life generally."[35] The notion of character, however, is more comprehensive. Character implies continuity and coherence in a historically situated moral agent. It implies not only dispositions or the skills to navigate life; the virtues understood as traits of moral character "influence how we describe the activities in which we engage, what we think we are doing and what we think important about what we are doing. . . . [They] not only suit us for life but shape our vision of life, helping to determine not only who we are but what world we see."[36]

Virtue, in this vein, has to do with the kind of person one is, and the kind of person one is in turn influences how we understand the world and our place in it.

This notion of character, and its relationship to how one envisions life, implies a narrative rendering of the concept of virtue. As we saw earlier, virtue implies some preestablished understanding of the good: the virtue of the knife is known by its capability to cut well. But the case is more complicated when we turn to the question of the excellence of a human life. The meaning of human virtue requires that we define a transcendent goal, a *telos* that constitutes "the good of a whole human life, the good of a human life conceived as a unity."[37]This unity, moreover, is not the unity of abstract principles but the unity of a good story. As some writers have argued, we are already disposed to structure how we understand ourselves in storied terms, even before we actually acquire language. A child learning to understand herself as an active agent in her world seeks out narrative meanings, and these are fashioned from a limited number of stories accepted by the culture in which she lives.[38] The *telos* of human life, the good toward which the perfection of human existence aspires, is defined by a culture's stock of stories. The virtues, understood narratively, are those qualities that, when exercised, direct human life toward these culturally defined ends.

Any given culture, of course, possesses several such stories, some more comprehensive and some less. The postmodern temper is less an abandonment of metanarratives than their democratization. All hierarchy is to be removed from between stories, and our allegiance to them is to be freely given. Once that choice is made, however, the story becomes authoritative, at least for a time, defining for us the virtues appropriate to it. If, for example, one submits to a therapeutic narrative that defines self-fulfillment as the good of a human life, then the courage to leave a stagnant relationship will be defined as a higher virtue than the commitment to an uncertain future. Such a construction is supported by a particular "culture of healing" that trains its clients in how to think and act in terms of its own core narratives. This is similar to what Alasdair MacIntyre refers to as a "living tradition," or "an historically extended, socially embodied argument, and an argument precisely in part about the goods which constitute that tradition." A particular individual's understanding of both the good and her own life history are shaped by the traditions of which she is a part. But as MacIntyre notes, traditions may "decay, disintegrate and disappear" when the relevant virtues are not practiced.[39] Thus the virtues both sustain and are sustained by moral communities that embody narrative traditions.

The church, of course, is that community formed by the story revealed to us in Scripture.[40] It is a story that runs from creation through fall and covenant to incarnation, salvation and eventually the consummation of a kingdom that is already partially present in the believing church.[41] The Christian virtues are those qualities that fit Christians for the kingdom. The most fundamental of these are known as the "theological" or "supernatural" virtues of faith, hope and love. It cannot be the goal of this book to give exhaustive accounts of each. The aim is far more modest: to suggest a narrative interpretation of the virtues that will provide a starting point for a new discussion of the church's relationship to the family in a postmodern society. MacIntyre portrays our current era as one in which the disorder of moral language has created a new "dark ages," and he holds out the renewal of virtue and community as our hope:

> What matters at this stage is the construction of local forms of community within which civility and the intellectual and moral life can be sustained through the new dark ages which are already upon us. And if the tradition of the virtues was able to survive the horrors of the last dark ages, we are not entirely without grounds for hope. This time however the barbarians are not waiting beyond the frontiers; they have already been governing us for quite some time.[42]

MacIntyre pays scant attention to the church, but we should take note of his view nonetheless. If the argument of this book is at all valid, then the church has uncritically adopted a variety of cultural narratives and symbols that assume goals alien to the Christian story. Our discourse, particularly about the family, betrays the inconsistent nature of our values. We will best serve Christian families by first revitalizing the community that has primary responsibility for bearing the narrative of God's reign: the church. That revitalization will in turn require a renewed appreciation for the place of the Christian virtues. The remaining chapters explore the meaning of faith, hope and love for Christian families living in a world increasingly governed by postmodern ideals.

Seven

INDWELLING
THE STORY

The Virtue of Faith

· · · · · · · · · · · · · · · · · · ·

*Even though the divine mystery is inexhaustible,
so that no finite mind can ever be capable of comprehensively knowing it,
the saints in heaven will pass beyond that deficient mode of knowledge which,
in humanity's present state of pilgrimage, goes by the name of faith.*
AVERY DULLES, *The Assurance of Things Hoped For*[1]

*Faith in Jesus means retelling the Jesus stories so that
the life of the teller is interwoven with the tale.
The core of the process is the interaction of two stories—
the life story of the individual and the inherited story of Jesus. . . .
We must take our lives to his and think, feel, and act out of the interaction.*
JOHN SHEA, *Stories of Faith*[2]

Mommy, Daddy, tell me a story." What parent hasn't been plied
by that request? I remember when my children were younger and I
would sit on the floor of their darkened bedroom, spinning new
adventures to make them laugh. For us, as for many families, storytelling
became something of a nightly ritual. Having spent the bulk of my
waking hours in the pursuits of academia, I enjoyed the chance to
indulge in a bit of whimsy with my delightfully receptive son and
daughter. But as has already been suggested, stories and narratives are
not mere fictions for the undisciplined imagination; they are the shape
of imagination itself, giving us a sense of being active agents in a world

with a past, present and future. As Donald Polkinghorne writes:

Narrative is a scheme by means of which human beings give meaning to their experience of temporality and personal actions. Narrative meaning functions to give form to the understanding of a purpose to life and to join everyday actions and events into episodic units. It provides a framework for understanding the past events of one's life and for planning future actions. It is the primary scheme by means of which human existence is rendered meaningful.[3]

Stories can evoke a full range of emotional responses, and some make us think and wonder about life not only as it is but as it could be. Good stories give us the vision of the character to which we aspire, the goals worthy of a life well lived.

As we have seen in chapter three, stories have come to occupy a peculiar place in the postmodern world. On the one hand, they have grown in personal importance. Our very sense of self is held to be narrative in its contours; the telling of a coherent story pulls together and gives meaning to the various experiences of our world and the people in it. We become the stories that we tell about ourselves, and the avant-garde of psychotherapy promotes an understanding whereby problems in life may be edited out by a judicious rewrite. On the other hand, even while the category of narrative takes central stage in our understanding of self, the radicalization of modern ideals engenders a postmodern suspicion of metanarratives.

All of us are heir to the grand stories of our own culture, which define everything from our national identity to the nature of the good life. These cultural stories transcend individual constructions, providing the social stock of knowledge from which individual narratives are constructed. But those of a postmodern temper are wary of the received authority of such stories. Having been socially transmitted rather than individually chosen, metanarratives are suspected of working an unconscious and oppressive influence. Any narrative that makes universal truth-claims is understood as inherently oppressive, and it is assumed that we must maintain our freedom in the face of such stories. The truly enlightened soul will accept their demise and take up the heroic task of constructing her own meanings.

Such postmodern suspicion would seem to be justified by the way some stories are used to manipulate the emotions of children. Looking

again at William Bennett's *The Book of Virtues,* for example, we read
stories illustrating the virtue of self-discipline, in which the improper
behavior of children brings dire consequences. In "The Story of
Augustus, Who Would Not Have Any Soup," Heinrich Hoffmann tells
in verse of a boy who always ate what was put before him.[4] One day,
however, Augustus stubbornly refused to eat his soup, and he continued in this behavior for four days. On the fifth day the poor disobedient
boy died of starvation! We can note in passing the sheer implausibility
of the story itself. Are we really meant to suppose that a formerly robust
boy would persist in this type of rebellion to the point of death? Then
what are we to learn of virtue from this sad tale? The one-dimensionality
of Hoffmann's portrayal suggests parody rather than edification: the
verse may have been written more for the amusement of frustrated
parents than for the moral instruction of recalcitrant children. But let
us assume, as Bennett does, that the story serves to illustrate "the
inevitable result of not eating enough of the right stuff."[5] If this was
Hoffmann's intent, then the moral weight of the story does not seem
to lie in its capability to inspire virtue by positive example but in the
fear it provokes in an unreasoning child.

   This is even more the case with Hilaire Belloc's "Jim."[6] The story is
of a spoiled little boy who refuses to hold on to his caretaker's hand
during a trip to the zoo. A lion springs at young Jim and begins to eat
him. Nearly half of the verse is taken up by a tongue-in-cheek yet grisly
description of Jim's fate. The lion begins with the feet and eats the child
bit by bit; by the time the animal's keeper forces the beast to release
the child, only the head is left. Jim's father, presumably a model of
self-discipline himself, gathers his children around to use their unfor-
tunate brother's story as an example of the importance of obeying
adults. Bennett's commentary, likewise, adopts the same moral position
that Belloc assigns to the father: what happened to Jim illustrates "the
kind of gruesome end that comes to children . . . who in general cannot
bring themselves to hold on to the hand they are told to hold."[7] Here,
too, though Belloc was known in part for his comic verse, Bennett's
brief commentary seems to miss the possibility of parody.

   As potential examples of the narrative aspects of moral instruction,
these stories and Bennett's interpretation of them seem to achieve little
more than frightening children into compliance. Do we as parents lack

the ability to articulate a more compelling story? Why would we tell our children a story like Laura Richards's "To the Little Girl Who Wriggles," in which the parents suggest that if their daughter doesn't stop squirming in her seat, she will turn into an eel and be swallowed by a shark?[8] This is not to say that fear is never justified. There is good reason for children not to run out into the street heedlessly; nor can we allow young children to wander off by themselves in a zoo or amusement park. But compliance is not yet self-discipline, and obedience born of fear is not virtue. If this is all there is to the relationship between story and moral instruction, then postmodern theorists have good reason to be skeptical.

The matter becomes particularly important when considering the religious stories that parents tell their children. Can the religious parent pass on a tradition without "oppressing" children, depriving them of the right to freely choose? Christians who were interviewed for the RVP were asked to respond to the statement "Parents should let their children decide for themselves what religion they will follow, if any." The majority of the interviewees stated that they must provide guidance for their children by word and deed while they are young, but that their children will have to make up their own minds when they come of age. What is interesting is the way in which the language of choice itself was largely unquestioned. Many parents automatically reacted to the statement by remarking that they could not "force" their children to believe; they could only "expose" them to the gospel and hope they make the right choice. But this is an extremely limiting moral framework for understanding the transmission of a tradition. It is a far cry, for example, from the words of Moses delivering the law to the Israelites on the eve of their crossing over into the land of promise. Preparing to deliver the Ten Commandments to a new generation, he addresses them with these words:

> Hear, O Israel, the statutes and ordinances that I am addressing to you today; you shall learn them and observe them diligently. The LORD our God made a covenant with us at Horeb. Not with our ancestors did the LORD make this covenant, but with us, who are all of us here alive today. (Deut 5:1-3)

The fact is that it *was* the previous generation with whom the Lord made the covenant recorded in the book of Exodus. It is important that Moses did not say, "The Lord made a covenant with your ancestors; I will therefore expose you to this covenant, and you must choose whether or not to follow it." This does not mean, of course, that the Israelites were not free to choose disobedience. But Moses establishes the moral horizon for the current generation by recalling the history of God's relationship to his people and setting his audience firmly and confidently within that narrative context.[9]

Curiosity about the boundaries and meaning of human existence seems natural to young minds. In their attempts to construct meaning, however, children are not born postmodernists. Much to the consternation of the agnostic parent, the innocent but direct questions of their children may slice straight through even the most carefully nuanced and politically correct of answers. Martha Fay relates this honest story about an interaction with her daughter:

> You never really understand how handy the story of Adam and Eve is until, barely grasping the matter yourself, you've explained evolution to a four-year-old and been rewarded with "But how did the first person get born?" Nor is it possible to fully appreciate what a social lubricant the assumption of a shared piety is until you've tried to climb back out of the hole you've dug for yourself by broad-mindedly announcing, "No, we don't believe in God, but lots of other people do." "Why do they?" was her initial follow-up, later to alternate with the equally blunt, but surely more pertinent, "Why don't you?"[10]

But is the "shared piety" to which Fay refers only a "social lubricant," a useful escape hatch for parents who are stymied by their children's spiritual queries? Of what significance are religious stories to the relationship between parents and their children?

A narrative perspective on virtue, and more particularly the virtue of faith, must go beyond the mere usefulness of stories in the moral education of children, situated in a moral framework of individual choice. Let us begin by making the assumptions of a narrative approach more explicit. As in the preceding quotation from Polkinghorne, narrative is to be understood as a fundamental means by which we organize human experience.[11] We are predisposed to gather together the events of our lives into a coherent whole by integrating them into a plot, an organizing theme, from which the events derive their meaning and significance.[12] We understand ourselves as active in history, bringing past experience to bear on present situations, orienting ourselves toward immediate or distant future goals. Narratives, in other words, give order to what Jerome Bruner calls "the vicissitudes of human intentions" by organizing our goal-directed activity into a coherent plot.[13]

There is no single plot or story that is logically *demanded* by any particular set of experiences, regardless of how passionately we might defend our own narrative interpretations. But not all narratives are possible, because individuals are born into social groups that exhibit two limiting characteristics. First, cultures provide a preexisting stock of prototypical stories and characters that form the basis for individual variations.[14] Second, cultures tend to be conservative, reinterpreting deviations from established patterns of belief in such a way that they fit within accepted narrative norms.[15] The upshot is that the construction of the narrative of one's life is not first of all an individual accomplishment but a process of socialization. As Bruner argues,

> While we have an "innate" and primitive predisposition to narrative organization that allows us quickly and easily to comprehend and use it, the culture soon equips us with new powers of narration through its tool kit and through the traditions of telling and interpreting in which we soon come to participate.[16]

It is the task of our key social institutions to preserve and transmit these narrative traditions. The family, in particular, is the site not simply of biological reproduction but of *social* reproduction, through which the values and traditions of one generation of a society are preserved to the next.[17]

It follows from this and the discussion of the preceding chapter that the virtues are narrative-dependent. The cultural stock of stories defines a limited number of understandings of the *telos* of a human life, and the virtues in general are those qualities that best equip a person to achieve such ends. If the good life is defined by the copious consumption of consumer goods, for example, then the relevant virtues are those that fit a person for success in the marketplace, such as industriousness, competitiveness and even, to an extent, greed. This is parodied in postmodern popular culture by the interplanetary multiculturalism of the television series *Star Trek: Deep Space Nine*, set aboard a space station populated by an assortment of beings from around the galaxy. One of the regular characters is a bartender named Quark, from a race known as the Ferengi. To the Ferengi the world of commerce is the ultimate moral horizon, and profit is the motive that drives all decisions. They live by a moral code, committed to memory, called "The Rules of Acquisition," which includes such sage aphorisms as "Once you have their money, never give it back." Pure fantasy? No, because we find the character humorous. Were we completely unable to identify with the moral context that drives Quark's profit-mongering, we would simply find him bizarre. The point is that even greed, which traditionally would be classed among the deadly sins, can be treated as virtuous given the proper cultural (or planetary?) narrative.

Faith, Virtue and Narrative

If, then the virtues are narrative-dependent, how should we understand the virtue of faith? As the foregoing would suggest, the word *faith* has a broader application than *Christian faith*. In the wider sense the term refers to "a constant feature of human cognition and existence" in which convictions rest "upon a free and trusting commitment."[18] More specifically, Brian Walsh and J. Richard Middleton identify faith as a *commitment to a worldview* that "shapes our vision for a way of life."[19] That worldview is narrative in form, framed by four basic questions that provide the basic elements of the story. The first question, "Who am I?" defines the identity of the protagonist and by extension the other characters of the story. The answer to the question reveals an underlying anthropology or theory of human nature. The second question, "Where am I?" provides the setting for the story and depends upon metabeliefs about the nature of reality and the world we inhabit. Third is the question "What's wrong?" indicating the conflict or dramatic tension that drives the story, implying broader beliefs about the nature of evil. Finally, the question "What's the remedy?" suggests the way in which the dramatic conflict is to be resolved, relying upon implicit images of redemption or salvation.[20] They suggest, for example, that a prototypical cultural narrative for the United States could be rendered as follows:

> I am me, an individual, the free and independent master of my own destiny. I stand in a world full of natural potential, and my task is to utilize that potential to economic good. While I am hindered in this task by ignorance of nature and lack of tools for controlling it, nevertheless my hope rests in the good life of progress wherein nature yields its bounty for human benefit. Only then will all find happiness

in a life of material affluence, with no needs and no dependence.[21] We can see in this generic narrative glimpses of the moral horizons discussed in previous chapters. Our culture, of course, supplies a variety of possibilities for constructing more specific life stories that carry similar themes. For the present it is sufficient to note that commitment to such a narrative context constitutes an incipient form of faith.

Within our cultural context, the stories we encounter through novels, television and the movies may evoke a powerful narrative resonance in us, a palpable experience of religious significance. Robert Jewett, for example, reflects on the immense popularity of the movie *Star Wars,* first released in 1977 and then rereleased twenty years later to a new generation of enthusiastic fans. He observes that many Christian families attended the movie several times, viewing it as a cinematic embodiment of the Christian story of the triumph of good over evil. One woman saw the movie more than forty times, using it as an emotional pick-me-up when she felt depressed. Jewett argues that this involves "more than mere entertainment. It involves a ritualistic reenactment of a story of salvation, comparable to the function of religious rituals studied by anthropologists and theologians."[22] The *Star Wars* gospel even has its own therapeutically minded religion: we have the power to accomplish miracles, if we will only let go of conscious intention and stretch out with our feelings to unite with the Force that pervades all living things.

Again the objection might be anticipated: is Christian faith, then, no different from belief in the Force? Are we to adopt a postmodern stance that all faiths are equal? If it is true that human experience is narratively structured, then all faiths are indeed *structurally* equivalent inasmuch as they involve commitment to a story, to which general categories of literary analysis might be applied. It must be added, of course, that the uniqueness of Christian faith is bound up with the unique claims of its story, the so-called scandal of particularity that the sole Creator-God has chosen to reveal himself through the singular person of Jesus Christ. This said, however, we must recognize that other stories also make unique claims, and none can be completely legitimated on the context-free basis of universal reason. This is not to say that the criteria of reason do not apply, only that the authority of a particular story does not ultimately rest upon the rational demonstration of its truth.

choose?

All narratives, the Christian story included, require a response of faith. There are, and always will be, a variety of stories available to which a person may give allegiance. A person may reject Christ and embrace some vague New Age notion of an all-pervasive life force, a higher power or even a highly personalized religion such as "Sheilaism." What we must come to terms with is that in the end, to uphold the necessity of faith in a pluralistic world means that we cannot eliminate rival traditions, for to do so would dismiss the very need for faith itself.

What then is Christian faith? We may approach the answer with three interpenetrating concepts: faith as surrender, as vision and finally as the commitment to indwell the Christian story, the narrative of the reign of God inaugurated in Christ. Understood first as a gift of grace, faith is "a self-surrender to God as he reveals himself. . . . Faith in its full and integral reality is more than a merely intellectual assent or an act of blind trust. It is a complex act in which assent, trust, obedience, and loving self-commitment are interwoven."[23] It is a personal act in response to the revelation of a personal God: "Faith in its proper and active sense describes the response of one person to another in trust and obedience. . . . Theological faith is the response by a human being to the call of God."[24] Again, although there is rational content to the revelation, faith itself is not merely the intellectual acknowledgment of that content but a response to personal disclosure of God:

> In speaking to men God does not cause them to know objective facts, but He does throw open to them His own being. The subject matter which forms the essential content of revelation—that man has been elected to participate in the divine life; that that divine life has been offered to him, in fact already given—this subject matter owes its reality to nothing but the fact that it is pronounced by God. It is real in that God reveals it. . . . Divine revelation is not an announcement of a report on reality, but the "imparting" of reality itself.[25]

Second, faith involves a renewal of our vision. Paul tells the Corinthian church that "we walk by faith, not by sight" (2 Cor 5:7). This does not mean the sightlessness of blind obedience, but the adoption of an alternative vision that challenges worldly empiricism: "We look not at what can be seen but at what cannot be seen; for what can be seen is temporary, but what cannot be seen is eternal" (2 Cor 4:18). A similar theme is struck by the writer of Hebrews, for whom the metaphor of vision is central to the understanding of faith: "Faith is the assurance of things hoped for, the conviction of things not seen" (Heb 11:1). The roll call of biblical exemplars of faith shows that these men and women trusted in the promises of God despite what they could see with their eyes. Noah, for example, built the ark without any external evidence of an impending flood, while Abraham set out for the Promised Land without so much as a map. The author of Hebrews reminds us that

all of these died in faith without having received the promises, but from a distance they saw and greeted them. They confessed that they were strangers and foreigners on the earth, for people who speak in this way make it clear that they are seeking a homeland. If they had been thinking of the land that they had left behind, they would have had opportunity to return. But as it is, they desire a better country, that is, a heavenly one. Therefore God is not ashamed to be called their God; indeed, he has prepared a city for them. (Heb 11:13-16)

Faith is not blindness to reality but the ability "to see reality from God's perspective."[26] Whereas the empiricism of human reason declares "I'll believe it when I see it," by faith we see when we believe.

Furthermore, faith maintains its vision even in the absence of signs. Faith is a favorite theme of John the Evangelist. He places the account of Jesus' cleansing of the temple at the beginning of his public ministry, after which the Jewish leaders press for a sign to authenticate what seems to be a forthrightly messianic act (Jn 2:13-22). But would such a sign have elicited true faith? The only sign that Jesus would grant them was his resurrection, which was understood only by those who already believed in him, and even they did not fully comprehend the magnitude of the event. As Lesslie Newbigin comments, "The demand for a visible sign means that the one who makes the demand keeps ultimate sovereignty in his own hands. He has himself prescribed the tests by which divinity must prove itself."[27] John, for his part, portrays signs as an inadequate basis for faith (e.g., Jn 2:23-25). Nevertheless, there are signs given by grace to the faithful. The healing of the official's son, for example, is counted a sign in the face of the official's faithful and obedient response to Jesus' command to return home (Jn 4:46-54). Again to quote Newbigin:

Faith begins with obedience to the words of Jesus. But to those who take that path there are indeed "signs" which lead believers on to a fuller and more understanding faith. . . . Within a context of obedient discipleship Jesus does graciously grant signs which enable the disciple to go forward on the path of faith.[28]

Faith is a surrender in trust and obedience to God's self-revelation, in which we come by degrees to see the world and our place in it as God does. While faith is not dependent on signs, God may yet in his grace grant signs to encourage faith where it already exists.

We may enfold this discussion into a narrative perspective by conceiving of faith as the virtue by which we are committed to "indwelling" the story of the reign of God. What does this mean? First, as already suggested, faith implies the ability to see the world differently, which raises the question of how to live in the world that is thus disclosed. As Stephen Fowl and L. Gregory Jones have observed,

> It is true that becoming a Christian involves living in a "new" world. . . . Scripture does not "create" anything *de novo;* in the encounter with Scripture, believers' "old" selves and perceptions of reality are confronted with that new world. Hence the emphasis must be placed on *learning* to live in that world, for it involves not only discerning the "new" world but also diagnosing what is wrong and corrupting about the "old" one.[29]

Faith, in other words, provides an alternative rationality; it creates a new moral horizon that exists in tension with the previous horizons by which we have understood the nature of the world and how we should act within it. But if the assumptions outlined earlier are valid, then this rationality by which we learn to live in the world disclosed by faith will necessarily have narrative contours. Faith does not draw us into a raw world of images, ideas or sense impressions, but a new story. John Shea writes:

> Faith in Jesus is a process of relating our own lives to his life story. . . . [It] entails a process of handing power over to his story and receiving it back into our own. We allow the life story of Jesus to focus the areas of importance in human life and to give perspective on those areas.[30]

Similarly, Newbigin stresses the narrative context of discipleship:

> There is no way by which we come to know a person except by dwelling in his or her story and, in the measure that may be possible, becoming part of it. The person who allows the biblical story to be the all-surrounding ambience of daily life and who continually seeks to place all experiences in this context finds that daily life is a

continuous conversation with the one whose character is revealed in the biblical story taken as a whole.[31]

Newbigin's language of "dwelling in" a story draws on the epistemological theories of Michael Polanyi, who openly declares that "only a Christian who stands in the service of his faith can understand Christian theology and only he can enter into the religious meaning of the Bible."[32] Polanyi's notion of indwelling relies on his distinction between *focal* and *subsidiary awareness*, which he illustrates by reference to the use of tools. When I drive a nail with a hammer, I am focally aware of the nail but only subsidiarily aware of the hammer. In a sense I focus on the nail *through* the hammer, as the tool becomes an extension of my arm; I *indwell* the hammer. Were I to shift my focus to the feel of the hammer, I would no longer be able to hit the nail properly. More generally, Polanyi contends that any act of focal awareness depends on a background of subsidiary particulars to which we are personally committed but only tacitly aware.[33]

Thus it might be said that we indwell not only tools but languages and moral horizons. When asked to focus on questions of family values, Christians respond on the basis of tacit moral commitments that may escape their immediate conscious awareness. In a pluralistic and postmodern world we indwell competing rationalities, of which the Christian story is only one. But it is precisely here that our description of the virtue of faith as the commitment to indwell the Christian story becomes relevant. The community of faith seeks in all aspects of its life to submit its understandings to the horizon of the biblical narrative. In the New Testament the record of the Acts of the Apostles runs to twenty-eight chapters; (the church should see itself as living in the unfolding of the twenty-ninth chapter.) This is less the critical appropriation of principles from the Scripture than it is an act of narrative imagination. As Newbigin writes:

> Our proper relation to the Bible is not that we examine it from the outside, but that we *indwell* it and from within it seek to understand and cope with what is out there. In other words, the Bible furnishes us with our plausibility structure. This structure is in the form of a story. . . . If we follow these suggestions we get a picture of the Christian life as one in which we live *in* the biblical story as part of the community whose story it is, find in the story the clues to knowing God

as his character becomes manifest in the story, and from within that indwelling try to understand and cope with the events of our time and the world about us and so carry the story forward.[34]

Note the assumption that the faith narrative is first the story of a people, a community, and not of individual Christians. It is, from one angle of vision, the story of God's reign, or what Jesus frequently referred to as the kingdom of heaven. The life of the church is a sign of the moral authority of the kingdom in a pluralistic world. Where the church has settled for a privatized faith, it is an ambiguous sign at best.[35] Annie Dillard recalls her religious education by adults who failed to take the transforming narrative of Scripture seriously:

> The adult members of society adverted to the Bible unreasonably often. What arcana! Why did they spread this scandalous document before our eyes? If they had read it, I thought, they would have hid it. They didn't recognize the vivid danger that we would, through repeated exposure, catch a case of its wild opposition to their world. Instead they bade us study great chunks of it, and think about those chunks, and commit them to memory, and ignore them. By dipping us children in the Bible so often, they hoped, I think, to give our lives a serious tint, and to provide us with quaintly magnificent snatches of prayer to produce charms while, say, being mugged for our cash or jewels.[36]

This may shed some light on what Jesus meant when he told his disciples, "Let the little children come to me, and do not stop them; for it is to such as these that the kingdom of heaven belongs" (Mt 19:14). The child is able to see the radical nature of the story of the kingdom in a way that adults long accustomed to other horizons may not. The virtue of faith requires more than just respect for Scripture. It requires commitment to indwelling the narrative in such a way that all other moral horizons are thereby challenged.

The church that bears the story is called to witness through its own life to the authority of that story, in a world in which the moral authority of communal narratives is rapidly dissolving. The postmodern rejection of transcendent authority, ironically, does not eliminate the yearning to receive the meaning of one's life from beyond the self. The consequence is idolatry, where one seeks redemption through the created order.

Idolatry is a way of responding to existence which says that the world we see is all there is. Idolatry flees the terror of contingency and attempts to seize hold of life as a possession. Faith is the response to existence which says that the one who is not seen is most real, and that although contingent, we are established in being every moment by the power of God.[37]

Christian faith must therefore hold fast to the "conviction of things not seen," resisting the temptation to despair of transcendence and set up false gods through the worship of money, the family or any other created thing. But it must also do this in a way that is not "otherworldly." For the present it is in *this* world that we are called to make manifest the authority of the kingdom. Faith does not engage in a "prideful attempt to free ourselves from a finite location within nature and history."[38] God has created us as finite creatures; the faith appropriate to such beings is a continual learning process whereby we seek to live transformed lives in the real contexts of our families and other groups. These settings are to be understood as "schools of virtue," where God "sets before us others who need our care and faithful commitment."[39] The virtue of faith, in short, exhibits confidence that the kingdom of God is to be made manifest in the particularities of our lived history, while we simultaneously receive the authority of the narrative as a gift from beyond ourselves.

Faithful Families

In what way might the virtue of faith, then, apply to Christian families living in a postmodern society? The Bible does not provide us with a manual on contemporary family life. To expect that it should is to read our modern preoccupation with the family back into the Scripture. If, as we have seen, our concerns about the family are often framed by moral horizons that would seem alien to the American colonists, then they may be even more foreign to the first-century world of the New Testament.

From the standpoint of faith understood as indwelling the story, the question should be what role the social institution of the family plays in nurturing, or possibly hindering, a kingdom perspective. It is instructive to note how, in the vision of the Old Testament, the strongly intergenerational understanding of family and clan creates a joint moral stake between parents and children. The book of Proverbs, for example, is cast in the form of parental instruction, in which the "fear of the LORD" is taught as the foundation of wisdom (see, for example, Prov

1:7; 2:1-6). But more concretely, parents serve an *anamnestic* function. The Greek word *anamnesis* is translated as "remembrance" and is best known to Christians in the words of institution for the Lord's Supper: "Do this in remembrance of me" (1 Cor 11:24-25). Thus, specifically with regard to the ritual observances of the people of God, parents are to teach their children the stories of God's reign.

The Israelites were repeatedly commanded to commemorate the mighty acts of God with monuments and ritual celebrations, which served as exercises in communal memory. The price of forgetting would be to relinquish their very identity as a people. The first Passover, for example, was instituted on the evening just before the Israelites made their exodus from Egypt, when God struck the Egyptians with the last of ten plagues. The Lord instructed Moses that the Israelites were to eat the Passover lamb hurriedly, with their loins girded for travel. They were to mark the doorways to their houses with the blood of the lamb, so that the Lord would pass over their homes when he struck down the firstborn throughout Egypt. Even before the final plague had come, however, God decreed that this day was to be celebrated as a remembrance throughout the generations to come. Thus Moses directed the people:

> You shall observe this rite as a perpetual ordinance for you and your children. When you come to the land that the LORD will give you, as he has promised, you shall keep this observance. And when your children ask you, "What do you mean by this observance?" you shall say, "It is the passover sacrifice to the LORD, for he passed over the houses of the Israelites in Egypt, when struck down the Egyptians but spared our houses." (Ex 12:24-27)

It is assumed that the life of the household will be marked by ritual events that commemorate the mighty acts of God and that the children will naturally express curiosity as to the meaning of these events. When children ask why Israel celebrates the Festival of Unleavened Bread, parents are to respond, "It is because of what the LORD did for me when I came out of Egypt" (Ex 13:8). When they inquire about the consecration of the firstborn, parents are to say, "By strength of hand the LORD brought us out of Egypt, from the house of slavery. When Pharaoh stubbornly refused to let us go, the LORD killed all the firstborn in the land of Egypt, from human firstborn to the firstborn of animals.

Therefore I sacrifice to the LORD every male that first opens the womb, but every firstborn of my sons I redeem" (Ex 13:14-15). When the Lord dammed up the waters of the river Jordan so that the Israelites could cross over on dry land, he commanded Joshua to erect a memorial of twelve stones, one for each of the tribes of Israel. When the memorial had been established in Gilgal, Joshua spoke these words to the people:

When your children ask their parents in time to come, "What do these stones mean?" then you shall let your children know, "Israel crossed over the Jordan here on dry ground." For the LORD your God dried up the waters of the Jordan for you until you crossed over, as the LORD your God did to the Red Sea, which he dried up for us until we crossed over, so that all the peoples of the earth may know that the hand of the LORD is mighty, and so that you may fear the LORD your God forever. (Josh 4:21-24)

The rituals of anamnesis, of remembrance, are the occasions for parents to tell again the story of God's grace and justice toward his people, a narrative act that endows not just the observances but the family itself with meaning and significance. Here shared piety is not the "social lubricant" of which Martha Fay writes. For Christians it is not merely the stories of the Passover or the crossing of the Jordan but the stories of the birth, ministry, death and resurrection of Jesus Christ, the coming of the Holy Spirit, and the acts of the church through the ages, that constitute the narrative backdrop for our particular life stories. Each individual's life is as a subplot within the grand narrative of God's creation and redemption of the world.

Such rituals, however, are not the exclusive occasions for remembrance: our day-to-day lives are to be saturated with the symbolic world of the kingdom. As Moses instructed the Israelites:

Hear, O Israel: The LORD is our God, the LORD alone. You shall love the LORD your God with all your heart, and with all your soul, and with all your might. Keep these words that I am commanding you today in your heart. Recite them to your children and talk about them when you are at home and when you are away, when you lie down and when you rise. Bind them as a sign on your hand, fix them as an emblem on your forehead, and write them on the doorposts of your house and on your gates.[40] (Deut 6:4-9)

The importance of this cannot be overstated. The anamnestic role, the

Request/demand?

responsibility of sustaining communal memory, is not simply a function of church worship and sacrament or of Christian education. It is the responsibility of all Christian parents not merely to tell the stories but to live in such a way that their truth is evident. As Stanley Hauerwas asserts:

> I think we should not admire religious or non-religious parents who are afraid to share their values and convictions with their children. It is a false and bad-faith position to think that if we do not teach them values our children will be free to "make up their own minds." What must be said, and said clearly, is that the refusal to ask our children to believe as we believe, to live as we live, to act as we act is a betrayal that derives from moral cowardice. For to ask this of our children requires that we have the courage to ask ourselves to live truthfully.[41]

Such truthful living is of the very essence of the virtue of faith. Paul Brockelman writes:

> The sacred, then, is experienced as the unconditional demand to transform ourselves and to live righteously or truly. . . . Faith is living in the light of an interpretive understanding of life made manifest narratively. . . . [It is] a mode of being, actively living out a personal story centered on such an interpretive understanding of what it means to be, a way of existing in a world.[42]

Applied to the family setting, this is not a matter of "forcing" children to believe what the parents believe. The range of choices we offer to children is bounded by what we perceive as the demands of the real world. We teach them the manners and customs of our society because we know implicitly that they will need these in the social world. We teach them rules of safety without worrying if we are forcing them to conform to our beliefs against their will. Why, then, should we hesitate to train our children to indwell the story, to see the world through the eyes of faith? Is it that the kingdom is less real, less immediate, less compelling to us? What other moral horizons compete to shape our vision?

Such questions pose important challenges for Christian families in today's world. Of all the social institutions in our culture, it is the family that is the locus of privatization par excellence. Contemporary American society looks to the family as an emotional and spiritual haven, the place where the affective and consumptive goods of life are to be enjoyed. In such a climate a family-centered religious privatism becomes common, particularly among those who have left the organized church, even if only for a time.[43] Religion becomes more and more of a subjective preference, sovereign in the family realm but with little authority beyond. But does a privatized religion have the power and authority to challenge the dominant moral horizons of our culture? In a world of consumer affluence and comfort it is easy to forget our spiritual heritage, the stories of faith that we are directed to retell and embody:

Take care that you do not forget the LORD your God, by failing to keep his commandments, his ordinances, and his statutes, which I am commanding you today. When you have eaten your fill and have built fine houses and live in them, and when your herds and flocks have multiplied, and your silver and gold is multiplied, and all that you have is multiplied, then do not exalt yourself, forgetting the LORD your God, who brought you out of the land of Egypt, out of the house of slavery, who led you through the great and terrible wilderness, an arid wasteland with poisonous snakes and scorpions. He made water flow for you from flint rock, and fed you in the wilderness with manna that your ancestors did not know, to humble you and test you, and in the end to do you good. Do not say to yourself, "My power and the might of my own hand have gotten me this wealth." But remember the LORD your God, for it is he who gives you power to get wealth, so that he may confirm his covenant that he swore to your ancestors, as he is doing today. If you do forget the LORD your God and follow other gods to serve and worship them, I solemnly warn you today that you shall surely perish. (Deut 8:11-19)

Such words should remind us that the commitment to live as a community of the faithful supersedes the seductively privatistic goals of family life. What it means to be a Christian family is not given by cultural definitions of family life with a biblical gloss. It is not to be taken for granted that the family as a social institution is an intrinsic moral good; like any other institution, it too needs to be transformed by being taken up into the reign of God.

To take this view of family life may require a shift in how we think about family ministry in the local church. Parents who come to educational seminars, for example, are typically seeking guidance on how to deal with their children's misbehavior, how to communicate more effectively and so on. To provide parents with skills in these areas is a good and worthwhile ministry, but it is not the central one, nor an end in itself. Parents must be encouraged to recognize and take up their role of discipling their children in the narratives of faith.[44] This is not to say that parents are not concerned about their children's moral and spiritual development. Yet it is too easy simply to accede to the twentieth-century answer: let the experts take care of it. Parents and churches alike rely too heavily on the assumption that Sunday school will be the primary vehicle, by design or default, by which the next generation of Christians are initiated into the divine history. Alternatively, some seem to hold that it is the youth pastor's job to disciple our children and the parent's job to get the kids to church. But is it the mission of the church to be the geographic location at which certain spiritual, educational or psychological services are provided to religiously minded consumers? These may serve the mission (and even this should not be taken for granted), but they are not themselves the mission. Rather, to use Hauerwas's phrase, the task of the church is "to be the kind of community that tells and tells rightly the story of Jesus."[45]

The existence of such a community, I would argue, is necessary if families are to maintain the virtue of faith. There should be an organic and interdependent relationship between the two communities of faith that we call church and family. From one side, we must consider whether or not we have squarely faced the central role of the family in telling the story rightly from one generation to the next. The Bible appears to take as unremarkable the natural role that parents play in the spiritual formation of their children, and local congregations would be wise to build their ministries around that fact. But from the other side, this must not degenerate into either putting the family on a spiritual pedestal to be worshiped or reducing the church to the role of service provider. The Lord is quite clear that the advent of the reign of God relativizes all human institutions, including the family.

To put the matter differently, if the task of faith is to indwell the story of the kingdom, then the church and the family have different and complementary roles in that task. In a broad sense it is the church that bears and legitimates the story; in a narrower sense it is the family that most naturally socializes children into the language and perceptions of that story. The family provides the first training ground in Christian virtue, of those habits and dispositions of thought and behavior that demonstrate the reality of God's reign. Reflecting on the parental discourses of the book of Proverbs, William Brown writes:

> Wisdom . . . serves as the vital link that bridges the generational chasm between parent and child, as well as the social domains of family and community. . . . In this way, the values and virtues of the father are extended into the community as the son is beckoned to make the transition from family to society in a responsible manner. . . . The family . . . provides the foundation and training ground for responsible communal life.[46]

On this last point many family scholars would agree. We must remember, however, that Proverbs comes to us in an era in which wisdom lacks the narrative context of "the fear of the Lord." The virtues specific to the church are not merely those that support civil society or democratic discourse, but those that make it possible to tell the story of Jesus rightly. In the preceding quotation it is the larger community of faith that undergirds and legitimates the moral lessons of parent to child, providing both a context and a reference point for training in virtue. The family is not an end in itself; those of the younger generation are not socialized merely to create more biological units but to take their place among the cloud of witnesses whose lives give testimony to the truth of the gospel.

The moral horizons of our culture exert a subtle and powerful influence over how we view the world and our families. The family is "a community of moral formation and conviction,"[47] whether we choose to recognize it as such or not; all families indwell some moral horizon and will transmit this faith to the next generation. But what of *Christian* faith, the commitment to live consistently within the biblical narrative and the continually unfolding reign of God? As Fowl and Jones declare, "faithfulness to God demands that we exhibit the courage needed to stand against the prevailing wisdom of the day."[48] But given the many cultural pressures described in this book, does the family have the resources on its own to effectively and consistently challenge our cultural narratives, to faithfully indwell the story of the kingdom? Family life is the center of a privatized, consumptive lifestyle; it would take a heroic effort for a family to sustain a different vision from within that center, without the support of a larger community.

This is where the complementarity between the church and the family is important. It is the church that bears the primary task of manifesting to the world the meaning of God's reign. Some of my students have asked, with skepticism and even annoyance, "What do you mean by church? I agree with you if you mean the church universal—but not the local congregation." Such comments, I surmise, stem from negative experiences with particular congregations or denominations that have soured people on the possibilities of true and abiding Christian fellowship in such settings. I agree wholeheartedly that the local congregation is not the only social form that the more universal notion of church can take. But I also am leery of those who settle too easily for criticizing the problem without being part of the solution. Many disgruntled Christians prefer to leave congregations to shop for ones that "meet their families' needs" better, rather than engage in the substantive dialogue that would challenge both them and their community.

Whether embodied in a local congregation or some other face-to-face community of Christians, the church must help parents to envision and carry out their spiritual task. This is done not only for the sake of the family but for the future vitality of the church itself. This is not accomplished by providing expert advice but by being the very community that exhibits within its life together the reign and the authority of the kingdom established by Christ. The living reality of this community stands as the alternative to the postmodern rejection of received authority, a cultural paradigm that has little place for the notion of a self-revealing, transcendent God. The church, in its life as a community, draws families out of their self-enclosed privatism, providing them with the ritual symbols and stories by which they come to interpret their own existence. Church life itself becomes a hermeneutical process by which the living Word of God speaks anew in each generation and in each situation. But the church itself does not replace or usurp the spiritual functions of its families, where children learn firsthand the meaning of Christian maturity, provided by the daily evidence of parents whose lives are demonstrations of God's reign.

Eight

LIVING TOWARD
THE PROMISE

The Virtue of Hope

● ● ● ● ● ● ● ● ● ● ● ● ● ● ● ● ● ● ● ●

Clearly, the dominant values of our culture . . . are values of hopelessness.
WALTER BRUEGGEMANN, *Hope Within History*[1]

*The glory of self-realization and the misery of self-estrangement alike
arise from hopelessness in a world of lost horizons.*
*To disclose to it the horizon of the future of the crucified Christ
is the task of the Christian Church.*
JÜRGEN MOLTMANN, *Theology of Hope*[2]

I was only about twelve years old when I first encountered J. R. R. Tolkien's majestic epic trilogy The Lord of the Rings. I had not been an avid reader as a child, preferring to while away idle moments in front of the television set. Nor had I read much in the fantasy genre; I recall having read only the first three volumes of C. S. Lewis's The Chronicles of Narnia in the fifth or sixth grade. But Tolkien the master storyteller did not simply write a book. He created an entire world called Middle Earth, an enchanted land of incredibly rich texture and history. Once I picked up Tolkien and began to read, I could scarcely put it down again. After school I would hurriedly finish my homework (or skip it altogether) and throw myself on the bed to read. Later, after a hastily eaten dinner, I would eagerly return again to Middle Earth, and there remain until bedtime, when I would close the book and continue the journey in my dreams. Even today, The Lord of the Rings and its predecessor, *The Hobbit,* have become much more than just interesting fairy tales I read in my youth; they have become something of a family tradition.

There is something compelling about a story regarding a noble quest. Tolkien's trilogy centers on a diminutive race known as hobbits. As a people, they are unremarkable, being largely overlooked in the wider cultural lore of Middle Earth. They are known chiefly for their love of creature comfort. One hobbit, by the name of Frodo Baggins, inherits a magical Ring of Power, which his uncle Bilbo had acquired in another story and which renders its wearer invisible.[3] Once he had finished with his adventures, old Bilbo had used the ring chiefly as a convenience, to escape the notice of unwanted visitors. The wizard Gandalf, however, tells Frodo of the ring's true significance: it was fashioned in ages past by the Dark Lord, the sorcerer Sauron, and is the key to his power. Sauron had been building his might through many long years and had thought the ring lost; now, newly aware that it still exists, he seeks to find it and place all of Middle Earth under his dominion. With this as background, Tolkien interweaves two narratives in his saga. One is Frodo's journey into Mordor to break Sauron's kingdom by destroying the Ring of Power. This can be accomplished only by entering into the heart of Mordor, Sauron's realm, and casting the ring into the fires of Mount Doom, where it was first forged. The other narrative strand concerns the return of the true king, who gathers his allies and prepares to engage the forces of the Dark Lord in battle.

How will the story end? And how shall we direct ourselves toward that end? These are ultimately the questions that give substance to the virtue of hope. Here, perhaps, we may learn something from hobbits. What hobbits share with the other races of Middle Earth, be they humans, elves or dwarves, is their love of a good story, poem or song that tells the lore of the past. But these are not idle tales for amusement; rather they are narratives that shape how the peoples of Middle Earth understand their history and destiny. It is the preservation and trans- mission of the stories that helps the free inhabitants of Middle Earth to recognize their peril and their duties; it is story and song that enable them to recognize and authenticate the true king when he comes.

And it is such narratives that supply hope in the most difficult days of the quest. Pausing to rest in a dreadful passageway leading into the land of Mordor, Frodo and his ever-faithful servant, a hobbit named Sam, reflect together on their dark journey. The very feel and smell of the passage is oppressive and evil, hinting at the terror that awaits them just ahead. But still the hobbits are determined to continue. Frodo remarks to Sam that such is the path that has been laid for them, and Sam agrees, though he admits that if they had known more about the quest from the beginning, they might never have set out upon it. Sam reflects further:

> But I suppose it's often that way. The brave things in the old tales and songs, Mr. Frodo . . . I used to think that they were things the wonderful folk of the stories went out and looked for. . . . But that's not the way of it with the tales that really mattered, or the ones that stay in the mind. Folk seem to have been just landed in them, usually—their paths were laid that way, as you put it. But I expect they had lots of chances, like us, of turning back, only they didn't. And if they had, we shouldn't know, because they'd have been forgotten. We hear about those as just went on—and not all to a good end, mind you; at least not to what folk inside a story and not outside it call a good end. You know, coming home, and finding things all right. . . . But those aren't always the best tales to hear, though they may be the best tales to get landed in! I wonder what sort of a tale we've fallen into?[4]

Frodo and Sam know implicitly that they have been "landed in" a great tale, and they must see their own parts through to the end, whatever may come. In the stories that "really matter," the characters must accept their roles, not turning back in the face of suffering or adversity. The hobbits have no way of knowing for certain if their own part in the tale will have a happy ending or a sad one. But such knowledge would not necessarily deter them from their adventure. They perceive that they have parts to play but that it is not "their" story. The legends they have learned from childhood stretch far back into antiquity, and they know that the story will continue after they have gone. Their destinies have been taken up into the narrative, and their actions are compelled by it.

They press onward, with only the dimmest hopes of success. It is not a cheerfully blind optimism that draws them forward. The landscape of Mordor is grim and bleak. Their endurance threatens to fail them at every new turn. The hobbits do not even have the benefit of a clear path to follow, having to trust to the guidance of the crafty Gollum, who once possessed the ring and is wracked with a consuming lust to have it back. They eventually realize that their food supply is barely enough to sustain them until they reach the fires of Mount Doom, and they have neither provision nor plan for a journey back. Nevertheless, Frodo, his will and body increasingly weighed down by the magic of the ring, at last completes his quest. The might of Mordor begins to collapse all about them, but the hobbits possess neither the strength nor the means to return home. Frodo, injured yet free of the ring's influence, lies down to die. He tells Sam, "It's like things are in the world. Hopes fail. An end comes. We have only a little time to wait now. We are lost in ruin and downfall, and there is no escape."[5] The steadfast Sam, however, refuses to give up hope. He gently coaxes his master to come farther down the mountain; but soon they find themselves surrounded on every side by flowing lava. The two hobbits finally collapse from exhaustion and the suffocating heat and fumes of the ruined mountain. But even then Sam continues to muse about how the story will continue after them, and raises his gaze to the sky, as if looking for their salvation.[6] This, then, is the posture of hope, a watchful expectancy that looks to the horizon while planted firmly and unflinchingly in the circumstances of the present. Sam does not know what he is looking for, and the situation appears hopeless. But having submitted himself to the story, he waits with uplifted eyes even when it seems that the very last page of his part in the drama is being turned.

The Virtue of Hope

As a stance of confident expectation, hope is grounded in faith. As discussed earlier, faith is the virtue that continually sets before us the narrative horizon of the kingdom of God, which Brueggemann calls "the core metaphor for a new social imagination."[7] As those who stand under that kingdom, we submit our personal stories, in trust and commitment, to the authority of that narrative, often over against the moral horizons of our culture. The virtue of hope begins here, recognizing that the promised kingdom has already been given in part through the life and work of Christ, the founding of the church and the gift of the Holy Spirit. But hope also looks forward to the future completion of that promise; indeed it eagerly anticipates it.

The author of the letter to the Hebrews tells us that "faith is the assurance of things hoped for, the conviction of things not seen," and that without faith "it is impossible to please God, for whoever would approach him must believe that he exists and that he rewards those who seek him" (Heb 11:1, 6). Within this context he cites Abraham as an example: "By faith Abraham obeyed when he was called to set out for a place that he was to receive as an inheritance; and he set out, not knowing where he was going" (v. 8). We should not take the subsequent statement that "he looked forward to the city that has foundations, whose architect and builder is God" (v. 10) to mean that he had a clear vision of his destination, only that he placed his confidence in God and his promises.

This is both a trusting faith and an active hope. Remember that having cited Abraham and other as exemplars of the faith, the writer of Hebrews declares that all of them "died in faith without having received the promises" (11:13). Abraham was obedient in faith, directing his life toward the fulfillment of God's promise to him:

> Hoping against hope, he believed that he would become "the father of many nations," according to what was said, "So numerous shall your descendants be." . . . No distrust made him waver concerning the promise of God, but he grew strong in his faith as he gave glory to God, being fully convinced that God was able to do what he had promised. (Rom 4:18, 20-21)

Abraham did not live to see the promise completely fulfilled. But he trusted God, and God revealed himself to be faithful through the gift of Isaac, born to Abraham when both he and his wife Sarah were well past their childbearing years. His faith and confident hope establish a narrative example for all who follow the same God of promise. Did Abraham know that in the generations to come Moses would retell his story to the children of Israel? Or that these children would be taught to understand themselves as characters in that continuing story of God's faithfulness to his covenant? Or that the apostle Paul and others would use his life as a great example of faith, after the coming of the Messiah? By faith Abraham knew that he had been landed in a story that had God as its author, and by faith we also come to see ourselves as part of the same unfolding drama.

Indwelling the story of the kingdom means coming to terms with its strikingly eschatological character and, in so doing, recognizing the importance of the virtue of hope. Christian hope begins with the affirmation that our God is the God of Abraham, the God of promise. Faith locates our lives within a horizon of promise; hope continually looks to that horizon and orders life accordingly. For Christians this means more than giving intellectual assent to the claim that Christ will someday return. Hope is an earnest expectation, for which Paul employs the graphic metaphor of a woman in labor, anticipating the birth of her child:

> We know that the whole creation has been groaning in labor pains until now; and not only the creation, but we ourselves, who have the first fruits of the Spirit, groan inwardly while we wait for adoption, the redemption of our bodies. For in hope we were saved. Now hope that is seen is not hope. For who hopes for what is seen? But if we hope for what we do not see, we wait for it with patience. (Rom 8:22-25)

The larger context here is one in which Paul addresses both suffering and the often-confusing struggle of Christians to live the life of the Spirit. The apostle recognizes how easily we become preoccupied with the difficulties of the Christian life, so that we lose perspective. Against this he sets the virtue of hope. He recognizes that the present state of the world is "not the way it's supposed to be."[8] For Paul, however, this does not count against the validity of the promise; he gives suffering meaning by identifying it with the suffering of Christ (cf. Rom 8:17). The present struggles of Christians are placed within a narrative context of hope. The inner witness of the Spirit attests that we are children of God and directs us in prayer toward the eventual fulfillment of the promise of being fully adopted into the kingdom (cf. Rom 8:16, 23, 26).

Gilbert Meilaender makes a similar point by distinguishing between two understandings of virtue.[9] On the one hand, a focus on moral character tends to lead us to think of the development of self-mastery, that somehow the moral life can be perfected by persistent human effort. On the other hand, such an understanding seems to eliminate the need for grace. Is, then, our virtue a human achievement or a gracious verdict of God by which he declares us righteous in spite of our sin? Meilaender follows Martin Luther in declaring that true virtue is not a human accomplishment. The formation of character through virtuous action has its place but can never make us righteous before God. True virtue stems first from the freedom that comes from having been justified by grace through the gift of faith.

Thus we live within the tensions that Paul addresses in his epistles, knowing that we have been redeemed but struggling daily to live the truth of that claim. There is a gap between the several virtues that we attempt to develop through forming the right habits and the unity of a virtuous character in which we, like Christ, are truly righteous before God. But it is precisely here that hope becomes central. Meilaender writes:

> The narrative of the Christian story which provides the contours for Christian living envisions a day when these several evaluations of our character meet, are reconciled, and no longer stand in tension. Until that day, however, we live within the constraints of a temporal narrative—adding virtues piecemeal, shaping being by doing, unable to see ourselves whole. And hence, until that day the virtue of hope must be the *leitmotif* of Christian existence, the fundamental shape of Christian character—hope that God can make of our piecemeal virtues more than we see or know and thus bring the plot of this story to a happy ending.[10]

The temporality of the narrative gives the Christian life the nature of a pilgrimage, a state of being on the way to a destination that eludes human grasp.[11] Consider again Paul's description of the Christian life in Romans 8. If we apply to it the questions posed by Brian J. Walsh and J. Richard Middleton in the preceding chapter,[12] we can better see the nature and role of hope. Recall that these two authors summarize the faith assumptions of worldviews with four questions: Where are we? Who are we? What's the problem? and What's the remedy? The answers to these questions supply the setting, characters, dramatic tension and plot resolution of the narrative. To begin with, Paul does not call Christians to an otherworldly orientation; the setting of the drama that he describes is *this* world, a world created by God yet characterized by suffering and decay. As the protagonists of Paul's story, Christians are the adopted children of God, the rightful heirs of the coming King. But the tension is given by the gap between the presence and absence of God.[13] We already have the sign and seal of the kingdom in the inner witness of the Spirit, who aids us in prayer and through whom we call out to God as our Father. But God has not yet returned to claim and redeem his creation or his heirs. This redemption is the resolution toward which the narrative drives, the future climax that gives meaning to present adversities.

The promise that God's reign and our adoption will be made manifest when Christ returns in glory is the horizon of Christian hope. This is not simply a culturally optimistic vision of the future of humanity in general, nor is it a privatized personal vision of life after death. As Lesslie Newbigin writes,

> What is made possible through the gospel is a life looking toward a horizon which is different than either of these. That horizon is defined in the words "He shall come again." For a Christian the horizon for all action is this. It is advent rather than future. He is coming to meet us, and whatever we do . . . is simply offered to him for whatever place it may have in his blessed kingdom. Here is the clue to meaningful action in a meaningful history: it is the translation into action of the prayer: "Your kingdom come, your will be done, as in heaven so on earth."[14]

It is significant that Jesus teaches his disciples to pray for the coming of the kingdom. We might well reflect on the substance of our prayers: how many of them are limited to petitioning God's help with the troubles of the day? This is not wrong, but it is a far more restricted vision than the Lord himself taught. And how can one earnestly pray for God's will to be done on earth, in the same way that it is done in heaven, without also crying out, "Lord, begin with me"?

Thus the virtue of hope does not merely anticipate the resolution of the narrative, it *lives toward it.* The promise is not given only as an inner assurance. It is the horizon of action. It is just such a horizon that makes Jesus' teachings on watchfulness intelligible. The parable of the wise and foolish bridesmaids is one example (Mt 25:1-13). The background setting is a wedding celebration, a metaphor that Jesus used more than once for the eschatological kingdom. There were ten bridesmaids, all of whom brought lamps or torches in anticipation of a torchlight procession to the banquet. Five of the bridesmaids were "wise" and well-prepared, having brought extra oil with which to keep their torches lit; the other five were "foolish" and brought only their

torches. Their carelessness is not explaine͏ ͏
some oil in the torches, but probably n͏
appreciable length of time. The bridegro͏
bridesmaids fell asleep. But at the strok͏
awakened by the announcement that the br͏
procession was ready to begin.

Then all those bridesmaids got up and t͏
foolish said to the wise, "Give us some of y͏ ͏, ͏ ͏ ͏ oil lamps are
going out." But the wise replied, "No! there will not be enough for
you and for us; you had better go to the dealers and buy some for
yourselves." And while they went to buy it, the bridegroom came,
and those who were ready went with him into the wedding banquet;
and the door was shut. Later the other bridesmaids came also, saying,
"Lord, lord, open to us." But he replied, "Truly I tell you, I do not
know you." Keep awake therefore, for you know neither the day
nor the hour. (Mt 25:7-13)

What are we to make of this? Those of us who have been nurtured on
a Christianity that teaches grace but no judgment, and that equates
Christian virtue with niceness, will find this parable difficult to accept.
The five wise bridesmaids would know that no oil dealers would be
open at midnight; they would have to be rousted from their beds.
Wouldn't sharing the oil be the proper thing to do, the *Christian*
response? Likewise, the response of the bridegroom to the foolish
bridesmaids' late arrival may seem unduly harsh. "You're late" and a
gentle remonstrance before letting them in would surely be more
gracious.

But if we respond to the parable in this manner, it may indicate that
we do not sufficiently appreciate the eschatological aspect of the gospel
narrative. Again, we do not know the exact reason for the carelessness
of the five bridesmaids who brought no oil, but perhaps we need know
nothing more than this. The five wise ones appear to have taken the
anticipated event far more seriously. It was important to them that
nothing hinder them from participating fully in the celebration, and
they prepared accordingly. Their refusal to divide their oil with the
other five demonstrates an important priority: sharing may be virtuous,
but it is not an end in itself. As Meilaender recognizes, it is possible to
focus on the development of Christian character in a way that empha-

perfectibility of the moral life to the virtual exclusion of grace.
not pursue virtue to perfect ourselves, for God alone can do
. Rather, we pursue virtue so that we may be found ready when he
calls. When the final summons comes, all programs of character
development are swept aside; we must immediately and without
hesitation join the procession that will bring us into the banquet of the
ages.

Thus the virtue of hope actively lives toward the fulfillment of God's
promise, the resolution of the dilemma of living in a kingdom that has
dawned but has not yet been completed. The church lives radically in
the present while directing its gaze toward the horizon of the future:
"Christianity is to be understood as the community of those who on
the ground of the resurrection of Christ wait for the kingdom of God
and whose life is determined by this expectation."[15] The wedding
banquet is but a metaphor that directs our imagination to the glorious
and celebratory consummation of God's reign. No human description
can completely capture that glory, and it is wrongheaded to attempt to
transform poetic apocalyptic imagery into the detailed certainties of
predicted events:

The biblical way of hope is to dream large dreams about the powerful
purposes of God, but they are not designs, blueprints, or programs.
To make them such is to deny God's free governance over the
future.[16] *Brueggeman*

Rather, we must accept Jesus' words that we know neither the day nor
the hour of his return. The character of Christian hope is that we must
hold ourselves "in readiness for a fulfillment which goes beyond every
imaginable human postulate," and in so doing we devote ourselves not
to "militantly promoting defined, planned goals and eschatological
aims" but "to doing daily whatever is prudent, good and just at the
time."[17]

But if hope does not deny God's free governance of the future,
neither does it deny his governance of this present life. Our hope is
not grounded in the promise itself but in the Lord who gives it, a
surprising God who frequently bursts our anticipation. In the eleventh
chapter of John's Gospel, we read the story of how Jesus raised his
friend Lazarus from the dead. While Lazarus was deathly ill, his sisters
Mary and Martha sent word from Bethany to Jesus to ask his help. Jesus

was not far away when he received the news, but he deliberately remained where he was until he knew that Lazarus was already dead. When he arrived in Bethany, Martha came out to meet him. John records their conversation:

> Martha said to Jesus, "Lord, if you had been here, my brother would not have died. But even now I know that God will give you whatever you ask of him." Jesus said to her, "Your brother will rise again." Martha said to him, "I know that he will rise again in the resurrection on the last day." Jesus said to her, "I am the resurrection and the life. Those who believe in me, even though they die, will live, and everyone who lives and believes in me will never die. Do you believe this?" She said to him, "Yes, Lord, I believe that you are the Messiah, the Son of God, the one coming into the world." (Jn 11:21-27)

It is easy to imagine what Mary and Martha had talked about while they awaited Jesus' arrival: when Mary came out to meet the Lord, she greeted him with exactly the same words as her sister had: "Lord, if you had been here, my brother would not have died" (Jn 11:32).[18] That in itself is a declaration of faith, even though it seems to take the death of their brother as a final and irrevocable loss.

Martha, however, goes even further in her expression of faith, declaring her confidence that God will give Jesus whatever he asks. Her faith is strong, and she specifically believes that Jesus is the long-awaited Messiah. Yet even so, she lacks the vision of what a God of hope can and will do. Jesus tells her that Lazarus will rise again, and Martha responds with an appropriate eschatological statement about a final resurrection. It is clear from the narrative that she has no idea what Jesus intends to do. When the Lord commands the stone to be taken away from the entrance of the tomb where Lazarus is buried, it is Martha who objects, because of the stench of decaying flesh that she assumes will be released (Jn 11:39). With that objection she disappears from John's retelling of the story. But how would she have reacted to the raising of her brother from the dead, not in the last days but before her very eyes? Martha already believes in the God of promise; now she encounters the God of surprise, who from time to time delights his children with foretastes of the glory that is to come.

Hope looks and lives toward the horizon of promise that is to be fulfilled in the future, while remaining open to the ways that God may in his grace grant signs of that fulfillment in our present sufferings. To what extent does this virtue characterize the church? To answer that question requires examining the horizons by which we order our lives and in what or whom we place our confidence. Our culture supplies many different narratives by which we understand both the tensions we experience and the remedies for them. If the truth be told, the only narrative solutions toward which many of us live are nothing more than the next paycheck, a more satisfying relationship or even the fabled "perfect" church. (Here it is wise to remember the popular adage "If you find the perfect church, don't join it—you'll ruin it.") But this is not Christian hope. As the quote from Brueggemann in the epigraph to this chapter suggests, it is hopelessness rather than hope that characterizes our culture. Understanding the outlines of that hopelessness may help us to see where the challenge lies for the church and for Christian families.

A World Without Hope?

Clearly the horizon of Christian hope is a transcendent one. But as we have seen, the values of the modern and postmodern world militate against such transcendence. The modern impulse discards a teleological vision in favor of an ordered universe of predictable causes and effects. This, in turn, undermines hope:

> The dominant intellectual tradition of the West . . . is not a tradition of hope. It is a tradition of *order* which seeks to discern, understand, decipher, know, and, if possible, master and control. . . . We are in a season when the *urge for order* seems nearly to squeeze out the *voice of hope.*[19]

Whereas hope lives toward a resolution that is "not at the disposal of the hoper,"[20] the modern metanarrative of mastery and progress defines problems and their solutions as lying within the grasp of human reason and technique, and thus dispenses with hope. The advent of postmodernism is the sign that the modern project has failed. The replacement of tradition with technique, hope with mastery, has not resulted in the fulfillment of our deepest human desires but has substituted superficial gratification. By squeezing out the transcendent, modernism leaves us rootless:

> The modern rationalization of consciousness has undermined the

plausibility of religious definitions of reality. . . . The final consequence of all of this can be put very simply (though the simplicity
is deceptive): *modern man has suffered from a deepening condition
of "homelessness."*[21]

Similarly, Albert Borgmann characterizes our postmodern society as
sullen, resentful and indolent on the one hand and on the other pouring
ourselves compulsively and hyperactively into our work.[22] These are
the characteristics that Josef Pieper identifies with *acedia,* or *sloth,*
which in turn is the root of despair, the antithesis of hope. As Pieper
argues, sloth, properly understood, is not simply laziness or the
opposite of industry, but the rejection of our true destiny:

It is a kind of anxious vertigo that befalls the human individual when
he becomes aware of the height to which God has raised him. One
who is trapped in acedia has neither the courage nor the will to be
as great as he really is. He would prefer to be less great in order thus
to avoid the obligation of greatness. . . . As a capital sin, sloth is
man's joyless, ill-tempered, and narrow-mindedly self-seeking rejection of the nobility of the children of God with all the obligations it
entails.[23]

Hopelessness is not merely an individual sin but the characteristic of
a society that turns away from transcendent narratives and poses its
own solutions. Philip Cushman argues that the erosion of communal
traditions that attended the advent of modernization has resulted in a
sense of inner emptiness. This "empty self" has been continually
exploited by the U.S. advertising industry from the years immediately
following World War II, when the nation was ready to pursue a new
American dream after decades of social unease. Conspicuous consumption, or what Borgmann calls "commodious individualism,"[24] was
proposed as the antidote to emptiness. Cushman calls this the "lifestyle solution":

One prominent type of ad offers the fantasy that the consumer's life
can be transformed into a glorious, problem-free life—the "life" of
the model who is featured in the ad. This can be accomplished by
purchasing and "ingesting" the product, which will magically transfer
the life-style of the model to the consumer.[25]

This constitutes an alternative narrative, in which we come to understand ourselves primarily as consumers in a world of mass-produced

goods. Consumption itself, not just the products consumed, is presented as the therapeutic solution to the anomie of the modern dissolution of transcendent meaning. As Neil Postman trenchantly observes with regard to television advertisements:

> The television commercial is not at all about the character of products to be consumed. It is about the character of the consumers of products. . . . What the advertiser needs to know is not what is right about the product but what is wrong about the buyer. . . . The television commercial has oriented business away from making products of value and toward making consumers feel valuable, which means that the business of business has now become pseudo-therapy. The consumer is a patient assured by psycho-dramas.[26]

This is, of course, more a way to keep the consumer economy afloat than it is a cure for the existential ills of modernity. Advertising deals only in images and, at best, fragments of stories. Thus it cannot provide the full narrative resources for a reconstruction or readjustment of cultural meanings. The lifestyle solution is, as Cushman calls it, a "pseudoculture" that promises more than it can actually deliver: "advertising can only offer the illusory exchange of one life for another."[27] Nevertheless, barring other viable alternatives, the fragmentary narrative of commodious individualism may represent a default standard in a society without hope.

In this vein it is important to remember that not all who are without hope would see themselves as being in despair. Hope is most visible in a context of suffering, but hopelessness can also characterize those who do not appear to be in any discomfort. Recall the passage quoted in the preceding chapter: "When you have eaten your fill and have built fine houses and live in them . . . and your silver and gold is multiplied . . . then do not exalt yourself, forgetting the LORD your God" (Deut 8:12-14). Hope was a central characteristic of the people of the exodus, a people who could look only to the coming of the mighty acts of God for their salvation.[28] Once the people had become settled and prosperous, the very real danger existed that they would no longer look to God and would instead begin to believe that their prosperity was a result of their own hard work. Similarly, Brueggemann writes:

> Because hope has such a revolutionary function, it is more likely

that failure to hope—hopelessness—happens among the affluent, the prosperous, the successful, the employable, the competent, for whom the present system works so well. . . . The more one benefits from the rewards of the system, the more one is enraptured with the system, until it feels like the only game in town and the whole game. Our "well-offness" leads us finally to absolutize, so that we may say "the system is the solution."[29]

Hopelessness, therefore, is not simply the failure of hope in the face of suffering but the restriction of our moral horizons to that which is immanent in the created world. It is a visionless conformity to things as they are, rather than the challenging of the status quo and the pursuit of what should be. When the system itself is the solution, life becomes the pursuit of success. This is the situation of Christians for whom hope is manifested chiefly in prayers for help when the system breaks down. When our careers or our relationships or our health seem unproblematic, they are taken for granted and there is little felt need to pray about them. But a radical, forward-looking hope means accepting the call to be more than simply successful by the world's standards. Instead of asking "Is my career going OK?" we ask, "How can I begin to show myself to be a child of God in the midst of my work?" Instead of wondering "How are my relationships doing?" we ask, "In what way can I demonstrate the presence of Christ's Spirit to someone else?" These are questions put to us by the virtue of hope, because behind them lies a more fundamental question about our lives: "What will Jesus find when he returns?"

Hope, then, reorients our existence so that we live toward the promise of a consummated kingdom. We enter the narrative by faith, and in hope we actively direct ourselves toward its climax. But we must recognize that this story differs radically from the moral fragments that can be gleaned from a culture of homelessness and hopelessness. Let us end this chapter, therefore, with a consideration of some of the challenges of hope for Christian families and the church.

Christian Families in a Hopeless Culture
Perhaps it is less accurate to say that hope is absent from our culture than to say that hope has been robbed of much of its moral content. In common usage a person may say that she "hopes" something will

come to pass, expressing what may be little more than an idle wish. The meaning of such a vacant word becomes fluid when held captive within different moral horizons. This is illustrated by a radio advertisement for a home loan agency that aired during the Christmas shopping season two or three years ago. It was targeted to desperate consumers who were already wondering how they would pay the massive credit card bills that would reach their mailboxes in January. The solution, of course, was to take out a home equity loan to consolidate debts. Whatever one may think of this kind of economic reasoning, the proposal itself is so commonplace as to be unremarkable. What was striking, however, was the moral language that constituted the loan company's closing slogan: "We fund hope." This is all that remains of the virtue of hope, it would seem, when it has been evacuated by the logic of the marketplace. The salvation offered is not even capable of getting us off the treadmill of indebtedness.

The example is not trivial. The ad reflects what can happen to the language of virtue when it is submitted to cultural norms. More to the point, what happens in Christian families during the Christmas season may be as good an indicator as any of the moral horizons that characterize their lives, and thus also the status of hope. I remember vividly a conversation with a man who was a much-loved soloist at a church where my wife and I were formerly members. His warm baritone had graced many a worship service with soaring songs of the faith. One Sunday morning I found him standing outside the church, without his usual gregarious smile. Innocently I asked him how he was doing, whereupon he burst into tears. After some moments he told me the cause of his distress: his anxiety and frustration over how he was going to finish his Christmas shopping on time. I am not, of course, minimizing the stress of shopping for the right presents. More fundamentally I am questioning why the consumption-saturated interpretation of Christmas should be so compelling to Christians, and whether it is inaccessible to hope. Here was a man who had sung hymns of hope and praise to uplift an entire congregation, but for whom such lyrics seemed to offer little solace in the face of market-induced despair.

When considering the relevance of virtue language to Christian families, we must always begin with the realities of our historical situation and its values. In contemporary American culture the private domain of family life is the primary location for living out the ideals of commodious consumption. This is easily taken for granted, even in Christian homes. We do not question these ideals too stringently, provided that our lifestyles do not display conspicuous greed, at least by neighborhood standards. But we fail to notice how the goods and technology with which we surround ourselves have the power to reshape what we do and how we live. As Borgmann insists, our technological devices are not merely instrumental conveniences for those who use them; rather, they intrude into already-existing household practices and remold those practices around them. He illustrates:

> Once a television set is in the house, the daily decision whether to read a book, or write a letter, or play a game, or tell stories, or go for a walk, or sit down to dinner, or watch television no longer really ranges over seven possibilities. The presence of television has compressed all alternatives to one whose subalternatives are contained in the question: What are we going to watch tonight?[30]

There are, of course, many families whose lives are not so thoroughly compelled by the television set. Borgmann's point is not to criticize a particular piece of technology but to indicate the typically transparent way that technology shapes our lives.[31] We should not forget that it was in large part the invention of techniques of mass production that gave rise to the need to create markets for the goods thus produced. The creation of such markets in turn required the moral reeducation of a population, to make customers into consumers. We have come to indwell the horizon of consumption to such an extent that, as Borgmann concludes, the "moral fabric of family life is typically patterned not so much by practices as by acquisitions, by material decisions."[32] Thus we are once again confronted with the question of the moral horizons by which our families tacitly live. The values of the consumer marketplace that are embedded in contemporary family life are examples of the false hopes or even hopelessness of our modern and postmodern culture. Other horizons could be cited and have been discussed in previous chapters. The point is not to equate the embodiment of Christian hope with a rejection of consumerism, though in part it may well take this form. More generally, we must become more critically aware of how our participation in the values and images of our culture predisposes us to narrate our lives in such a way as to render the promises of God irrelevant.

A vital Christian hope requires that we recapture the narrative imagery of what it means to be a pilgrim people, an exodus people on a lifelong journey to the promised kingdom. This is true first of all for those who suffer. The Gospels demonstrate that with the ministry of Jesus came a kingdom characterized by compassion for the afflicted. Jesus healed people of their distress, even in cases where there would appear to be no corresponding profession of faith (e.g., Lk 17:11-19; Jn 5:1-15). Further, when the imprisoned John the Baptist sent word to ask if Jesus was in fact the Messiah, Jesus did not reply directly. Instead he asked John to consider the character of the emerging kingdom: "Go and tell John what you hear and see: the blind receive their sight, the lame walk, the lepers are cleansed, the deaf hear, the dead are raised, and the poor have good news brought to them" (Mt 11:4-5). Those who suffer may confidently place their hope in such a merciful and compassionate God, the One who surprised Martha with an unanticipated gift of life.

But we should also be careful to remember the difference between cultural and biblical perspectives on suffering. Our culture tends to view nearly any obstacle to self-fulfillment and self-determination as a type of suffering and seeks legal, therapeutic or lifestyle solutions. In the biblical narrative, however, *suffering* describes not only physical affliction but also the consequence for God's people who stand over against the values, structures and ideologies of the world.[33] It is assumed that those who truly seek the kingdom, who in Jesus' words "hunger and thirst for righteousness" (Mt 5:6), will be persecuted. In this vein Paul tells the Roman church:

> Therefore, since we are justified by faith, we have peace with God through our Lord Jesus Christ, through whom we have obtained access to this grace in which we stand; and we boast in our hope of sharing the glory of God. And not only that, but we also boast in our sufferings, knowing that suffering produces endurance, and endurance produces character, and character produces hope, and hope does not disappoint us, because God's love has been poured into our hearts through the Holy Spirit that has been given to us. (Rom 5:1-5)

It is significant that this passage immediately follows his retelling of the story of Abraham's faith and hope. Abraham looked to the promise that he would be the father of innumerable descendants, a promise that would await its fulfillment in the generations after his death. But the miraculous birth of a son to an aged and childless couple signified that his trust was not misplaced. He believed, and in so doing Abraham could see in the boy Isaac the realization of the promise. So, too, Paul's hope of glory is clearly eschatological. Yet two things are present to him: his suffering and his experience of the love of God through the Spirit. Hope does not disappoint, because Paul bears the sign that the promised kingdom is already under way. This hope, therefore, affords him a new narrative context for his suffering, a way of making suffering meaningful and thus endurable.

Hope, however, does not apply only to Christians whose suffering is of the magnitude of Paul's. What counts as suffering or persecution is not determined by a scale of severity. A pilgrim people can stand against the ideologies of the surrounding culture in homely ways. We have already mentioned the captivity of Christian families to a consumer-oriented Christmas. What resistance would we encounter in our families if we decided to do things differently this year? Or consider the parents who are feeling trapped in the neighborhood birthday circuit of elaborate parties and expensive gifts. What would the other families say if they decided to break the mold? Consider, too, the child who feels she must have the latest toy or other fad that it seems all of her friends already have. The unquestioned values of our therapeutic and consumer culture seem to say: If you want it and you can afford it, there is no reason not to buy it.

> Children learn these things from ads: that they are the most important person in the universe, that impulses should not be denied, that pain should not be tolerated and that the cure for any kind of pain is a product. They learn a weird mix of dissatisfaction and entitlement. . . . We may try to protect our own children from such nonsense, but they live in a world with children who have been socialized into this value system. . . . Their peers will teach them to be consumers even if they do not learn from the primary sources.[54]

"We can't afford it" sometimes seems the only legitimate excuse to children who are pestering their parents to buy them something. What other reason might a parent give that is consistent with virtues of faith and hope? How do we help our children to understand these values, so that they have an answer for their incredulous friends, who wonder why their parents won't let them have the prized commodity? To stand for the kingdom, and thus against many of our most cherished cultural axioms, is to invite derision and conflict, to risk being marginalized. Only a hope that looks beyond earthly goals will sustain us in this pursuit.

Thus a Christian understanding of hope is not only an encouragement to the persecuted; it is also a wake-up call to the complacent. By what narratives do we define what constitute "problems" in our lives, and where do we look for the solution? The temptation of our culture is to define tension and resolution in such a way that redemption, in principle at least, is within our reach. We strive to be able to say that we have "arrived," whether financially, psychologically or by some other cultural standard that befits whatever is left of the American dream. But this is to turn our backs on the transcendent hope and pilgrimage that should characterize the lives of the children of God. As Moltmann asserts, family life is a calling, as are other social roles and functions. But every such calling must be subsumed under the more central call to discipleship, "the call to join in working for the kingdom of God that is to come."[35] The kingdom is, in part, already here; but still we are taught to pray for the fullness of the kingdom that is yet to come. That is the horizon of our hope, which is beyond all human achievement.

To Stanley Hauerwas the moral significance of the family is that it serves as a sign of this hope. Families represent a limit to the ideals of free choice and self-determination:

> For the most inescapable fact about families, regardless of their different forms and customs, is that we do not choose to be part of them. We do not choose our relatives; they are simply given. . . . To be part of a family is to understand what it means to be "stuck with" a history and a people.[36]

Children do not choose their parents but owe them a debt of loyalty nonetheless.[37] Likewise, siblings do not choose each other but must learn to coexist peacefully. Parents may choose whether or not to have children but do not normally choose what children will be born to them.[38] As Hauerwas argues, the decision to have children is of great moral significance from the standpoint of Christian hope:

A child represents our willingness to go on in the face of difficulties, suffering, and the ambiguity of modern life and is thus our claim that we have something worthwhile to pass on. The refusal to have children can be an act of ultimate despair. . . . Fear and rejection of parenthood, the tendency to view family as nothing more than companionable marriage, and the understanding of marriage as one of a series of nonbinding commitments, are but indications that our society has a growing distrust of our ability to deal with the future.[39] It is not that family and parenthood are the only social institutions that reflect hope. To lean in this direction is to accede to our culture's idealization of the family. The underlying issue is, to use Moltmann's distinction again, a matter of calling and call: within our culture and historical setting the social calling of family life is to be taken up into the call to discipleship. In this way "marriage and the family, like the life of singleness, becomes a vocation for the upbuilding of a particular kind of community."[40]

Further, if Hauerwas is correct about the moral significance of the involuntary relationships of family life, then what shall we say about the church? If we accept that we do not "shop" for children, do we still "shop" for churches? It is a tremendous irony when Christians move from congregation to congregation for the sake of their families and yet never commit themselves in any of those settings to pursue the virtues that would sustain communal life. Do we on the one hand decry the decline of commitment and family values but on the other hand speak glibly of our "church family" and then divorce them over a change in the worship style?

The community that sustains the virtue of hope is not abstract community but a specific group, in a specific place, where regular face-to-face personal interaction occurs. If Christian families are to sustain their calling, they must be part of a local body of believers for whom the biblical narrative is or is becoming the dominant moral horizon. Newbigin writes:

> It is only as we are truly "indwelling" the gospel story, only as we are so deeply involved in the life of the community which is shaped by this story that it becomes our real "plausibility structure," that we are able steadily and confidently to live in this attitude of eager hope.[41]

But how often do our conversations at church display more of hopelessness and resignation? When friends tell us of their family difficulties, do we simply nod sympathetically and commiserate with them, or do we together consider how we might understand such situations from within the horizon of Christian hope? Even the disciples, who had witnessed firsthand the miracles of Jesus, would lose confidence in the face of obstacles. With a crowd of thousands coming up the hillside, Jesus turned to Philip and asked a question that tested his vision: "Where are we to buy bread for these people to eat?" Philip's answer was less than exemplary: "Six months' wages would not buy enough bread for each of them to get a little" (Jn 6:5-7). The latter-day equivalent of his response would be "But Lord, it's not in the budget." Andrew's response is a bit more hopeful. He offers Jesus a poor boy's lunch of bread and fish but struggles to understand how it could possibly serve the purpose: "But what are they among so many people?" (Jn 6:9). But once again, of course, the God of surprise takes over. The enormous crowd is miraculously fed, and the leftover pieces of bread are more than the five loaves with which they started.

The question for us is this: When Jesus turns to us to ask how we will feed those who come to him, what is our response?[42] We look at what seem to be the hopelessly meager resources at our disposal and compare them to the magnitude of the ministry to which he has directed us. A quick mental calculation may leave us skeptical at best. But Jesus asks only that we bring to him what we have and trust that he will multiply it as needed to complete the task. Recall the story from chapter three about the church that baptized a fourteen-year-old teenage mother and her infant and committed themselves to care for them both. What makes it possible to extend this kind of compassion? Is it confidence in their own talents and resources? Or is it a confident hope in the God of promise and the God of surprise?

Such counsels of hope are but foolishness to a world that posits its own solutions to human need and desire. "We experience and practice the American dream as a rush too easily taken toward new children, bright tomorrows, more security, and new energy resources, all within reach."[43] How well does this describe the horizon of daily life within Christian families and the church? The American dream is a fragile social creation that has shown signs of deterioration in recent decades. We find ourselves living toward that cultural promise when we bend our energies to fill our emptiness with consumer goods and their associated images. But this is to betray our call to be a people of hope.

To be a Christian family in a hopeless culture requires that our lives exhibit a different narrative, one that stands over against the ideologies of our day. There are many circumstances in family life that threaten to shatter our hope: marital discord, adultery, delinquency and the specter of unemployment, to name just a few. Any of these at once gives the lie to the ghost of the 1950s family of the Golden Age, which still maintains its ideological influence somewhere in the recesses of our popular imagination. We cannot and should not attempt to resurrect the American dream.[44] Rather, we must come to full terms with human sinfulness, knowing that broken relationships are to be expected in a broken world of false hopes and empty promises. As a pilgrim people, we have confidence and hope that do not reside in any thing, person or institution in the created world, not even the family itself. Our hope resides in the God of promise, who is at once both faithful and surprising. The people who follow that God live within the horizon of his story, practicing a social imagination that challenges the status quo. To do this earnestly invites being pushed to the margins of society. Yet it is from that vantage point that we might finally and truly learn the depth of the virtue of hope.

Nine

THE MARK
OF THE KINGDOM

The Virtue of Love

. . . .

I give you a new commandment, that you love one another.
Just as I have loved you, you also should love one another.
By this everyone will know that you are my disciples,
if you have love for one another.
JOHN 13:34-35

And now faith, hope, and love abide, these three;
and the greatest of these is love.
1 CORINTHIANS 13:13

We have come to the third and last of the theological virtues, one the church has recognized throughout its history as a central characteristic of the Christian life. The word *love*, of course, elicits many associations, many of which have nothing directly to do with the Christian faith. The family images of couples walking hand in hand on the beach, mothers and fathers nuzzling their babies, or children hugging their parents' knees are not the exclusive domain of the church or any other cultural group. Is there anything distinct about the Christian understanding of love?

As we see in the well-known texts cited in the preceding epigraphs, Paul holds love to be the greatest of the three virtues, while Jesus himself declares love to be the mark by which his disciples are to be known. On one occasion the Pharisees tried to discredit Jesus by asking him which was the greatest commandment in the law. They expected, no doubt, that he would entangle himself in endless rabbinic controversy no matter what answer he gave. His answer, however, silenced them by taking a completely unexpected tack: the first and greatest commandment is to "love the Lord your God with all your heart, and with all your soul, and with all your mind" (Mt 22:37). The directive, of course, was not original with Jesus. It was already part of the Mosaic tradition, which would have been well-known to devout Jews (Deut 6:5). Nevertheless, Jesus' legally minded opponents apparently did not anticipate such a reply. Nor did Jesus remain content to end the discussion there. He cited a second commandment, "You shall love your neighbor as yourself," with the bold statement that "on these two commandments hang all the law and the prophets" (Mt 22:39-40; cf. also Lev 19:18). On the basis of such texts, it is small wonder that the church has emphasized the priority of love through the centuries.

We might question, however, whether the word *love* denotes the same thing to us as it did to Jesus or the early church. With what do we associate love? We are accustomed here to thinking of family relationships, of the love of spouses for each other, of parents for their children and of children for their parents.

Obviously, however, our culture teaches us to use the term much more broadly than this. *Love* describes everything from the self-sacrificial devotion of the late Mother Teresa to the mass-market fantasies of paperback romance novels. In our modern consumer society we love not only people but also our technology and material possessions. "I love what you do for me," exclaims the advertising slogan, as the happy Toyota owner jumps for joy. A more tongue-in-cheek magazine advertisement for John Deere tractors depicts a peaceful scene in which a handsome retired couple relaxes together on the porch of their white clapboard home. The sun is setting as they serenely gaze off into the distance together. "I have two loves," the caption reads. "I married one, and I mow with the other." This is not just a tribute to riding mowers, nor just an insulting jab at marital devotion. It is an indication of how shallow the very notion of love itself has become. Within such a social climate, how is love to be understood within the church?

More precisely, what do we mean when we speak of love as a specifically Christian virtue? Is the church's vision of love uniquely formed by the biblical narrative? The diversity of writing in this area precludes a simple answer. The following section has a much more modest goal: to show that cultural narratives have considerable leverage in how Christians think about love. Of the moral horizons discussed in chapter four, it is particularly the horizon of the therapeutic that has exerted the greatest influence in this regard. This will be illustrated here by a close examination of a recent Christian book dealing with the topic of love in the context of the family.

Love Within the Limits of a Therapeutic Horizon

As has already been suggested in earlier chapters, the values intrinsic to American family life have changed significantly since the first days of the colonies. Even during the years just prior to the Revolutionary War, popular conceptions were already moving away from notions of the economically based patriarchal household and toward the centrality of love in family life. Readers of the fiction of that era, for example, learned that

> love was superior to property as a basis for marriage; that marriage should be based on mutual sympathy, affection, and friendship; that parental example was more effective than coercion in governing children; and that the ideal parent sought to cultivate children's natural talents and abilities through love.[1]

Companionate ideals would increasingly become the norm with the advent of industrialization, and they were later institutionalized and democratized in the family norms of the Golden Era of the 1950s.[2] Although that era is now behind us, its mythmaking vision of the private and intimate domestic sphere, the haven in the heartless world, is still very much a part of the cultural imagination.

As Robert Bellah and his colleagues observe, the norms of expressive individualism and the therapeutic horizon have reshaped how Americans think about love and commitment. We cherish love but often seem to cherish autonomous selfhood even more. The understanding of love as the free sharing of one's true self in an intimate relationship clashes with ideals of permanent commitment:

> Americans are, then, torn between love as an expression of spontaneous inner freedom, a deeply personal, but necessarily somewhat

arbitrary, choice, and the image of love as a firmly planted, permanent commitment, embodying obligations that transcend the immediate feelings or wishes of the partners in a love relationship.[3]

Like other members of our society, Christians find themselves wrestling with these competing views. As Bellah notes, the Christian tradition favors an ethic of obligation, in which love is more than just a feeling; it is an action, a matter of the will. In this way "love involves placing duty and obligation above the ebb and flow of feeling, and, in the end, finding freedom in willing sacrifice of one's own interest to others."[4] Nevertheless the ideological tension remains, for as Bellah also observes,

> while the evangelical Christians welcomed the idea of sacrifice as an expression of Christian love, many others were uncomfortable with the idea. It was not that they were unwilling to make compromises or sacrifices for their spouses, but they were troubled by the ideal of self-denial the term "sacrifice" implied.[5]

In other words, Christians in a therapeutically oriented society struggle to articulate how a biblical ethic of love can be viable in a culture that prizes individual freedom.

An example of the struggle between biblical and therapeutic understandings of love may be found in a recent book by family therapist Alfred Ells.[6] *Family Love* presents an interesting and somewhat uneasy alliance of themes drawn from the recovery/codependency movement and biblical texts. Ells begins with the familiar observation of family decline: "Today's families are in crisis. The media constantly herald the difficulties of single-parent homes, blended families, couples in conflict, and the breakdown of traditional family values."[7] His perception of the root of the problem, which he calls *love hunger,* is clearly framed by the perspectives of the recovery literature. Ells writes:

> The problems we experience today are tied to the past—the family past. Nothing affects the way we think, feel, act, and react as much as our families do. . . . The problems and negative patterns of behavior we experience today are directly related to who raised us and how we were raised. . . . Most relationship problems stem from unquenched family love hungers—deep unfulfilled needs to receive and give love that come from the family past.[8]

A similar perspective is adopted by Harville Hendrix, who argues that individuals bring unconscious motivations to the process of selecting a mate, including the expectation that their partners "are going to love them the way their parents never did."[9] Ells, for his part, goes on to cite the standard array of social problems: drugs, violence, sexual abuse, divorce and so on. Rather than examine cultural factors and contexts, he prefers to trace these problems to deficits in the affective dimension of family relationships. There is little doubt that some of our social ills are at least associated with family variables, but this is a far cry from establishing causality, and Ells offers nothing to support his generalization. More broadly his approach already seems to presume the modern cultural definition of the family as a haven, together with the popular idea that society's problems are the unidirectional result of family decline. One wonders, for example, how families of earlier ages would have responded to his statement that "the patterns of love in a family are the glue holding the family together."[10] Would the early Puritans have agreed that love patterns, in the sense of how people give and receive affection, are the core of the family?

The perspective also appears to be controlled more closely by narratives of codependence and recovery than biblical horizons. Even when biblical stories are used, they stand only as illustrations of dysfunctional family patterns. The stories of Abraham, Sarah, Isaac, Rebekah and Jacob are used as case studies, lifted out of their larger narrative context of faith, grace, destiny and the acts of God in history. In fairness, Ells's observations about the family dynamics portrayed in the stories are probably valid as far as they go. After all, the characters given to us in the Bible are real people: sneaky, conniving and manipulative, just like many of us. The point is that Ells's *use* of the stories, ironically, shows that it is the recovery literature and not the biblical narrative that is the dominant moral horizon. The stories of Abraham and the others are treated as examples drawn from the cultural stock of available stories. As such, they have illustrative and not normative force. This is akin to a "Bible as literature" approach, with the Scripture providing case studies in codependence and dysfunctional family "love patterns."[11]

This is not to say, of course, that love is unimportant. But we must ask if the understanding of love that Ells advances is adequate to the virtue of love that is portrayed in the biblical story. As already suggested,

Ells's treatise on love and family hews more closely to the narrative forms of the recovery movement. We can summarize the elements of that narrative by again using the fourfold scheme of character, setting, tension and resolution. First, the element of character is given by Ells's anthropological assumptions. The central theme here is emotional need: "Every child has deep needs for belonging, acceptance, approval, attention, and affection."[12] In particular human beings are born with an emotional need for attachment to a loving adult:

> We are social beings. Deep within every child is the need to be intimately connected to a caretaker. . . . For healthy development to take place, the young child must be emotionally close or bonded. This closeness opens the person's developing inner being to life.[13]

Second, the primary setting for the drama of the developing self is, of course, the family. Third, the dramatic tension is given by the mishandling of this inborn need for connection, which emerges in imbalanced patterns of disengagement (too little closeness) or enmeshment (too much closeness).[14] The mishandling results in love hunger. This sense of emotional deficit in turn leads to the mismanagement of closeness in subsequent generations. Fourth and finally, what is the narrative resolution? The horizon of hope is the achievement of what Ells calls the "family dream," a composite inner vision of what we want and don't want in a family, of "how we want to be loved" and how we expect others to fulfill our expectations.[15]

Is there anything specifically Christian about Ells's perspective? His goal of healthier patterns of intimacy is largely a therapeutic one, as are his strategies for achieving them. He outlines five steps toward this end: both spouses must recognize their own contributions to the dysfunctional pattern in their relationship; each must resolve the emotional issues of the past; the couple must adopt a healthier style of relating; they must commit themselves to a balance of closeness and distance; and they must learn better communication and conflict resolution.[16] Again, there is nothing wrong with such strategies and goals as far as they go. But what role do Christian norms and beliefs play in this approach to relationships?

Ells does address this issue, albeit inconsistently. In some passages it is clear that religious language and even the portrayal of God have been taken captive by therapeutic metaphors. The family is described as "God's profound and enduring plan for creation." With that as a moral context, Ells renders God almost as a heavenly family therapist:

> Our mission is to resist recreating the negative patterns of relationship that keep us from getting and giving the love we so desperately need. It is also to reach out to God, asking Him to create in us new and healthy patterns of care, concern, and love.[17]

Elsewhere God is portrayed as the perfect parent. Even here the language of a therapeutic horizon predominates:

> I have discovered that there is one perfect Parent. In relationship with God, we have found a Father who understands and loves us perfectly, even when we don't deserve it. Through His grace, many of the wounds of childhood have been healed. Through His mercy, our faults and shortcomings have been forgiven. Through His wisdom, we are learning together how to love each other and our children.[18]

It is not that God cannot and does not heal our emotional wounds. But neither should we press theology into a therapeutic mold. Ells recommends that those who have suffered from a family history of disengagement pray the following: "Please, Father, help me to release the pain of my past and recreate enduring patterns of healthy love for the future. Be the close and caring parent to me that I have never had."[19] I have no doubt that many of his clients have indeed found this prayer to be emotionally healing. But is God more than the caring father or the divine therapist?

To his credit, Ells does in places invoke a more demanding moral horizon. It is not simply that we determine the family dream that we desire and then seek God's help in attaining it. Rather, "our dreams must always be ones that God values."[20] He writes:

> Dreams are too important to leave to our whims. We need God's guidance and direction for our lives. Our love hungers can easily distort our vision and produce failed dreams. Biblical truth and prayer must anchor the expression of our dreams, or we will risk their failure. . . . For a good dream to come true, we must prayerfully submit to God the dream and the steps we take to fulfill it. . . . God will always help us achieve what He desires for our lives—but only if we cooperate with Him in its pursuit.[21]

Here Ells introduces an important qualification to the self-help perspec-

tive that permeates the earlier part of the book. He recognizes the
possibility of idolatry:

> Re-creating family requires that we embrace a healthy dream of
> fulfillment. But even then the dream, no matter how fine or good,
> can never compete with our desire for God. If it does, the dream
> will not fulfill our deepest needs. Love hunger can make the need
> for love an idol in our lives. . . . As we continue to pursue the insights
> and methods of healthy family love, let us not forget that His love
> and desires must be first.[22]

Moreover, he clearly states that the "biblical concept of love . . . involves
sacrificial giving and unwavering commitment."[23] The practical upshot
of this recognition is that while we must admit our needs for love and
affection, our primary task is to focus on our responsibility to love the
other. As Ells asserts, "Needs should not be turned into demands and
expectations of others. Rather, they should be reviewed in light of the
past and surrendered to God for healing and fulfillment."[24]

Even here, however, we should be careful to recognize the extent
to which the therapeutic horizon prevails. While the *content* of one's
family dream must be reexamined in the light of divine guidance, the
legitimacy of the *role* of dreams is taken for granted, based on the
somewhat dubious assertion that dreams "are God's way of directing
the human spirit toward accomplishment and fulfillment."[25] The language of fulfillment represents the more dominant horizon. Even the
preceding passage on idolatry seems to be motivated by the concern
that dreams that usurp God's place in our affections "will not fulfill our
deepest needs." It is possible, of course, to assert that a rightly ordered
love for God is itself a human "need," the fulfillment of our deepest
longings, even when not recognized as such. But to make this assertion
in the present context would require a more carefully nuanced anthropology, one that distinguishes the need for affection that arises from
our social nature from our spiritual need for communion with our
Creator. At times Ells seems to run these together:

> If you are feeling the hurt of not being loved the way you need to
> be, offer your pain to God. Reach out to Him. The love hunger within
> can be satiated when you partake of His goodness and experience
> His touch. An intimate relationship with God will fulfill the deep
> need for perfect love, acceptance, and attachment.[26]

This is the therapeutic gospel par excellence. Here God is the perfect intimate partner, the one who meets the emotional needs that go unmet in our mortal relationships. We might note that this idea that we must fill our needs by being related to God is a consequence of Ells's understanding of the biblical concept of love. We might paraphrase the logic of the argument as follows. The family dream is one of both giving and getting love. But the biblical standard is giving, not getting. Therefore we should focus on giving in our relationships. Where, then, can we turn to get the love we need but to God?

This sits a bit uneasily, of course, with the therapeutic strategies for improving intimate relationships. Moreover, Ells's argument would be greatly helped by adopting a more communal perspective, whereby self-sacrifice is an ethic for the church and not merely for individual Christians. It is the Christian community that maintains the plausibility structures that sustain self-sacrificial love in Christian couples and families. Without this the notion of Christian love becomes restricted to the sphere of private family life, and when this fails, there is no recourse except the wounded individual's relationship to God as the Great Therapist.

In sum, Ells's book represents the ideological tension of which Bellah writes, between the competing understandings of love that derive from therapeutic and biblical horizons. One might object that I am taking Ells to task for not having written an ethics or theology text instead of a self-help book for emotionally wounded Christians. No doubt, readers who suspect that they have been raised in dysfunctional families will find more concrete help in his book than in the present work. The purpose of this extended critique has been to illustrate that popular Christian discourse about love and family is often controlled by a therapeutic horizon. I have singled out Ells because the title and subject of his book are particularly appropriate for our present purposes, not because I believe his book to be an unusually egregious example of therapized Christian discourse.

In fact I agree with Ells that humans are intrinsically social and that certain patterns of relationship can have negative repercussions. I also do not doubt that many of his relationship strategies have therapeutic value. Ells did not write his book as a theological treatise on Christian love but as a self-help book for Christians needing assistance with the expression of love in their families. This is a valid and laudable goal. But can one write such a book without making normative claims about the nature of love and of the family? Probably not. Inevitably such claims must be made, and they are made against some narrative backdrop. In Ells's case the controlling horizon is the recovery and codependence literature, which provides powerful narrative resources for reimagining family relationships. Such power has a dangerous side, as Mary Pipher observes:

> Therapy's worst offense is to reframe love as something negative, such as codependency, controlling behavior, emotional incest or even an "addiction to people." We have confused people about the healthiness of loving their own families. . . . When love is labeled in negative ways, we hurt people who are trying to help each other.[27]

Ells, for his part, stays mostly on the more positive side and does not engage in the excesses that Pipher describes. But the question is whether or not such narratives adequately represent the nature of Christian love or its relationship to the family.

The biblical understanding of the virtue of love goes far beyond notions of the need for affection and belonging. Volumes have been written on this topic, and we can only hope to scratch the surface here. I hope to demonstrate, however, that what the Bible teaches about love must first be understood as an ethical mandate for the entire Christian community before it can be rightly appropriated by the family.

The Virtue of Love

The Bible speaks of love in many guises. God's love for humanity is shown by the very message of the gospel itself. As John the Evangelist declares, "For God so loved the world that he gave his only Son, so that everyone who believes in him may not perish but may have eternal life" (Jn 3:16). Similarly, Paul writes that "God proves his love for us in that while we still were sinners Christ died for us" (Rom 5:8). John also tells us of Christ's love for individuals, such as Lazarus (Jn 11:3, 36), as well as his love for his disciples, which reflects the Father's love for him (Jn 15:9). Furthermore, as we already have seen, Jesus supports and extends Jewish tradition by declaring that to love God wholeheartedly is the first and greatest commandment and the fulfillment of the law (Mt 22:37-38; Mk 12:29-30; Lk 10:27). It is love on the horizontal

plane of human interaction, however, that seems to receive the greatest
ethical emphasis in the New Testament. These teachings can be
grouped under three headings: the love of Christians for one another,
the more general principle of neighbor-love and the distinctive extension of neighbor-love that expresses itself in love for one's enemies.
We will briefly examine each in turn by sampling a selection of key
texts.

Jesus teaches that his disciples are to love one another and that this
is the mark of their discipleship (Jn 13:34-35; 15:12). Perhaps one of
the best-known texts on the love that is to be expressed within the
body of Christ is found in the thirteenth chapter of Paul's first letter to
the Corinthian church. Throughout his letters Paul associates the virtues
of faith, hope and love, but here in particular he asserts that love is the
greatest of the three (1 Cor 13:13). How should we understand this? In
the final section of this chapter we will consider how the virtue of love
depends on the virtues of faith and hope for its sustenance. For the
moment, however, we must examine the meaning of Paul's claim. On
a casual first reading, the love chapter may appear to break the flow
of Paul's argument. It is almost as if, reminded somehow of the beauty
of love, he breaks into a spontaneous hymn of praise. To separate the
chapter thus from the rest of the letter tempts us to view it as an
extended definition of Christian love, independent of its context.

But this would do violence to Paul's apparent intent. We must
remember that Paul was dealing with a particular problem in the
Corinthian church, a divisiveness born of religious pride. One manifestation of this was religious name-dropping, the concern with which
Paul opens the letter. Individuals in the church had created factions by
proudly asserting their allegiance to a particular leader. "I belong to
Paul," claimed some, while others countered with "I belong to Apollos,"
or "I belong to Cephas" or even "I belong to Christ" (1 Cor 1:12). Another
sign of spiritual self-interest was the tendency of the Corinthian
Christians to treat spiritual gifts as ends in themselves, a problem that
Paul addresses in the twelfth chapter. Such arrogance had led to the
formation of a social hierarchy in which some gifts, such as prophecy
or speaking in tongues, were being defined as more valuable than
others. This led naturally to self-aggrandizement on the part of those
who appeared to possess the desirable gifts and self-denigration on the

part of those who did not. Against this tendency Paul teaches that the individuals in the church are members of a single body, the body of Christ, and that the various gifts have their unity in the one Spirit who is their source. It is in this context that Paul desires to teach them the larger ethical context in which to properly understand spiritual gifts: the "more excellent way" of love (1 Cor 12:31).

Paul's chapter on love presents three related ideas. First, he begins by asserting the supremacy of love over spiritual gifts. Whatever gifts they might have, they come to nothing without love (1 Cor 13:1-3). Second, he describes the characteristics of love in a series of positive and negative assertions. Rather than take these as a definition of love as such, we should probably understand what Paul is saying here as primarily a corrective application of the principle of love to the particular flaws he found in Corinth. Paul writes, for example, that love "is not envious or boastful or arrogant or rude," and it is easy to imagine that he specifically has in mind the problems described in the preceding chapter of the letter. At any rate, the description of love is broad indeed, actually saying more about what love is *not* than what it *is*. Paul appears to be pointing to specific attitudes he finds in the Corinthian church, to show them that they are not following the way of love.

Paul brings the matter to a point by placing it into a larger eschatological perspective:

> Love never ends. But as for prophecies, they will come to an end; as for tongues, they will cease; as for knowledge, it will come to an end. For we know only in part, and we prophesy only in part; but when the complete comes, the partial will come to an end. (1 Cor 13:8-10)

How can believers treat spiritual gifts as ends in themselves, when even the most cherished gifts are given only for a season? They are genuine manifestations of the Spirit, but they belong to the age that is passing away. The gifts cannot be taken as a sign that the kingdom of God has already been completed. Rather, the church is an eschatological community that lives in hope toward a promised future. Spiritual gifts, then, are given for the purpose of building up the eschatological church in the present (e.g., 1 Cor 14:12), and they will pass away when God's purposes have been fulfilled. Even Paul's personal "favorite" among the gifts, prophecy, will also come to an end (1 Cor 13:8; 14:1-5).

But not so love. When all else has passed away, love will remain, for love is of the very character of God (1 Jn 4:8, 16). This, finally, is why love is the greatest of the theological virtues. It is the very nature of faith and hope to be characteristic of the present time, when the Spirit is present but the kingdom has not yet been fully revealed. Love does not replace these; rather, it assumes them and is the form of their concrete expression in the life of the church. But when the reign of God is at last fully and finally consummated, faith and hope will dissolve into a relationship in which we know God fully and are fully known by him. Only love, the reflection of God's nature, will endure into eternity.

Love is not only a defining characteristic of how we as Christians are to relate to each other but also of how we are to relate to our neighbors. As noted earlier, Jesus teaches that the second greatest commandment, after full devotion to God, is that we love our neighbors as ourselves (Mt 22:39; Mk 12:31). In a parallel passage in Luke 10:25-37, an expert in the law asks Jesus what he must do to inherit eternal life. Jesus responds by turning the question back to him: "What is written in the law? What do you read there?" The lawyer responds correctly with the two greatest commandments (spoken by Jesus in the other two Synoptic accounts), and Jesus affirms his answer. But Luke portrays the man as uncertain about his performance on the second commandment. The lawyer therefore poses another question to Jesus, a technicality behind which to hide his ethical shortcomings: "And who is my neighbor?" Jesus responds with the parable of the good Samaritan. The plot is familiar to us. A man is beaten by robbers and left for dead. Both a priest and a Levite happen by, but neither demonstrates compassion by coming to the victim's aid. It is only a Samaritan man, a hated ethnic rival of the Jews, who shows mercy by tending his wounds and paying for his lodging while he recuperates. Jesus then poses a question to the lawyer: which of the three was a neighbor to the victim? Again the lawyer answers correctly; it is the Samaritan, the one who showed mercy. Jesus therefore commands the lawyer to do likewise.

As Paul Ramsey observes, what is significant about the parable is that Jesus sidesteps the original question and leaves no loophole for escaping the commandment to love. The lawyer's self-justifying question "Who is my neighbor?" is ignored by Jesus and replaced by the more ethically pertinent question "Who was neighborly?" Ramsey writes:

> No answer at all is given to the request for a general definition of "neighbor" which might justify loving a certain man if he falls within the definition or failure to love him if he does not. . . . Proving neighborly is one thing; setting up tests for proving the neighbor another. . . . This parable tells us something about neighbor-love, nothing about the neighbor. What the parable does is to demand that the questioner revise entirely his point of view, reformulating the question first asked so as to require neighborliness of himself rather than anything of his neighbor.[28]

Jesus resists the lawyer's attempt to reduce neighbor-love to a rule that dies the death of a thousand qualifications and instead offers a narrative paradigm, a model of the kind of love the commandment envisions.[29] This understanding of neighbor-love has a necessary corollary. If the question "Who is my neighbor?" is not allowed, then I may not separate the world into neighbors and nonneighbors. The result is that even those I consider to be enemies are to be recipients of neighbor-love.

Showing love for one's enemies is an important mark of the kingdom. In the Sermon on the Mount Jesus teaches his followers,

> You have heard that it was said, "You shall love your neighbor and hate your enemy." But I say to you, Love your enemies and pray for those who persecute you, so that you may be children of your Father in heaven. (Mt 5:43-45)

The first part, regarding love for one's neighbor, is already familiar. But nowhere does the Old Testament teach hatred for one's enemies; one can only suppose that this was a cultural addition to the tradition. Here love for one's enemies, expressed concretely in the act of prayer for one's persecutors, is the mark of the children of God. Jesus goes on to highlight the distinctiveness of this kind of love:

> For if you love those who love you, what reward do you have? Do not even the tax collectors do the same? And if you greet only your brothers and sisters, what more are you doing than others? Do not even the Gentiles do the same? Be perfect, therefore, as your heavenly Father is perfect. (Mt 5:46-48)

Here again the uniqueness of this kind of love marks one as a child of the heavenly Father. We should probably read the last statement eschatologically, similar in intent to the Lord's Prayer, in which Jesus teaches his disciples to pray for the coming of the kingdom (Mt 6:10). To be perfect is to have achieved one's *telos,* the goal to which all virtue points.

Those who claim to be disciples of Jesus are therefore to love one another and to show a love for their neighbors that extends even to their enemies. Of what does such love consist? What actions and qualities befit the virtue of Christian love? The passages previously cited give some indication. Paul, for example, teaches that love, among other things, is to be patient and kind (1 Cor 13:4), while Jesus teaches that love for one's enemies includes praying for them (Mt 5:44). But we should be wary of attempting to catalog a specific list of virtuous behaviors, lest we fall into the same error as the lawyer to whom Jesus directed the parable of the good Samaritan. The *telos* of the Christian life and our eschatological hope is not conformity to a set of behaviors but to be molded into the likeness of our Lord (cf. Rom 8:29; 1 Cor 15:49; 2 Cor 3:18; 1 Jn 3:2), who alone demonstrates true sinless humanity. Jesus himself is the *telos* toward which our virtues strive.

Recognizing this, we should avoid trying to encapsulate the life and character of Jesus by reducing them to rules and principles. While this may make for a tidier ethical system, it fails to do justice to the rich narrative world of the Scriptures. As Joseph Kotva observes:

> The most common example of this reduction is seeing Jesus as bearer of the law of love. Following Jesus' example, we are to love God and neighbor. This view is, however, an inadequate expression of Jesus' paradigmatic humanity. . . It is as if we totally understand what love is without his specific example. . . It is unlikely that we can encapsulate and communicate such a life in a single principle like "love."[30]

This said, however, we should also acknowledge that the problem does not lie in how the word *love* is used by the biblical writers. The difficulty arises instead from our modern penchant for a kind of definitional precision that transcends the ambiguities of narrative context. When Paul speaks of love as patient and kind, it is against the larger background of love, patience and kindness together being manifestations of the fruit of the Spirit, along with joy, peace, generosity, faithfulness, gentleness and self-control (Gal 5:22-23). We would not, I hope, read this list as exhausting the possibilities of the Spirit-filled life, any more than we would read Paul's preceding inventory of "the works of the flesh" as exhausting the possibilities of sin (Gal 5:19-21). In addition, as has been frequently observed, the word translated *fruit* is singular, which should discourage us from making any kind of checklist from the qualities Paul describes.

To put the matter differently, both Paul and the early church understand the Spirit to be the Spirit of Christ himself (e.g., Acts 16:7; Rom 8:9; Gal 4:6; Phil 1:19; 1 Pet 1:11). In this light, patience and kindness are not predicates that *define* love as an abstract quality. Rather love, patience and kindness are but three characteristics among many that Paul predicates of a life lived in the Spirit of Christ. If love has any moral priority, it is not because of its own intrinsic conceptual or ethical merit. Nor is it because the Greek word *agapē,* the most common term used for love by Paul and the Gospel writers, has its own unique definition, distinct from other terms. The importance of love stems from the fact that some, but not all, of the New Testament writers press this earthly term into service to describe the character of God and the Son, and thus by extension the church.[31] While there may in principle be some continuity between human understandings of love and a biblical one, our cultural models and beliefs do not establish the primary horizon by which the church understands love. It is the life of Jesus in its narrative wholeness that provides the paradigm against which all other understandings are to be examined.

The virtue of love, then, is grounded in the imitation of Christ, who is also our *telos,* the goal of our perfection. When the apostle Paul looks to Jesus, he sees the love of God displayed on the cross (Rom 5:8). Our love is but a response to the sacrificial love of Christ: "Therefore be imitators of God, as beloved children, and live in love, as Christ loved us and gave himself up for us, a fragrant offering and sacrifice to God" (Eph 5:1-2). Moreover, it is this very attitude of self-giving sacrifice that Paul calls the church to emulate. Christians show their unity and love for one another by humbly considering the interests of others ahead of their own, just as Christ humbled himself on the cross (Phil 2:1-8). Thus the love to which Christians are called is always premised on the love of God shown to us in Christ. When we truly understand the nature of

God's love for us, the natural response is to love God in return; but this is most concretely expressed in extending his love to others (1 Jn 4:10-21), an imitation of the self-denying love of Jesus.

How, then, does an ethic of self-denying neighbor-love apply to Christian families? Given what has been said in previous chapters about the private domain of family life being characterized by an expressive and commodious individualism, coupled with the "hard sayings" of Jesus that seem to undermine family devotion (Mt 10:34-39), are Christians to marginalize the family and its relationships of love? I do not believe so, but it is of the utmost importance that we learn to get our priorities straight. Jesus does not set aside the family but relativizes it, as Stephen Post explains:

> Jesus demonstrated an exceptional reverence for the family. . . .
> Often in his preaching the family provides the nearest human
> analogy to that divine order he sought to reveal. The hard sayings
> do not contradict this; rather, they simply put familial loves on a
> penultimate level because of the urgency of spreading the news of
> the kingdom.[32]

But how are we to understand this urgency, unless we already exhibit the virtues of faith and hope? It is only as we come to indwell the story of the kingdom and eagerly seek its completion that we can appreciate the penultimate position in which Jesus places the family. As we turn, therefore, to a final consideration of Christian love and family life, let us keep in mind that for Paul any discussion of love must presuppose horizons of faith and hope, and that we should do likewise.

Love and the Christian Family

It is Sunday morning, and the faithful of First Church are gathered for worship. All eyes are forward as the preacher pounds out an exhortation to love our neighbors. Who is in attendance this morning? There's Mrs. A, whose husband left her and their children a year ago for another woman. She has tried to remain hopeful of her husband's return, but her friends at First Church are telling her to forget him and get on with her life. As she listens to the sermon, Mrs. A is confused about how to love a husband who has abandoned her.

A few rows back sits Mr. B, who two days ago had a shouting match with his teenage son over his choice of friends. The boy left the house in disgust, and the parents do not know where he is. Mr. B regrets some of the things he said but believes that in the main he was right. As the pastor presses on, Mr. B wonders to himself, *How do I love a boy who seems bent on defying me and doing things that I know will harm him?*

To the left are Mr. and Mrs. C, well-regarded members of the church who give generously and are always ready to help. They married at an early age, full of youthful enthusiasm and romantic dreams. That was twenty years ago. Today both are successful professionals but in separate fields. They have little in common save the roof they share. Each feels somewhat bitter about the marriage, and petty annoyances add daily to their resentment and simmering discontent. Both have thought about divorce, but neither is willing to speak the word. The sermon falls lifeless into a hollow place in their emotions, like a stone in a dry well.

Love is self-emptying, the preacher says. Love is self-denial. Love is self-sacrifice. Mrs. A weeps quietly. *I already feel empty. I feel like I've been sacrificed,* she thinks to herself. *What more can I do?* Mr. B sits rigidly, avoiding catching anyone's eye. *I've given that boy everything,* he repeats to himself, as he has done so many times in the past two days. *He's done nothing but take advantage of me.* But for a moment remorse overcomes his defensiveness. *I just wish he'd come home,* Mr. B thinks sadly as he reaches over for a touch of his wife's hand. *We could work things out.* Mr. and Mrs. C are watching the minister but by now are hearing nothing. They are reviewing in their minds the list of things each of them must do as soon as church is over.

The fictional First Church, of course, could be anyone's congregation. We accept the commandment to love as a Christian ideal but are not always sure how to put it into practice. The message seems to be "You have to be like Christ. It doesn't matter whether you feel loving or not. Just try harder." Love not only fulfills the law, it becomes a new law. We look at the fractures in our relationships and our families and know immediately that we don't measure up. What does it mean for the sacrificial love of Christ to be the model of virtue? Is my need for affection nothing more than selfishness, unworthy of being called by the name of love? And how do I follow the call to love when relationships have stagnated or split apart?

Is Christian love an unattainable virtue? Neighbor-love is indiscriminate. The call to imitate Jesus extends to all of our relationships in our families, workplaces, neighborhoods and congregations. It is often much easier, however, to show love to people with whom you do not have to live. In his novel *The Brothers Karamazov* Fyodor Dostoyevsky expresses a similar sentiment through the melancholy character of Ivan Karamazov. Ivan is explaining his doubts about God and humanity to his younger brother Alyosha, who has entered the novitiate at a Russian monastery:

> To my thinking, Christ-like love for men is a miracle impossible on earth. He was God. But we are not gods. . . . One can love one's neighbors in the abstract, or even at a distance, but at close quarters it's almost impossible.[33]

Is it easier to show love for a child who lives in another country by donating to hunger relief or to consistently love the child in your own home who defies you openly? Is it easier to listen compassionately to someone else's marital woes or to squarely face your own?

Love will not allow us to take refuge in distant acts of kindness. I have spoken at length in this book about the cultural ideal of the family as an emotional haven and of the danger of making the family into an idol. Our modern society has taught us that emotional fulfillment and security are the *telos* of our existence and that the family serves this goal. Christians who indwell the story of God's reign, in faith and hope, rightly reject this cultural myth. This said, we must also distinguish the family ideal from the reality with which many live. Love is not bounded by our family relationships, but neither does it push them aside. It is in our families that we are most vulnerable. The ones who are closest to us, who live with us and know our weaknesses, are the ones whose love seems irreplaceable and who hurt us the most deeply. C. S. Lewis describes the dilemma of love:

> To love at all is to be vulnerable. Love anything, and your heart will certainly be wrung and possibly be broken. If you want to make sure of keeping it intact, you must give your heart to no one, not even to an animal. Wrap it carefully round with hobbies and little luxuries; avoid all entanglements; lock it up safe in the casket or coffin of your selfishness. But in that casket . . . it will change. It will not be broken; it will become unbreakable, impenetrable, irredeemable. The alternative to tragedy, or at least to the risk of tragedy, is

damnation. The only place outside Heaven where you can be perfectly safe from all the dangers and perturbations of love is Hell.[34] Lewis suggests here that to fail to love, to avoid the risk of giving of oneself in love, is to turn aside from our *telos* and descend into hell. To love is to open oneself to suffering. To love our families with the love of Christ is to risk the most painful form of rejection and betrayal.

But is this just one more way of bringing the therapeutic horizon back into the discussion? Aren't we talking about a need for acceptance and affection within our families, what Alfred Ells calls a "love hunger"? What is the value of this kind of love in the face of the incomparable sacrifice of Jesus on the cross? Some theologians and ethicists promote a view of Christian *agape* that sets sacrificial neighbor-love over against all human loves, and particularly the love of oneself.[35] In this view human loves, including the love of family, have a self-oriented component; put simply, there is something in it for us. This element of self-love must be redirected by an act of the will toward a pure interest in the welfare of others. Christian love involves a "disinterested regard for another person" that seeks a way of "disentangling self-regarding from other-regarding motives in concrete human relationships."[36] This is clearly the opposite emphasis from a therapeutic view that begins with the needs of the self.

Our family loves are not purely selfless. We do not primarily love our spouses, children, siblings or parents disinterestedly, as if we had no special relationship to them. We presume these loves to be mutual. In love I choose my spouse, but with the hope that my spouse also chooses me. I sacrifice for my children in ways that they cannot reciprocate, but I look expectantly for the signs that they know and love me in return. If family loves are not selfless, then, of what value are they to the Christian? If they are not self*less*, are they therefore self*ish* and undeserving of the name *love?* Josef Pieper puts the problem this way:

> The real question, the one on which opinions divide, runs as follows: Whenever someone says, "It's good that you exist, good for me, because I cannot be happy without you," is this always a distortion of love? Is it unworthy for anyone, or at least any *Christian,* to love in such a fashion?[37]

We might begin to construct an answer to Pieper's question by borrowing Lewis's distinction between *need-love* and *gift-love*.[38]

Lewis illustrates the first with the image of the frightened child running to her mother's arms. He illustrates the second with the example of parents who save for their children's future well-being, knowing that they will not share in that future personally. Lewis proposes that gift-love partakes of the divine nature, while need-love describes only our human finitude. In the introduction to his book Lewis confesses that he had originally intended to take the "highroad" on the subject, "that human loves deserved to be called loves at all just in so far as they resembled that Love which is God."[39] Having examined the matter more closely, however, he came to realize the legitimacy of our all-too-human need-love:

> I was looking forward to writing some fairly easy panegyrics on the first sort of love and disparagements of the second. . . . I still think that if all we mean by our love is a craving to be loved, we are in a very deplorable state. But I would not now say . . . that if we mean only this craving we are mistaking for love something that is not love at all. I cannot now deny the name *love* to Need-love.[40]

Thus though we might critique Ells's therapeutic emphasis on need-love within the Christian family, this does not mean that the "love hunger" of which he writes is only about selfishness and not at all about love. It can, of course, degenerate into selfishness without some broader moral horizon to redeem it. But it is not necessary to denigrate human love from the start simply because it falls short of embodying the sacrificial example of Christ.

Lewis recognizes that in a significant way need-love constitutes our present human existence. This applies particularly to our love for God:

> Man's love for God, from the very nature of the case, must always be very largely, and must often be entirely, a Need-love. . . . Our whole being by its very nature is one vast need; incomplete, preparatory, empty yet cluttered, crying out for Him who can untie things that are now knotted together and tie up things that are still dangling loose.[41]

But our family relationships, too, involve need-love. Children's dependence on their parents is an incipient form of love. Parents care for their children not only out of gift-love but out of need-love, a desire to have their affection reciprocated or at least recognized in some way. Some parents, of course, consistently put their needs ahead of their children's, manipulating their children's affections to their own ends. In such cases we might well ask whether this deserves the name of love. But even then we should probably understand this as legitimate love that has been corrupted, and not identify need-love directly and necessarily with selfishness.

Need-love, in other words, is an aspect of our created humanity. The idea that we are social beings means that we cannot realize our humanity in isolation. In a very real sense we *need* God and we *need* each other. It is a mistake to try to have one without the other. The fact that the Bible uses family metaphors to convey our relationship to God and to each other suggests that our earthly understandings of love are not obliterated by the coming of the kingdom. We do not cease being human. Self-denying gift-love, in other words, is not the only legitimate form of love for Christians. The virtue of love does not deny the passions that are part of our created nature.[42] If we cannot reduce the Christian life to the single principle of love, then neither can we reduce love to the single principle of self-sacrifice.

Nevertheless, self-sacrificial love is normative for Christians. Our need-loves do not disappear, but they must be relativized by being taken up into the narrative of the divine gift-love in Christ. Not all love is self-denying, but it is in self-denial that our loves are made subject to the kingdom. This is where the virtues of faith and hope must establish the horizon for our view of love. When I indwell the story of God's reign, I come to see others differently. They are not merely the objects of my affection, nor the source of my affirmation, but the ones for whom Christ died. Neither their cruelty nor their indifference to us can bar them from the love that calls from the cross. Moreover, when we can see others through the eyes of Jesus, we may also see ourselves truthfully and repent of the ways in which we too have betrayed those we love.

And how shall we continue in this love without hope? A steely determination to love merely because it is "the right thing to do" will not last long by itself. It is hope that sustains love when moral resolve fails. In hope we submit ourselves to the God of the promise and the God of surprise. As Jürgen Moltmann writes: "For love, we always require hope and assurance of the future, for love looks to the as yet unrealized possibilities of the other, and thus grants him freedom and

allows him a future in recognition of his possibilities."[43] Sacrificial love
is eschatological. It rejoices over love that is requited in the present,
but its horizon is the future, when "God will wipe away the tears from
all faces" (Is 25:8).

What can we say to the members of First Church? If what has been
said in this book is at all valid, then this is the wrong question to ask,
if it suggests that the solution lies in the giving of moral directives. The
more important question is, what kind of community is First Church?
Mrs. A does not want simply to be told either to forget her philandering
husband or to diligently pray for his return. Indeed if the other members
of First Church were to confront themselves honestly, they might
recognize that much of the advice they have so freely offered is meant
to assuage their own outrage or anxiety. "Forget him and move on,"
they say. "The relationship is dead, you need to grieve it; you need
closure." For her to continue to pray for reconciliation seems unrealistic,
and they are uncomfortable with such a naive display. This is a
community that kills hope in the name of a loving realism. True love
awakens, restores and builds up hope. Certainly if Mrs. A has her eyes
set solely on the return of her husband, then her hope needs to be
refocused. But this is not accomplished in the company of those who
merely counsel her to be more realistic. She needs a community of
people who are committed to love her and weep with her. She needs
the company of those whose own hopes are rightly ordered and thus
are not afraid to extend to her the love that she needs.

Mr. B lacks the support and challenge of people who are seeking to
encourage right living but always within a context of forgiveness and
vulnerability. For such a community the narrative of the prodigal son
is particularly poignant, for even the father who has good reason to be
angry at adolescent foolishness is not exempt from the rule of love (Lk
15:11-32). And what love! The father, with reckless abandon and
throwing decorum to the wind, runs across the fields to embrace his
wayward son. But how can Mr. B enact this story except in the context
of other disciples who encourage one another to set aside their rights
in the name of love? Many other parents at First Church have had
conflicts with their teenage children. Will they merely commiserate with
Mr. B, saying, "Yes, well, you know how teenagers are these days"?
Will they do this in the name of being supportive? Or does someone

but ain't we all sinners?

love him enough to help him understand what the depth of God's love truly means?

Mr. and Mrs. C need the fellowship of those whose horizons extend beyond the sphere of intimate relationships, where their disillusionment can be put in its proper context and transcended. They do not simply need new principles by which they might add marital satisfaction to their list of successes; they need the very idea of success itself to be brought under the authority of the kingdom in which they profess to believe. Neither of them needs the kind of fellowship in which Christians gather to study the Bible and then complain about their spouses over coffee. To raise concerns about one's marriage in the company of believers is valid in itself; it may even represent an especially admirable measure of vulnerability. But what then? Will we respond in such a way as to remind each other that love, in the biblical sense, far transcends either romance or marital happiness? That the love of believers for each other, as brothers and sisters in the body of Christ, is, in the kingdom view, more primary than family affections?

In all of these cases it is the church, as a community of moral formation, that embodies the virtues of faith and hope needed to move Christians out of a despairing preoccupation with their family relationships. Jesus taught his disciples: "This is my commandment, that you love one another as I have loved you. No one has greater love than this, to lay down one's life for one's friends" (Jn 15:12-13). For the church the supreme symbol of love is the cross. But that sacrifice was not an end in itself. The crucifixion leads to the resurrection, and the resurrection to Pentecost. The gift of the Spirit of Christ, in turn, is promissory, pointing away from itself to the time when God's children will be revealed and Christ is glorified (Rom 8:17-19). The imitation of Christ's self-emptying is a virtue appropriate to an age that lives between the presence and absence of God, an emptying that anticipates the fullness of future communion. Love that is not completely self-denying is not for that reason selfish. We may accept as a gift the affections of others and be grateful for requited love. But these are incomplete loves that too easily put themselves forward as idols for us to worship. To cling too tightly to our human loves, as our culture is apt to encourage us to do, is to narrow and impoverish our horizons. We need the encouragement of communities of moral formation that make sacrifice meaningful and rescue us from folding our ultimate concerns back upon ourselves.

To put it differently, the sacrificial love of the cross is both the central symbol and the culmination of an earthly life of self-forgetfulness. Dostoyevsky exhorts his readers to Christian love through the character of Father Zosima, the monastic elder who takes Alyosha Karamazov under his charge. The monk receives a visit from a Madame Kokhlakov, who confesses to Father Zosima that she lacks faith and lives in terror of the afterlife. The priest does not attempt to reassure her with platitudes about the certainty of her salvation. Instead he counsels her to let go of her anxious self-concern through the active pursuit of neighbor-love:

> Strive to love your neighbor actively and constantly. . . . Never be frightened at your own faint-heartedness in attaining love. . . . Love in action is a harsh and dreadful thing compared with love in dreams. . . . Active love is labor and fortitude. . . . But I predict that just when you see with horror that in spite of all your efforts you are getting further from your goal instead of nearer to it—at that very moment I predict that you will reach it and behold clearly the miraculous power of the Lord who has been all the time loving and mysteriously guiding you.[44]

Love as a supernatural virtue is not the sentimental attachments of the private family haven. It is "labor and fortitude," but in the company of a community of hope. We may have a natural affection for our family members, and Christian love does not set this aside. But the neighbor-love that imitates Jesus is not natural. It is a gift wrought by the Spirit of Christ himself. When the family has been freed from its self-concern by having its life taken up into the narrative of God's reign, it will learn to receive its own imperfect affections as a gift of grace.

Postscript

Contemporary American Christians are citizens of at least two realms. The first is the modern/postmodern secular culture, which shapes our values, language and ideals in ways that we take for granted. Part of our modern inheritance is a privatized image of family life that differs markedly from the premodern household. This vision of the family as emotional and spiritual haven can be found on both sides of the culture war, as can the moral horizons of individual rights, consumer capitalism and therapeutic fulfillment associated with it. When Christians attempt to articulate their so-called family values, they frequently resort to language and thought-forms appropriate to these horizons. Distinctively Christian perspectives and ideas may still be found, but often they are reinterpreted to fit other worldviews.

The other realm—the one Christians profess to inhabit—is the kingdom of God. The thesis of this book has been that the language of family values is inadequate to the task of demonstrating what this second kind of citizenship entails. For that only the reappropriation and embodiment of Christian virtue will do. I doubt, actually, that the thesis can be satisfactorily *proven* true on intellectual grounds. The truth of it must be lived, and the evidence will be found in the quality of the communities that display the virtues of faith, hope and love.

What we are seeking is a change of vision—a change in the way we look at culture and in the way we look at the relationship between the family and the church. The first change requires recognizing the full extent to which the ideals of our culture dominate our moral horizons. We are so accustomed to the norms of a rights-saturated, consumer-oriented, therapeutic society that the ethics of the kingdom of God seem alien to us. But the pursuit of Christian virtue does not mean trying harder to be better while leaving our worldview intact. Rather, by the gift of faith we come to see ourselves as citizens and heirs of a different kingdom. We learn to take a critical stance toward the narratives transmitted through our cultural stock of knowledge and their definitions of the good life. In hope we direct our lives toward a new vision of the good, the promised fulfillment of God's reign in our world. The sign of the reality of that kingdom is love that aspires to the self-giving of Christ, risking our own security and comfort for the good of others inside and outside our families. Faith and hope culminate in love, and love cannot long survive without them.

This first change of vision entails the second. The virtues are not techniques through which we build happier and healthier Christian families. They are an organic unity that both grows from and shapes the life of a new eschatological community. The church therefore must be willing to commit the culturally inappropriate transgression of drawing families out of their privatism. As suggested in an earlier chapter, this includes rethinking our philosophy of family ministry. The church is not simply the site where goods and services are provided to families in the role of religious consumers. Rather, the church is the body of Christ: a community of moral formation that articulates and embodies the narrative of God's reign and in so doing brings families face to face with their idolatrous attachments.

But even this language is inadequate, for it suggests that "church" and "family" are somehow distinct or even at odds with one another. The renewal of our vision includes recognition of the limited and ambiguous nature of these social distinctions. As anthropologists remind us, there are cultures in the world whose "family" arrangements bear no resemblance whatsoever to the Western arrangement. What would it mean for the gospel to dwell there? Would it require that they reorder their society into economically independent family units? Or that these families be defined as places of consumption, separated from productive work? And what form of "church" would we consider right? All these questions are meant to raise the same point. When we use the language of "family" or "church," we do so against a tacit background of social assumptions which must therefore be subjected to the authority of the reign of God. In this way, we come to understand better what Jesus meant when he taught that we must hate our families to be his disciples (Lk 14:26; cf. also Mt 10:37). Ultimately, to speak of the kingdom is to attempt in human language to represent the movement of the Spirit of Christ in our lives and in our world. Our task is to cooperate and follow, not to press the Spirit into preexisting institutional forms.

Pragmatically, of course, we must begin with what is before us: the several families and congregations of which we are a part. The consequences of a renewed vision must be worked out case by case in local communities of moral formation. How-to advice is no substitute for the honest and open dialogue of a people who are striving to discern together what God is doing in their midst. As we saw earlier, one church was called to challenge the logic of abortion by baptizing and raising teenage mothers and their infants. To do so requires redefining and revisioning the meaning of family: this young woman and her child are a family; we receive them gladly into our family household, which is no longer our private preserve; we do so because we are part of a larger family, the family of God. Such a position cannot and should not be transmuted into an instant formula for virtue: not all congregations will take up such a ministry. But we should expect that as congregations discover their unique callings, the world will be presented with a rich and varied display of the manifestations of the kingdom.

The language of family values can no longer serve Christians living in a postmodern society. We live in an uncertain age, when truths formerly taken for granted are challenged on many fronts. But as children of late modernity we have already internalized the fractured moral horizons reflected in our culture's understanding of "values." Can the language be rehabilitated? I do not know, but I believe that the effort would direct our energies away from where they are truly needed. The call of the kingdom is to respond in faith to the grace of God and to be transformed bit by bit into the likeness of Jesus. The movement of the Spirit does not follow our preordained plans, nor can it be captured within certainties that define for us what are right or wrong family values. We are called primarily not to create and defend a set of religious rules and principles but to be part of an unfolding story that surprises us with twists of the plot as it moves toward its climax. We must therefore wrestle with the ambiguities of how these many families of ours can be knit together into a community that by the Spirit of Christ is "in full accord and of one mind" (Phil 2:2). But we do so with a sense of both gratitude and adventure, knowing that at the close of the ages there will be but one family, one congregation, together praising the Lord of all.

Appendix A

VALUES RELATED TO MARITAL PERMANENCE

. . . .

Items correlated with permanence as belief

Item	Type*	r	p
The Bible	DcF	.2620	.000
Following a strict moral code	FmV	.2523	.000
Having faith in God	FmV	.2518	.000
Trying to obey God	DcF	.2482	.000
Opposing abortion	FmV	.2432	.000
Respecting authority	FmV	.2390	.000
Your relationship to God	SfW	.2056	.000
Prayer	Beh	.1808	.000
Having a happy marriage	FmV	.1798	.000
Having children	FmV	.1680	.000
Your moral standards	SfW	.1654	.000
Your family	SfW	.1632	.000
Reading the Bible	Beh	.1615	.000
Being married	FmV	.1494	.001
Respecting one's parents	FmV	.1486	.001
Attending religious services	Beh	.1371	.002
How your family would react	DcF	.1254	.004

Being in favor of prayer in school	FmV	.1206	.006
The teachings of your church	DcF	.1131	.010

Items correlated with permanence as value

Item	Type*	*r*	**p**
Having a happy marriage	FmV	.3506	.000
Having good relationships with your extended family	FmV	.3386	.000
Being married	FmV	.3172	.000
Following a strict moral code	FmV	.2833	.000
The Bible	DcF	.2769	.000
Opposing abortion	FmV	.2745	.000
Respecting authority	FmV	.2406	.000
Being in favor of prayer in school	FmV	.2378	.000
Your moral standards	SfW	.2020	.000
Having children	FmV	.1993	.000
Having faith in God	FmV	.1973	.000
The teachings of your church	DcF	.1689	.000
Your relationship to God	SfW	.1667	.000
Reading the Bible	Beh	.1599	.000
Helping people in need	SfW	.1587	.000
Attending religious services	Beh	.1572	.000
Respecting one's parents	FmV	.1568	.000
Respecting one's children	FmV	.1532	.000
Your family	SfW	.1525	.000
How your family would react	DcF	.1436	.001
Being able to provide emotional support to your family	FmV	.1331	.002
Trying to obey God	DcF	.1292	.003
Being able to communicate your feelings to your family	FmV	.1213	.005

*Key to item type: Beh = religious behavior (frequency); DcF = decision factor; FmV = family value (Mellman et al.); SfW = self-worth factor

n = 523; all correlations positive

Appendix B

VALUES RELATED TO SUPPORT FOR DIVORCE

. . . .

Item	Type*	r	p
Positive correlations			
Being able to do what you want to do	SfW	+.2657	.000
Being successful	SfW	+.2151	.000
Being independent	FmV	+.2101	.000
Your personal rights	DcF	+.2085	.000
Being well-educated and cultured	FmV	+.2083	.000
Making a lot of money	SfW	+.1971	.000
Whether you would feel good about it	DcF	+.1798	.000
What would benefit you the most	DcF	+.1680	.000
Your personal needs	DcF	+.1631	.000
Paying attention to your feelings	SfW	+.1590	.000
Being financially secure	FmV	+.1563	.000
Living a comfortable life	SfW	+.1502	.000
Having a rewarding job	FmV	+.1459	.001
Your personal judgment	DcF	+.1371	.002
Having leisure time for recreational activities	FmV	+.1364	.002
Earning a good living	FmV	+.1320	.002
Having nice things	FmV	+.1222	.005

Negative correlations

Opposing abortion	FmV	-.3296	.000
Being married to the same person for life	FmV	-.3222	.000
Reading the Bible	Beh	-.2877	.000
The Bible	DcF	-.2690	.000
Being in favor of prayer in school	FmV	-.2366	.000
Respecting authority	FmV	-.2125	.000
Following a strict moral code	FmV	-.2084	.000
Attending religious services	Beh	-.1988	.000
Having faith in God	FmV	-.1758	.000
Your moral standards	SfW	-.1635	.000
Having a happy marriage	FmV	-.1627	.000
Your relation to God	SfW	-.1571	.000
Trying to obey God	DcF	-.1487	.001
Helping people in need	SfW	-.1397	.001
Prayer	Beh	-.1342	.002
Respecting one's parents	FmV	-.1287	.003
Being married	FmV	-.1250	.004

*Key to item type: Beh = religious behavior; DcF = decision factor; FmV = family value; SfW = self-worth factor

n = 523

Notes

Preface

[1] John Leo, "A Pox on Dan and Murphy," *U.S. News & World Report,* June 1, 1992, p. 19.

[2] Robin Knight, "An Unmarried Woman and a Political Fight," *U.S. News & World Report,* June 1, 1992, p. 10.

[3] Lance Morrow, "But Seriously, Folks . . ." *Time,* June 1, 1992, p. 29.

[4] Eleanor Clift, "The Murphy Brown Policy," *Newsweek,* June 1, 1992, p. 46.

[5] Barbara Dafoe Whitehead, "Dan Quayle Was Right," *The Atlantic Monthly,* April 1993. The article generated a flood of correspondence, much of it castigatory.

[6] Jonathan Alter, "Thinking of Family Values," *Newsweek,* December 30, 1996/January 6, 1997, p. 32.

[7] Dan Quayle and Diane Medved, *The American Family: Discovering the Values That Make Us Strong* (New York: HarperCollins, 1996), p. 2.

[8] Stephanie Coontz, *The Way We Really Are: Coming to Terms with America's Changing Families* (New York: BasicBooks, 1997).

[9] Phyllis Burke, *Family Values* (New York: Random House, 1993).

[10] William Bennett, ed., *The Book of Virtues* (New York: Simon & Schuster, 1993), p. 14.

[11] William Bennett, *The Moral Compass* (New York: Simon & Schuster, 1995), and *The Children's Book of Virtues* (New York: Simon & Schuster, 1995); Robin Getzen and Erik Bruun, eds., *The Book of American Values and Virtues* (New York: Black Dog & Leventhal, 1996).

[12] Stephen Carter, *Integrity* (New York: BasicBooks, 1996).

[13] Gertrude Himmelfarb, *The Demoralization of Society: From Victorian Virtues to Modern Values* (New York: Vintage, 1994), pp. 9, 11-12.

[14] Alasdair MacIntyre, *After Virtue,* 2nd ed. (Notre Dame, Ind.: University of Notre Dame Press, 1984), pp. 2, 7.

[15] Barbara Dafoe Whitehead, *The Divorce Culture* (New York: Alfred A. Knopf, 1997); cf. also David Blankenhorn, *Fatherless America* (New York: BasicBooks, 1995).

[16] For such a construal of the task of theology, see Luke Timothy Johnson, *Scripture and Discernment: Decision Making in the Church* (Nashville: Abingdon, 1996); also Stanley Hauerwas, *A Community of Character: Toward a Constructive Christian Social Ethic* (Notre Dame, Ind.: University of Notre Dame Press, 1981).

[17] The ten-page RVP questionnaires were sent in packets of 20 or 30 to pastors who volunteered to distribute them to adults attending their churches. No church was sent more than 30 questionnaires. Respondents were required to be married or formerly married, and experience in raising children was preferred. Responses were also screened to ensure that they met at least one of two criteria: they had to agree to the designation of "born again" or else be regular members of the church where they received the questionnaire. A total of 541 completed questionnaires were returned, of which 523 were usable. Counting the number of questionnaires mailed to churches that returned at least one completed questionnaire yields a maximum response rate of 49

percent. Sixty percent of the respondents were female, and 40 percent were male; they ranged in age from 25 to 92 years old, with a mean age of 48. Ninety-one percent agreed that they had been born again; eighty-eight were regular members of local churches. One-third of the sample had a high-school education or less, and just under one-half completed a bachelor's or higher degree. The median total pretax household income was between forty and fifty thousand dollars per year. Regarding marital status, three-fourths of the sample were married; 14 percent were divorced and remarried; 5 percent were divorced but not remarried, and another 5 percent widowed; the remaining 1 percent were separated. Nondenominational and independent congregations were best represented, at 17 percent of the sample. The next three most frequently represented, in order, were Assemblies of God (14 percent), American Baptist (14 percent) and Presbyterian Church U.S.A. (13 percent). No other denomination represented more than 4 percent of the sample. Geographically the volunteer sample favored the West at 38 percent (of which 28 percent was represented by the three coastal states alone), followed by the Midwest (32 percent), the South (21 percent) and finally the East Coast (9 percent).

Chapter 1: What Are Family Values?
[1] David Popenoe, "American Family Decline, 1960-1990: A Review and Appraisal," *Journal of Marriage and the Family* 55 (August 1993): 527, 529, 540.
[2] David Popenoe, *Disturbing the Nest: Family Change and Family Decline in Modern Societies* (New York: Aldine de Gruyter, 1988).
[3] David Popenoe, "Family Decline in America," in *Rebuilding the Nest: A New Commitment to the American Family,* ed. David Blankenhorn, Steven Bayme and Jean Bethke Elshtain (Milwaukee: Family Service America, 1990), pp. 39-51; and David Popenoe, *Life Without Father* (New York: Free Press, 1996).
[4] Popenoe, "Family Decline in America," p. 43.
[5] David Popenoe, "The Roots of Declining Social Virtue: Family, Community and the Need for a 'Natural Communities Policy,' " in *Seedbeds of Virtue: Sources of Competence, Character and Citizenship in American Society,* ed. Mary Ann Glendon and David Blankenhorn (Lanham, Md.: Madison, 1995), p. 72.
[6] Jack Kemp, foreword to Jerry Falwell, *The New American Family: The Rebirth of the American Dream* (Dallas: Word, 1992), p. xiii.
[7] Robert Lewis, *Real Family Values* (Gresham, Ore.: Vision House, 1995), p. 92.
[8] Ibid., p. 23. Capitals in original; italic emphasis added.
[9] Falwell, *New American Family,* p. 17.
[10] As David Popenoe remarks in his rejoinder to critiques of the article cited, the fact that his critics do not "seriously challenge the trend data is a sign of progress. . . . Thus we are seeing a new agreement on the basic, empirical family trend of our time which was, after all, the fundamental focus of my article." David Popenoe, "The National Family Wars," *Journal of Marriage and the Family* 55 (August 1993), p. 555.
[11] Stephanie Coontz, *The Way We Never Were: American Families and the Nostalgia Trap* (New York: BasicBooks, 1992), and *The Way We Really Are: Coming to Terms with America's Changing Families* (New York: BasicBooks, 1997); Judith Stacey, *Brave New Families: Stories of Domestic Upheaval in Late Twentieth Century America* (New York: BasicBooks, 1990), and *In the Name of the Family: Rethinking Family Values in the Postmodern Age* (Boston: Beacon, 1996).
[12] Stacey, *In the Name of the Family,* p. 99.

[13]See especially Coontz, *The Way We Never Were,* and Elaine Tyler May, *Homeward Bound: American Families in the Cold War Era* (New York: BasicBooks, 1988).

[14]Coontz, *The Way We Really Are,* p. 47.

[15]Jonathan Kozol, *Amazing Grace: The Lives of Children and the Conscience of a Nation* (New York: HarperPerennial, 1996), p. 180.

[16]Popenoe, "Family Decline in America."

[17]Popenoe, "American Family Decline," p. 529.

[18]Two other points must be recognized. First, Judith Stacey regards this attempt at a more inclusive definition as "well-intentioned" but "myopic." Her criticism, from a feminist perspective, is that he fails to address the potential internal contradiction for a democratic polity that wishes to promote justice, freedom and equality, on the one hand, and yet also stem marital decline by restricting access to divorce, on the other hand. See Judith Stacey, "Good Riddance to 'The Family': A Response to David Popenoe," *Journal of Marriage and the Family* 55 (August 1993): 547. Second, Popenoe and others who may not formally define the family according to more traditional and nuclear family norms may nevertheless argue the unique value of these forms for society, as over against other alternatives. See, for example, Brigitte Berger and Peter L. Berger, *The War over the Family: Capturing the Middle Ground* (Garden City, N.Y.: Doubleday/Anchor, 1984).

[19]Edward L. Kain, *The Myth of Family Decline: Understanding Families in a World of Rapid Social Change* (Lexington, Mass.: Lexington, 1990), p. 152.

[20]Cited by George Barna in *The Future of the American Family* (Chicago: Moody Press, 1993), p. 31.

[21]The results are summarized in Mark Mellman, Edward Lazarus and Allan Rivlin, "Family Time, Family Values," in *Rebuilding the Nest,* ed. Blankenhorn, Bayme and Elshtain, pp. 73-92.

[22]These response categories are taken from a similar set of questions used by Robert Wuthnow in his research for the book *God and Mammon in America* (New York: Free Press, 1994). Wuthnow's items were used in a separate section of the RVP.

[23]Richard Mouw and Sander Griffioen, *Pluralisms and Horizons* (Grand Rapids, Mich.: Eerdmans, 1993).

[24]This is the title of a well-known book by Christopher Lasch, *Haven in a Heartless World: The Family Besieged* (New York: Basic Books, 1977).

[25]John R. Gillis, *A World of Their Own Making: Myth, Ritual and the Quest for Family Values* (New York: BasicBooks, 1996), p. 40.

[26]Mellman, Lazarus and Rivlin, "Family Time, Family Values." The theme of time also emerges in the RVP study. See also Arlie Russell Hochschild, *The Time Bind: When Work Becomes Home and Home Becomes Work* (New York: Metropolitan, 1997).

[27]See, for example, James Davison Hunter, *Culture Wars: The Struggle to Define America* (New York: BasicBooks, 1991), especially chapter 7.

Chapter 2: The More Things Change

[1]John R. Gillis, *A World of Their Own Making: Myth, Ritual and the Quest for Family Values* (New York: BasicBooks, 1996), pp. xvi-xvii.

[2]Steven Mintz and Susan Kellogg, *Domestic Revolutions: A Social History of American Family Life* (New York: Free Press, 1988). These themes run throughout the text; for an introductory overview, see pp. xvii-xx.

[3]Stanley Hauerwas, *A Community of Character: Toward a Constructive Christian Social*

Ethic (Notre Dame, Ind.: University of Notre Dame Press, 1981).

4. Stanley Hauerwas and William Willimon, *Where Resident Aliens Live* (Nashville: Abingdon, 1996), p. 48.

5. See especially Stephanie Coontz, *The Way We Never Were: American Families and the Nostalgia Trap* (New York: BasicBooks, 1992), for an extended argument of this thesis. It is also worth noting how television portrayals of families have changed since the 1950s. Harry Waters, reviewing the new television season in 1993 for *Newsweek* magazine, summarized the family messages presented by these new programs in three observations: "Parents rarely come in pairs," "Father knows least," and finally, "Parents are just overgrown kids." H. F. Waters, "Fractured Family Ties," *Newsweek*, August 30, 1993, p. 50.

6. Quoted in Elaine Tyler May, *Homeward Bound: American Families in the Cold War Era* (New York: BasicBooks, 1988), p. 17.

7. Ibid., pp. 17-18.

8. Coontz, *The Way We Never Were*, pp. 37-38.

9. Mintz and Kellogg, *Domestic Revolutions*, p. 8.

10. As quoted in Edmund S. Morgan, *The Puritan Family: Religion and Domestic Relations in Seventeenth-Century New England*, rev. ed. (New York: Harper & Row, 1966), p. 143.

11. Ibid., pp. 150-51.

12. Ibid., pp. 103-4.

13. Ibid., p. 108.

14. Beatrice Gottlieb, *The Family in the Western World: From the Black Death to the Industrial Age* (New York: Oxford University Press, 1993), p. 7.

15. Morgan, *Puritan Family*, pp. 143-44.

16. Ibid., pp. 38-39.

17. Stephanie Coontz, *The Social Origins of Private Life* (London: Verso, 1988), p. 75.

18. As quoted in Morgan, *Puritan Family*, pp. 145-46.

19. Gottlieb, *Family in the Western World*, pp. 54, 60.

20. Edmund S. Morgan, *Virginians at Home: Family Life in the Eighteenth Century* (Williamsburg, Va.: Colonial Williamsburg Foundation, 1952), p. 33.

21. Ibid., pp. 32-33, as well as Elizabeth Goesel, *Courtship and Marriage of the 1700s* (Williamsburg, Va.: Bicast, 1993), p. 21.

22. Morgan, *Virginians at Home*, p. 31; Goesel, *Courtship and Marriage*, p. 26.

23. Mintz and Kellogg, *Domestic Revolutions*, p. 23.

24. Jan Dizard and Howard Gadlin, *The Minimal Family* (Amherst: University of Massachusetts Press, 1990), p. 6.

25. Ibid., p. 8.

26. Morgan, *Puritan Family*, p. 64.

27. Ibid., p. 172, quoting Benjamin Wadsworth's *The Well-Ordered Family*, written 1712.

28. Ibid., p. 173, quoting Cotton Mather's *A Family Well-Ordered*, written 1699.

29. Ibid., p. 173.

30. Ibid., p. 173.

31. Ibid., p. 185.

32. Tim Dearborn, *Taste and See: Awakening Our Spiritual Senses* (Downers Grove, Ill.: InterVarsity Press, 1996), p. 25.

33. Brigitte Berger and Peter L. Berger, *The War over the Family: Capturing the Middle Ground* (Garden City, N.Y.: Doubleday/Anchor, 1984), p. 92.

34. Barbara Welter, as quoted in Arlene Skolnick, *Embattled Paradise: The American Family*

in an Age of Uncertainty (New York: BasicBooks, 1991), p. 32.

[35] Gillis, *World of Their Own Making,* pp. 126, 116.

[36] Cultural pessimism is also a tradition of Western discourse with its own history; see Arthur Herman, *The Idea of Decline in Western History* (New York: Free Press, 1997).

[37] Stephanie Coontz, *The Way We Really Are: Coming to Terms with America's Changing Families* (New York: BasicBooks, 1997), p. 47.

[38] Ibid., p. 60. As Coontz notes, "it's possible to cut back in some areas," and families should well consider in what ways they might question their own levels of consumption. Realistically, however, she also observes that "there are limits to how fully most of us can opt out of the great American marketplace," and there are important economic consequences that may result from any such decisions.

[39] Gillis, *World of Their Own Making,* pp. xv, passim.

[40] Janet Fishburn, *Confronting the Idolatry of Family: A New Vision for the Household of God* (Nashville: Abingdon, 1991), pp. 35-36.

[41] Ibid., p. 86.

[42] Ibid., p. 54.

[43] I. Howard Marshall, *The Gospel of Luke: A Commentary on the Greek Text* (Grand Rapids, Mich.: Eerdmans, 1978), p. 411.

[44] Stanley Hauerwas, *Unleashing the Scripture: Freeing the Bible from Captivity to America* (Nashville: Abingdon, 1993), p.43.

[45] Rodney Clapp, *Families at the Crossroads: Beyond Traditional and Modern Options* (Downers Grove, Ill.: InterVarsity Press, 1993), p. 68.

[46] Ibid., pp. 76-77.

[47] Hauerwas, *Unleashing the Scripture,* p. 123.

[48] Mark DeVries, *Family-Based Youth Ministry* (Downers Grove, Ill.: InterVarsity Press, 1994), p. 171.

[49] Gilbert Meilaender, *Faith and Faithfulness: Basic Themes in Christian Ethics* (Notre Dame, Ind.: University of Notre Dame Press, 1991), p. 134.

[50] Ibid., p. 135.

[51] Ibid., p. 173.

Chapter 3: Family Values Go Postmodern

[1] Larry Rasmussen, *Moral Fragments and Moral Community: A Proposal for Church in Society* (Minneapolis: Fortress, 1993), p. 11.

[2] Brigitte Berger and Peter L. Berger, *The War over the Family: Capturing the Middle Ground* (Garden City, N.Y.: Doubleday/Anchor, 1983), p. 127.

[3] Richard B. Hays, *The Moral Vision of the New Testament: A Contemporary Introduction to New Testament Ethics* (San Francisco: HarperSanFrancisco, 1996), p. 458.

[4] Ibid., p. 459. Italics added.

[5] For the facts/artifacts distinction, see James B. Miller, "The Emerging Postmodern World," in *Postmodern Theology: Christian Faith in a Pluralist World,* ed. Frederic B. Burnham (New York: Harper & Row, 1989), p. 11.

[6] Maureen O'Hara and Walter Truett Anderson, "Welcome to the Postmodern World," *Family Therapy Networker* 15 (September/October 1991): 22.

[7] Ibid., p. 20.

[8] George Barna, *What Americans Believe* (Ventura, Calif.: Regal, 1991), pp. 83-85.

[9] The distinctions used here follow those made by Mike Featherstone, in *Consumer Culture and Postmodernism* (London: Sage, 1991), chapter 1.

[10] Stanley J. Grenz, *A Primer on Postmodernism* (Grand Rapids, Mich.: Eerdmans, 1996), p. 12.

[11] See Kenneth J. Gergen, *The Saturated Self: Dilemmas of Identity in Contemporary Life* (New York: BasicBooks, 1991), especially chapter 3.

[12] Kenneth J. Gergen, "The Saturated Family," *Family Therapy Networker* 15 (September/October 1991): 28.

[13] See Daniel Bell, *The Cultural Contradictions of Capitalism*, 20th anniversary ed. (New York: BasicBooks, 1996), pp. 63-72.

[14] Quoted by Rasmussen in *Moral Fragments and Moral Community*, p. 91.

[15] Judith Stacey, *Brave New Families: Stories of Domestic Upheaval in Late Twentieth Century America* (New York: BasicBooks, 1990).

[16] See James Q. Wilson, "The Family-Values Debate," *Commentary* 95, no. 4 (1993): 24-31; David Popenoe, "Scholars Should Worry About the Disintegration of the American Family," *Chronicle of Higher Education* 14 (April 1993): A48; Christopher Lasch, "Misreading the Facts About Families," *Commonweal* 22 (February 1991): 136.

[17] Judith Stacey, *In the Name of the Family: Rethinking Family Values in the Postmodern Age* (Boston: Beacon, 1996).

[18] Edward Shorter, *The Making of the Modern Family* (New York: BasicBooks, 1975).

[19] Stacey, *In the Name of the Family*, p. 7.

[20] Ibid., pp. 7-8.

[21] Ibid., p. 49.

[22] Ibid., p. 105. The title of her final chapter borrows from the gay rights slogan "We're here, we're queer, get used to it": "Gay and Lesbian Families Are Here; All Our Families Are Queer; Let's Get Used to It."

[23] Ibid., p. 37.

[24] As Berkeley sociologist Arlie Hochschild has argued, however, the homemaking function may still be primarily the wife's responsibility. See Arlie Russell Hochschild, *The Second Shift* (New York: Avon, 1989).

[25] Stacey, *In the Name of the Family*, p. 49.

[26] The former draw heavily upon the writings of Humberto Maturana and Francisco J. Varela, e.g., *Autopoiesis and Cognition: The Realization of the Living* (Boston: D. Reidel, 1980). The most thorough attempt to translate Maturana and Varela's biological theory into a therapeutic modality can be found in Jay Efran, Robert Lukens and Michael Lukens's *Language, Structure and Change* (New York: W. W. Norton, 1990). The latter are best represented by the social constructionist and narrative approaches to therapy. See, for example, Harold Goolishian and Harlene Anderson, "Human Systems as Linguistic Systems: Preliminary and Evolving Ideas About the Implications for Clinical Theory," *Family Process* 27 (1988): 371-93; Michael White and David Epston, *Narrative Means to Therapeutic Ends* (New York: W. W. Norton, 1990).

[27] Alan Parry and Robert E. Doan, *Story Re-visions: Narrative Therapy in the Postmodern World* (New York: Guilford, 1994), p. 6.

[28] Jean-François Lyotard, *The Postmodern Condition*, as quoted in Grenz, *Primer*, p. 46.

[29] Parry and Doan, *Re-visions*, p. 10.

[30] Ibid., p. 9.

[31] Ibid., p. 25.

[32] Ibid., p. 27.

[33] Ibid., p. 43.

[34] For a similar and more developed understanding of the transmission of meaning

between the generations, see Peter Berger and Thomas Luckmann, *The Social Construction of Reality: A Treatise in the Sociology of Knowledge* (Garden City, N.Y.: Doubleday/Anchor, 1967).

[35]Parry and Doan, *Story Re-visions,* p. 44.

[36]Ibid., pp. 40, 41.

[37]Ibid., p. 26.

[38]Ibid., p. 46. Italics added.

[39]William J. Doherty, "Family Therapy Goes Postmodern," *Family Therapy Networker* 15 (September/October 1991): 42.

[40]See especially Gergen, *Saturated Self.*

[41]Kenneth J. Gergen, "The Healthy, Happy Human Being Wears Many Masks," reprinted in *The Truth About the Truth: De-confusing and Re-constructing the Postmodern World,* ed. Walter Truett Anderson (New York: Tarcher/Putnam, 1995), p. 143.

[42]Gergen, "Saturated Family," p. 29.

[43]Ibid., p. 30.

[44]Ibid., p. 31.

[45]Ibid., pp. 31, 32.

[46]Ibid., p. 32.

[47]Ibid., p. 33.

[48]Ibid., p. 35.

[49]Ibid., p. 35.

[50]O'Hara and Anderson, "Welcome to the Postmodern World," p. 25.

[51]Gergen, "Saturated Family," p. 35.

[52]See especially Berger and Berger, *The War over the Family,* pp. 118-27.

[53]Robert Bellah, "Christian Faithfulness in a Pluralist World," in *Postmodern Theology,* ed. Burnham, p. 79.

Chapter 4: Moral Horizons

[1]Richard B. Hays, *Moral Vision of the New Testament: A Contemporary Introduction to New Testament Ethics* (San Francisco: HarperSanFrancisco, 1996), p. 2.

[2]Philip Yancey, "Neat! Way Cool! Awesome!" *Christianity Today,* April 7, 1997, p. 72.

[3]Lesslie Newbigin, *Truth to Tell: The Gospel as Public Truth* (Grand Rapids, Mich.: Eerdmans, 1991), p. 49.

[4]Robert N. Bellah, Richard Madsen, William M. Sullivan, Ann Swidler and Steven M. Tipton, *Habits of the Heart: Individualism and Commitment in American Life* (New York: Harper & Row, 1985).

[5]Brigitte Berger and Peter L. Berger, *The War over the Family: Capturing the Middle Ground* (Garden City, N.Y.: Doubleday/Anchor, 1983), p. 120. The term is also employed by Rodney Clapp in *Families at the Crossroads: Beyond Traditional and Modern Options* (Downers Grove, Ill.: InterVarsity Press, 1993), p. 24.

[6]Robert Bellah, ". . . Bring Along Your Compass," *Family Therapy Networker* 16 (November/December, 1992): 53.

[7]Bruce C. Hafen, "Individualism in Family Law," in *Rebuilding the Nest: A New Commitment to the American Family,* ed. David B. Blankenhorn, Steven Bayme and Jean Bethke Elshtain (Milwaukee: Family Service America, 1990), p. 164.

[8]Mary Ann Glendon, *Rights Talk: The Impoverishment of Political Discourse* (New York: Free Press, 1991).

[9]Alexis de Tocqueville, *Democracy in America,* trans. George Lawrence, ed. J. P. Mayer

(Garden City, N.Y.: Doubleday/Anchor, 1969), 1:270.

[10]Glendon, *Rights Talk*, p. 3.

[11]Ibid., p. 49. The history of the right to privacy is taken mostly from Glendon's text; the details of the *Bowers v. Hardwick* case are drawn from Hafen, "Individualism in Family Law."

[12]Glendon, *Rights Talk*, p. 52.

[13]Ibid., p. 55.

[14]Hafen, "Individualism in Family Law," pp. 174-75.

[15]The matter is far from simple. On the one hand, of course, there are numerous egregious examples of opportunistic abuses of rights language by individuals seeking compensation on highly questionable grounds—see Charles J. Sykes, *A Nation of Victims: The Decay of the American Character* (New York: St. Martin's, 1992). On the other hand, however, are the often chilling violations of Fourth Amendment rights as chronicled by Ellen Alderman and Caroline Kennedy, *The Right to Privacy* (New York: Alfred A. Knopf, 1995).

[16]Glendon, *Rights Talk*, p. xi.

[17]Robert N. Bellah, "The Invasion of the Money World," in *Rebuilding the Nest*, ed. Blankenhorn, Bayme and Elshtain, p. 229.

[18]Larry Rasmussen, *Moral Fragments and Moral Community: A Proposal for Church in Society* (Minneapolis: Fortress, 1993), p. 45.

[19]Daniel Bell, *The Cultural Contradictions of Capitalism*, 20th anniversary ed. (New York: BasicBooks, 1996), pp. 19-22.

[20]The substance of this argument in this paragraph is found in Jan E. Dizard and Howard Gadlin, *The Minimal Family* (Amherst: University of Massachusetts Press, 1990), chapter 2.

[21]Susan Strasser, *Satisfaction Guaranteed: The Making of the American Mass Market* (New York: Pantheon, 1989), p. 89.

[22]Ibid., p. 91.

[23]The history and quote are taken from Daniel J. Boorstin, *The Americans: The Democratic Experience* (New York: Vintage, 1974), pp. 373-76.

[24]See Strasser, *Satisfaction Guaranteed*, chapter 4.

[25]Mike Featherstone, *Consumer Culture and Postmodernism* (London: Sage, 1991), p. 86.

[26]Boorstin, *Americans*, pp. 145-46.

[27]Bellah et al., *Habits of the Heart*, pp. 32-35, passim.

[28]Bell, *Cultural Contradictions of Capitalism*, p. 22.

[29]Ibid., p. 21.

[30]This history of consumer credit is drawn from Boorstin, *Americans*, pp. 422-28.

[31]Ibid., p. 427.

[32]Bellah, "Invasion of the Money World," p. 231.

[33]Arlie Russell Hochschild, *The Time Bind: When Work Becomes Home and Home Becomes Work* (New York: Metropolitan, 1997), p. 232.

[34]Boorstin, *Americans*, p. 158.

[35]R. Laurence Moore, *Selling God: American Religion in the Marketplace of Culture* (New York: Oxford University Press, 1994), p. 205.

[36]Boorstin, *Americans*, p. 158.

[37]Moore, *Selling God*, p. 205.

[38]Boorstin, *Americans*, p. 159.

[39]Robert Wuthnow, *God and Mammon in America* (New York: Free Press, 1994), p. 133.

[40]Ibid., pp. 127-28.

[41]See James Davison Hunter, *Evangelicalism: The Coming Generation* (Chicago: University of Chicago Press, 1987), p. 74. Italics in original.

[42]Wuthnow, *God and Mammon in America*, pp. 188-89.

[43]Philip Rieff, *The Triumph of the Therapeutic: Uses of Faith after Freud* (Chicago: University of Chicago Press, 1966/1987), p. 18.

[44]Ibid., pp. 19-20.

[45]Christopher Lasch, *The Culture of Narcissism: American Life in an Age of Diminishing Expectations* (New York: W. W. Norton, 1979), p. 13.

[46]Bellah et al., *Habits of the Heart*, pp. 14-15.

[47]Ibid., p. 221.

[48]Joseph Veroff, Elizabeth Douvan and Richard A. Kulka, *The Inner American: A Self-Portrait from 1957 to 1976* (New York: Basic Books, 1981), p. 16.

[49]Charles Taylor, *The Ethics of Authenticity* (Cambridge, Mass.: Harvard University Press, 1991), p. 14.

[50]Veroff, Douvan and Kulka, *Inner American*, p. 18.

[51]Rieff, *Triumph of the Therapeutic*, p. 243.

[52]Judith Wallerstein and Sandra Blakeslee, *The Good Marriage: How and Why Love Lasts* (Boston: Houghton Mifflin, 1995), p. 337.

[53]Mary Sykes Wylie, "Consumer-Driven Therapy," *Family Therapy Networker* 21 (July/August 1997): 36.

[54]Ibid., p. 37.

[55]Rasmussen, *Moral Fragments and Moral Community*, p. 102.

[56]Sykes, *Nation of Victims*, p. 42.

[57]Taylor, *Ethics of Authenticity*, p. 69.

Chapter 5: Until Culture Do Us Part?

[1]Robert Bellah et al., *Habits of the Heart: Individualism and Commitment in American Life* (New York: Harper & Row, 1985), pp. 89-90.

[2]Constance Ahrons, *The Good Divorce: Keeping Your Family Together When Your Marriage Comes Apart* (New York: HarperCollins, 1994), p. ix.

[3]See, for example, Barbara Dafoe Whitehead, *The Divorce Culture* (New York: Alfred A. Knopf, 1996), and David Blankenhorn, *Fatherless America: Confronting Our Most Urgent Social Problem* (New York: BasicBooks, 1995). We should remember, however, that policy positions are not as simple as one might anticipate. Whitehead, for example, though concerned about the rise of a divorce culture, does not advocate the elimination of no-fault divorce. She suspects that the reestablishment of fault-based proceedings would not significantly deter divorce and would likely result in prolonging destructive legal conflicts. See Maggie Gallagher and Barbara Dafoe Whitehead, "End No-Fault Divorce?" *First Things* 75 (August/September 1997): 24-30.

[4]See, for example, Ahrons, *Good Divorce*, and Stephanie Coontz, *The Way We Really Are* (New York: BasicBooks, 1997).

[5]Michael Medved, *Hollywood vs. America: Popular Culture and the War on Traditional Values* (New York: HarperCollins/Zondervan, 1992), pp. 126-28.

[6]Blankenhorn, *Fatherless America*, p. 164.

[7]Whitehead, *Divorce Culture*, p. 145.

[8]Blankenhorn, *Fatherless America*, p. 167.

[9]Judith S. Wallerstein and Sandra Blakeslee, *Second Chances: Men, Women and Children*

[10] *a Decade After Divorce* (New York: Ticknor & Fields, 1989).

[10] Andrew J. Cherlin, *Public and Private Families: An Introduction* (New York: McGraw-Hill, 1996), p. 352.

[11] Ibid., p. 355.

[12] Whitehead, *Divorce Culture*, pp. 68-73.

[13] Ibid., p. 76.

[14] Ahrons, *Good Divorce*, p. 257.

[15] Ibid., p. 260.

[16] Blankenhorn, *Fatherless America*, p. 163. The phrase is used to describe the movie *Mrs. Doubtfire*.

[17] George Barna, *The Future of the American Family* (Chicago: Moody Press, 1993), p. 47.

[18] Participants were separated into three groups: those currently married but never divorced, those separated or divorced currently or in the past, and those who were currently unmarried due to the death of the spouse. The latter were removed from the sample for the purpose of this analysis. The results of the independent measures t-test were as follows: $t = 2.79$, df = 490, p = .006 (2-tailed).

[19] Mark Mellman, Edward Lazarus and Allan Rivlin, "Family Time, Family Values," in *Rebuilding the Nest*, ed. David Blankenhorn, Steven Bayme and Jean Bethke Elshtain (Milwaukee: Family Service America, 1990), pp. 73-92.

[20] The response categories are taken from items used by sociologist Robert Wuthnow in his Economic Values Survey. See Wuthnow's *God and Mammon in America* (New York: Free Press, 1994).

[21] The results of the independent measures t-test were as follows: $t = 7.72$, df = 490, p = .000 (2-tailed). The mean for the married group was 3.69.

[22] See Wuthnow, *God and Mammon in America*, p. 288; item 125 on the Economic Values Survey.

[23] Ibid., pp. 287-288, items 122 and 123. Wuthnow views the former statement as indicating a value orientation of *moral absolutism*, while the latter is evidence of an *emotivist* orientation (pp. 94-107). Regarding emotivism, see especially Alasdair MacIntyre, *After Virtue*, 2nd ed. (Notre Dame, Ind.: University of Notre Dame Press, 1984), chapters 2-3.

[24] Appendix A presents only the Pearson r correlation coefficients between the stated variables that are statistically significant. Because the large sample size makes even small to moderate correlations significant, the table uses a more stringent criterion than normal: only results that are significant at p .01 are reported. The table shows items correlated with the belief measure in a separate column from those correlated with permanence as a personal value. Each item is coded as to its type and listed in descending order from highest correlation to lowest. Forty-two positive correlations are reported. Only two statistically significant negative correlations were found in the analysis, both relatively small. Since these are an insufficient basis for observing general patterns, they are not reported.

[25] The distinction between *other-directed* versus *self-directed* values is found in Mellman, Lazarus and Rivlin, "Family Time, Family Values."

[26] Whitehead, *Divorce Culture*, pp. 140-45.

[27] Barna, *Future of the American Family*, p. 47.

[28] The name, of course, is fictitious, as it is for all the interview excerpts.

[29] Luke Timothy Johnson, *Scripture and Discernment: Decision Making in the Church* (Nashville: Abingdon, 1996), p. 43. Italics in original.

[30] Richard B. Hays, *The Moral Vision of the New Testament* (San Francisco: HarperSan-

Francisco, 1996), pp. 373-74.

Chapter 6: From Values to Virtue

[1]James Q. Wilson is quoted in an interview by Kenneth L. Woodward, "What Is Virtue?" *Newsweek,* June 13, 1994, p. 38.

[2]Stanley Hauerwas, "The Family as a School for Character," in *Perspectives on Marriage: A Reader,* ed. Kieran Scott and Michael Warren (New York: Oxford University Press, 1993), p. 152. The essay was reprinted from *Religious Education* 80 (1985): 272-85.

[3]David Blankenhorn, "The Possibility of Civil Society," in *Seedbeds of Virtue,* ed. Mary Ann Glendon and David Blankenhorn (Lanham, Md.: Madison, 1995), p. 277.

[4]Cited in Howard Fineman, "The Virtuecrats," *Newsweek,* June 13, 1994, p. 31. Poll conducted June 2-3, 1994.

[5]Stephen L. Carter, *Integrity* (New York: BasicBooks, 1996), p. 237. More extensively, C. S. Lewis has argued for a natural moral law, perceived by civilizations throughout history; see *The Abolition of Man* (New York: Macmillan, 1947).

[6]Gertrude Himmelfarb, *The Demoralization of Society: From Victorian Virtues to Modern Values* (New York: Vintage, 1994), p. 10.

[7]Alasdair MacIntyre, *After Virtue,* 2nd ed. (Notre Dame, Ind.: University of Notre Dame Press, 1984), p. 114.

[8]Charles Taylor, *The Ethics of Authenticity* (Cambridge, Mass.: Harvard University Press, 1994), p. 40. The phrase "horizons of significance" is found on p. 39.

[9]Ibid., p. 40. Taylor does not use the word *transcendent* here; I use it here and in this chapter to refer to horizons of significance that originate from outside the individual self. Thus the term need not be taken as implying an absolute transcendence beyond human experience or the limits of space and time.

[10]Anne Borrowdale, *Reconstructing Family Values* (London: SPCK, 1994), p. 56.

[11]James Davison Hunter, *Culture Wars: The Struggle to Define America* (New York: BasicBooks, 1991), p. 177.

[12]Diogenes Allen, *Christian Belief in a Postmodern World: The Full Wealth of Conviction* (Louisville, Ky.: Westminster John Knox, 1989).

[13]Robert T. Fancher, *Cultures of Healing: Correcting the Image of American Mental Health Care* (New York: W. H. Freeman, 1995), p. 328.

[14]Thomas S. Kuhn, *The Structure of Scientific Revolutions,* rev. ed. (Chicago: University of Chicago Press, 1962).

[15]Fancher, *Cultures of Healing,* p. 320.

[16]Ibid., p. 323.

[17]William J. Doherty, *Soul Searching: Why Psychotherapy Must Promote Moral Responsibility* (New York: BasicBooks, 1995), p. 24.

[18]Ibid., pp. 7-8.

[19]Ibid., p. 18.

[20]Ibid., p. 116.

[21]Ibid., p. 117.

[22]Ibid., pp. 187-90.

[23]Fineman, "Virtuecrats," pp. 30-33, 36.

[24]Ibid., pp. 33, 36.

[25]See Peggy Noonan, *Life, Liberty and the Pursuit of Happiness* (New York: Random House, 1994).

[26]Stanley Hauerwas, quoted during a discussion at a 1984 multidisciplinary conference

on virtue sponsored by the Rockford Institute in New York. See *Virtue—Public and Private,* ed. Richard John Neuhaus (Grand Rapids, Mich.: Eerdmans, 1986), pp. 58-59.

[27]William J. Bennett, ed., *The Book of Virtues: A Treasury of Great Moral Stories* (New York: Simon & Schuster, 1993), p. 12.

[28]Ibid., p. 21.

[29]See Robert Bellah et al., *Habits of the Heart: Individualism and Commitment in American Life* (New York: Harper & Row, 1985), pp. 71-75.

[30]The classic interpretation of this text by D. Martyn Lloyd-Jones is particularly apt in this regard. See his *Studies in the Sermon on the Mount* (Grand Rapids, Mich.: Eerdmans, 1959), 1:149-58. See also the treatment of the Beatitudes in Peter Kreeft's *Back to Virtue: Traditional Moral Wisdom for Modern Moral Confusion* (San Francisco: Ignatius, 1992), where they are contrasted with the seven deadly sins.

[31]For a related point regarding the interpretation of biblical texts, see Hans W. Frei, *The Eclipse of Biblical Narrative: A Study in Eighteenth and Nineteenth Century Hermeneutics* (New Haven, Conn.: Yale University Press, 1974).

[32]Over the years I have been challenged most by the thought of three individuals: Stanley Hauerwas, Alasdair MacIntyre and Gilbert Meilaender. From Hauerwas and MacIntyre one draws the connection between virtue ethics and the formative role of communal narrative. Meilaender, drawing from his Lutheran tradition, reminds us of the importance of preserving a strong doctrine of grace while formulating a Christian virtue ethic. Meilaender's *The Theory and Practice of Virtue* (Notre Dame, Ind.: University of Notre Dame Press, 1984) is also responsible for introducing me to the work of Josef Pieper, who is cited in later chapters. The best introduction that I have found to virtue ethics is Joseph Kotva, *The Christian Case for Virtue Ethics* (Washington, D.C.: Georgetown University Press, 1996), although his treatment of the role of narrative is necessarily brief.

[33]Stanley Hauerwas, *A Community of Character: Toward a Constructive Christian Social Ethic* (Notre Dame, Ind.: University of Notre Dame Press, 1981), p. 112.

[34]Bennett, *Book of Virtues,* p. 600.

[35]Meilaender, *Theory and Practice of Virtue,* p. 8.

[36]Ibid., pp. 10-11.

[37]MacIntyre, *After Virtue,* p. 203.

[38]See, for example, Jerome Bruner, *Acts of Meaning* (Cambridge, Mass.: Harvard University Press, 1990). A different angle is provided by Dan McAdams, who asserts that it is the emotional tone and basic imagery of later narrative constructions that are contributed in early childhood. See Dan McAdams, *The Stories We Live By: Personal Myths and the Making of the Self* (New York: William Morrow, 1993).

[39]MacIntyre, *After Virtue,* pp. 222-23.

[40]See Hauerwas's notion of the "story-formed community" in *Community of Character.*

[41]The categories of the synopsis from creation to consummation are adapted from Gabriel Fackre's *The Christian Story: A Narrative Interpretation of Basic Christian Doctrine,* vol. 1, 3rd ed. (Grand Rapids, Mich.: Eerdmans, 1996).

[42]MacIntyre, *After Virtue,* p. 263.

Chapter 7: Indwelling the Story

[1]Avery Dulles, *The Assurance of Things Hoped For: A Theology of Christian Faith* (New York: Oxford University Press, 1994), p. 281.

[2]John Shea, *Stories of Faith* (Chicago: Thomas More, 1980), pp. 160, 221.

[3]Donald E. Polkinghorne, *Narrative Knowing and the Human Sciences* (Albany: State University of New York Press, 1988), p. 11.

[4]In William J. Bennett, ed., *The Book of Virtues: A Treasury of Great Moral Stories* (New York: Simon & Schuster, 1993), pp. 45-46.

[5]Ibid., p. 45.

[6]Ibid., pp. 33-35.

[7]Ibid., p. 33.

[8]Ibid., pp. 32-33.

[9]In response to potential postmodern objections of the totalizing nature of the story, it may be useful to note that J. Richard Middleton and Brian Walsh argue that the Christian metanarrative contains "counterideological" elements that subvert "totalizing uses of the story": first, a "radical sensitivity to suffering," and second, a focus on God's "overarching creational intent." See *Truth Is Stranger Than It Used to Be: Biblical Faith in a Postmodern Age* (Downers Grove, Ill.: InterVarsity Press, 1995), p. 87.

[10]Martha Fay, *Do Children Need Religion?* (New York: Pantheon, 1993), pp. 8-9.

[11]This can be taken as an ontological assertion as over against the more limited heuristic claim of the usefulness of literary and linguistic concepts. Paul Brockelman writes that lived narrativity "is the ontological condition for human stories of any kind. Without that narrative condition of being an active agent, there could be no literature, history, religion, or even philosophy: These realms of discourse are built upon the human ability to tell and comprehend stories of various kinds, and only a being who in her very nature is acquainted and familiar with narrativity itself could possibly do that." Paul Brockelman, *The Inside Story: A Narrative Approach to Religious Understanding and Truth* (Albany: State University of New York Press, 1992), p. 96.

[12]See Paul Ricouer's treatment of the concept of "emplotment" in his *Time and Narrative*, vol. 1, trans. Kathleen McLaughlin and David Pellauer (Chicago: University of Chicago Press, 1984).

[13]Jerome Bruner, *Actual Minds, Possible Worlds* (Cambridge, Mass.: Harvard University Press, 1986), p. 16.

[14]See, for example, Peter Berger and Thomas Luckmann's discussion of the "social stock of knowledge" in *The Social Construction of Reality: A Treatise in the Sociology of Knowledge* (Garden City, N.Y.: Doubleday/Anchor, 1967).

[15]This is the concept of "canonicality" in Jerome Bruner's *Acts of Meaning* (Cambridge, Mass.: Harvard University Press, 1990).

[16]Ibid., p. 80.

[17]See, for example. Stephanie Coontz, *The Social Origins of Private Life* (London: Verso, 1988), chapter 1.

[18]Dulles, *Assurance of Things Hoped For,* p. 274.

[19]Brian J. Walsh and J. Richard Middleton, *The Transforming Vision: Shaping a Christian World View* (Downers Grove, Ill.: InterVarsity Press, 1984), p. 35.

[20]The four questions are already found in ibid., p. 35, but the more complete narrative interpretation of them is discussed in their later work. See Middleton and Walsh, *Truth Is Stranger Than It Used to Be,* especially chapter 4.

[21]Walsh and Middleton, *Transforming Vision,* p. 36.

[22]Robert Jewett, *Saint Paul at the Movies: The Apostle's Dialogue with American Culture* (Louisville, Ky.: Westminster John Knox, 1993), p. 20.

[23]Dulles, *Assurance of Things Hoped For,* p. 274.

[24]Luke Timothy Johnson, *Scripture and Discernment: Decision Making in the Church*

(Nashville: Abingdon, 1996), p. 23.

[25]Josef Pieper, *Belief and Faith: A Philosophical Tract,* trans. Richard Winston and Clara Winston (New York: Pantheon, 1963), pp. 90-91.

[26]Dulles, *Assurance of Things Hoped For,* p. 276.

[27]Lesslie Newbigin, *The Light Has Come: An Exposition of the Fourth Gospel* (Grand Rapids, Mich.: Eerdmans, 1982), p. 58.

[28]Ibid., p. 59.

[29]Stephen E. Fowl and L. Gregory Jones, *Reading in Communion: Scripture and Ethics in Christian Life* (Grand Rapids, Mich.: Eerdmans, 1991), p. 31. Italics in original.

[30]Shea, *Stories of Faith,* p. 156.

[31]Lesslie Newbigin, *Proper Confidence: Faith, Doubt and Certainty in Christian Discipleship* (Grand Rapids, Mich.: Eerdmans, 1995), p. 88.

[32]Michael Polanyi, *Personal Knowledge: Towards a Post-critical Philosophy* (Chicago: University of Chicago Press, 1962), p. 281.

[33]Ibid., pp. 55ff.

[34]Lesslie Newbigin, *The Gospel in a Pluralist Society* (Grand Rapids, Mich.: Eerdmans, 1989), pp. 98-99. Italics in original. Here also we should recognize that there are different ways in which Christians may appeal to the Scripture for ethical warrants. Richard Hays identifies the four modes of rules, principles, paradigms and symbolic world, the latter of which "creates the perceptual categories through which we interpret reality." The concept of indwelling a narrative world corresponds most closely to this fourth mode of appeal. See Richard Hays, *The Moral Vision of the New Testament* (San Francisco: HarperSanFrancisco, 1996), p. 209.

[35]See Paul Rowntree Clifford, *The Reality of the Kingdom: Making Sense of God's Reign in a World like Ours* (Grand Rapids, Mich.: Eerdmans, 1996), chapter 9.

[36]Annie Dillard, *An American Childhood* (New York: HarperPerennial, 1987), p. 134.

[37]Johnson, *Scripture and Discernment,* p. 23.

[38]The phrase is used by Gilbert Meilaender to refer to the universalizing aspirations of modern ethical theory. See his *Faith and Faithfulness: Basic Themes in Christian Ethics* (Notre Dame, Ind.: University of Notre Dame Press, 1991), p. 93.

[39]Ibid., p. 116.

[40]The passage, known as the *Shema,* became an important profession of faith, recited daily by pious Jews.

[41]Stanley Hauerwas, *A Community of Character* (Notre Dame, Ind.: University of Notre Dame Press, 1981), p. 166.

[42]Brockelman, *Inside Story,* pp. 137-39.

[43]See Wade Clark Roof, *A Generation of Seekers: The Spiritual Journeys of the Baby Boom Generation* (San Francisco: HarperSanFrancisco, 1993), especially pp. 194-200.

[44]See, for example, Cameron Lee, "Parenting as Discipleship: A Contextual Motif for Christian Parent Education," *Journal of Psychology and Theology* 19 (1991): 268-77.

[45]Hauerwas, *Community of Character,* p. 52.

[46]William P. Brown, *Character in Crisis: A Fresh Approach to the Wisdom Literature of the Old Testament* (Grand Rapids, Mich.: Eerdmans, 1996), p. 40.

[47]Larry Rasmussen, *Moral Fragments and Moral Community* (Minneapolis: Fortress, 1993), p. 169.

[48]Fowl and Jones, *Reading in Communion,* p. 101.

Chapter 8: Living Toward the Promise

[1] Walter Brueggemann, *Hope Within History* (Atlanta: John Knox, 1987), p. 5. The title of the chapter was inspired by Brueggemann's fourth chapter, "Living Toward a Vision," which was also the title of one of Brueggemann's earlier books.

[2] Jürgen Moltmann, *Theology of Hope,* trans. James Leitch (London: SCM Press, 1967), p. 338.

[3] J. R. R. Tolkien tells of Bilbo's adventures in the novel that preceded the trilogy, *The Hobbit* (New York: Ballantine, 1965).

[4] J. R. R. Tolkien, *The Two Towers* (New York: Ballantine, 1965), p. 407.

[5] J. R. R. Tolkien, *The Return of the King* (New York: Ballantine, 1965), p. 281.

[6] They are, of course, saved in the end; but for the benefit of those who have never read the books, I will leave it to you to discover the manner of their rescue. Jesuit scholar John Navone writes this about Tolkien's contribution to a theology of story: "Tolkien implies that we experience the Primary World at its deepest level only when we have made the willing suspension of disbelief whereby we enter into the wonderful and gracious Secondary World where the Gospel story is heard and believed." See John Navone, *Seeking God in Story* (Collegeville, Minn.: Liturgical, 1990), p. 250.

[7] Brueggemann, *Hope Within History,* p. 22.

[8] The phrase is used by Cornelius Plantinga to describe sin and brokenness, in contrast to the divine *shalom.* See Cornelius Plantinga, *Not the Way It's Supposed to Be: A Breviary of Sin* (Grand Rapids, Mich.: Eerdmans, 1995).

[9] See Gilbert C. Meilaender, *The Theory and Practice of Virtue* (Notre Dame, Ind.: University of Notre Dame Press, 1984), especially chapter 5.

[10] Ibid., p. 122.

[11] The theme of pilgrimage is key both to Moltmann's *Theology of Hope* and to Josef Pieper's *On Hope,* trans. Mary Frances McCarthy (San Francisco: Ignatius, 1986).

[12] See Brian J. Walsh and J. Richard Middleton, *The Transforming Vision* (Downers Grove, Ill.: InterVarsity Press, 1984), and Middleton and Walsh, *Truth Is Stranger Than It Used to Be* (Downers Grove, Ill.: InterVarsity Press, 1995).

[13] The language of presence and absence, for example, is used by John Shea, *Stories of Faith* (Chicago: Thomas More, 1980), p. 220.

[14] Lesslie Newbigin, *The Gospel in a Pluralist Society* (Grand Rapids, Mich.: Eerdmans, 1989), pp. 101-2.

[15] Moltmann, *Theology of Hope,* p. 326. Here it is useful to note that William Willimon criticizes Moltmann for reducing Christian ethics to the single overarching principle of hope: see Willimon, *The Service of God* (Nashville: Abingdon, 1983), pp. 210-11, n. 29. It is possible, however, to read Moltmann as a theological corrective to a cultural Christianity that has lost its forward-looking aspect. In this way the significance of eschatology can be recaptured without making it a solitary ethical principle.

[16] Brueggemann, *Hope Within History,* p. 77.

[17] Josef Pieper, *Hope and History* (New York: Herder and Herder, 1969), p. 91.

[18] There is a minor variation in the Greek text, but an insignificant one: the English translation of the two phrases is identical in the NRSV, as it is in the NIV, the KJV and the NAS.

[19] Brueggemann, *Hope Within History,* pp. 72-73. Italics in original.

[20] Pieper, *Hope and History,* p. 21.

[21] Peter Berger, Brigitte Berger and Hansfried Kellner, *The Homeless Mind: Modernization and Consciousness* (New York: Vintage, 1974), p. 82. Italics in original.

[22] See Albert Borgmann, *Crossing the Postmodern Divide* (Chicago: University of Chicago

[23] Press, 1992), chapter 1.

[23] Pieper, *On Hope*, pp. 55-57.

[24] Borgmann, *Crossing the Postmodern Divide*, p. 47.

[25] Philip Cushman, "Why the Self Is Empty: Toward a Historically Situated Psychology," *American Psychologist* 45 (1990): 605. See also his later work *Constructing the Self, Constructing America: A Cultural History of Psychotherapy* (Reading, Mass.: Addison-Wesley, 1995). A similar point is made by Robert Bellah and his colleagues: the "unencumbered" self is empty because it is first severed from communal traditions, and therefore chooses values as a means of expression. See Robert Bellah et al., *Habits of the Heart* (New York: Harper & Row, 1985), pp. 75-81.

[26] Neil Postman, *Amusing Ourselves to Death: Public Discourse in the Age of Show Business* (New York: Penguin, 1985), p. 128.

[27] Cushman, *Constructing the Self*, p. 81.

[28] The exodus narrative is key to both Moltmann's *(Theology of Hope)* and Brueggemann's *(Hope Within History)* treatment of hope and its relationship to the church.

[29] Brueggemann, *Hope Within History*, p. 80. He identifies the phrase "the system is the solution" as a phone company slogan.

[30] Borgmann, *Crossing the Postmodern Divide*, p. 112.

[31] Neil Postman makes a similar point regarding what he calls the "epistemology of television": the movement out of a typographic culture into a video culture has changed the way we think and process information; see his book *Amusing Ourselves to Death*.

[32] Borgmann, *Crossing the Postmodern Divide*, p. 112. On this point see also Larry Rasmussen, *Moral Fragments and Moral Community* (Minneapolis: Fortress, 1993), chapter 5.

[33] Accordingly Brueggemann suggests that the exodus narrative delineates three movements in the development of faith, beginning with a "critique of ideology which has shaped personhood according to dominant myths that reflect social interests." See *Hope Within History*, p. 24.

[34] Mary Pipher, *The Shelter of Each Other: Rebuilding our Families* (New York: Ballantine, 1996), p. 15.

[35] Moltmann, *Theology of Hope*, p. 333.

[36] Stanley Hauerwas, *A Community of Character* (Notre Dame, Ind.: University of Notre Dame Press, 1981), p. 165.

[37] See, for example, Ivan Boszormenyi-Nagy and Geraldine Spark, *Invisible Loyalties* (Hagerstown, Md.: Harper & Row Medical, 1973).

[38] Although the matter cannot be addressed here, this suggests an important angle on the ethical and theological debates over reproductive technology.

[39] Hauerwas, *Community of Character*, pp. 165-66.

[40] Ibid., p. 174.

[41] Newbigin, *Gospel in a Pluralist Society*, p. 232.

[42] There is, of course, a third response to Jesus: on the basis of the miraculous sign, the people conclude that he is the Prophet promised in Deuteronomy 18, and seek to make him king by force (Jn 6:14-15). This is less a failure of confidence than an alternative narrative of the kingdom, which the disciples apparently shared to some degree.

[43] Brueggemann, *Hope Within History*, p. 105.

[44] So Brueggemann: "The American dream we have lived is precarious, if not ending. It helps very little to offer technological or religious certitudes to cushion the break. The

church's ministry is not only prophetic, to *note the ending,* but also pastoral, to *embrace the ending.*" Ibid., p. 106.

Chapter 9: The Mark of the Kingdom

[1]Steven Mintz and Susan Kellogg, *Domestic Revolutions: A Social History of American Family Life* (New York: Free Press, 1988), p. 46.

[2]Ibid., pp. 186-90.

[3]Robert Bellah et al., *Habits of the Heart: Individualism and Commitment in American Life* (New York: Harper & Row, 1985), p. 93.

[4]Ibid., pp. 95-96.

[5]Ibid., p. 109.

[6]Alfred H. Ells, *Family Love* (Nashville: Thomas Nelson, 1995).

[7]Ibid., p. 8.

[8]Ibid., pp. 9-10.

[9]Harville Hendrix, *Getting the Love You Want: A Guide for Couples* (New York: HarperPerennial, 1990), p. 66.

[10]Ells, *Family Love,* p. 11.

[11]Ells defines a *love pattern* as a "recurring set of behaviors that you exhibit when giving or getting love." Ibid., p. 21.

[12]Ibid., p. 12.

[13]Ibid., p. 34.

[14]Although not cited, Ells draws the terms from the family therapy literature, particularly the work of Salvador Minuchin. See, for example, Salvador Minuchin, *Families and Family Therapy* (Cambridge, Mass.: Harvard University Press, 1974).

[15]Ells, *Family Love,* chapter 11.

[16]Ibid., pp. 113-17.

[17]Ibid., p. 48.

[18]Ibid., pp. 71-72.

[19]Ibid., p. 72.

[20]Ibid., p. 178.

[21]Ibid., pp. 178-79.

[22]Ibid., p. 181.

[23]Ibid., p. 95.

[24]Ibid., p. 97.

[25]Ibid., p. 171.

[26]Ibid., p. 98.

[27]Mary Pipher, *The Shelter of Each Other: Rebuilding Our Families* (New York: Ballantine, 1996), p. 119.

[28]Paul Ramsey, *Basic Christian Ethics* (Louisville, Ky.: Westminster John Knox, 1950/1993), pp. 92, 93.

[29]See Richard Hays, *The Moral Vision of the New Testament* (San Francisco: HarperSanFrancisco, 1996), p. 209.

[30]Joseph Kotva, *The Christian Case for Virtue Ethics* (Washington, D.C.: Georgetown University Press, 1996), pp. 87-88.

[31]Here we should note that Richard Hays, for example, argues that love is inadequate as a unifying theme for New Testament ethics. He observes that while love is fundamental to both Paul's and John's characterization of the Christian life, it is not a central emphasis in the Gospel of Mark, the book of Hebrews or Revelation, and the word is absent

entirely from the book of Acts. This reinforces the notion that the Christian life cannot
be reduced to the single principle of love, nor love reduced to simple characteristics.
See Hays, *The Moral Vision of the New Testament,* pp. 200-203.

[32]Stephen G. Post, *Spheres of Love: Toward a New Ethics of the Family* (Dallas: Southern
Methodist University Press, 1994), pp. 13-14.

[33]Fyodor Dostoyevsky, *The Brothers Karamazov,* trans. Constance Garnett, ed. Manuel
Komroff (New York: New American Library, 1957), pp. 218-19.

[34]C. S. Lewis, *The Four Loves* (New York: Harcourt Brace Jovanovich, 1960), p. 169.

[35]See, for example, Ramsey, *Basic Christian Ethics,* and Anders Nygren, *Agape and Eros:
A Study of the Christian Idea of Love,* 3 vols. (New York: Macmillan, 1932).

[36]Ramsey, *Basic Christian Ethics,* pp. 95, 97.

[37]Josef Pieper, *About Love,* trans. Richard Winston and Clara Winston (Chicago: Franciscan
Herald, 1974), p. 58.

[38]Lewis, *Four Loves,* pp. 11-21.

[39]Ibid., p. 11.

[40]Ibid., p. 12.

[41]Ibid., pp. 13-14.

[42]See, for example, G. Simon Harak, *Virtuous Passions: The Formation of Christian
Character* (New York: Paulist, 1993).

[43]Jürgen Moltmann, *Theology of Hope,* trans. James Leitch (London: SCM Press, 1967), p.
338.

[44]Dostoyevsky, *Brothers Karamazov,* pp. 60, 62.

Bibliography

Ahrons, Constance. *The Good Divorce: Keeping Your Family Together When Your Marriage Comes Apart*. New York: HarperCollins, 1994.

Alderman, Ellen, and Caroline Kennedy. *The Right to Privacy*. New York: Alfred A. Knopf, 1995.

Allen, Diogenes. *Christian Belief in a Postmodern World: The Full Wealth of Conviction*. Louisville, Ky.: Westminster John Knox, 1989.

Alter, Jonathan. "Thinking of Family Values." *Newsweek*, December 30, 1996/January 6, 1997, pp. 30-35.

Barna, George. *The Future of the American Family*. Chicago: Moody Press, 1993.

———. *What Americans Believe*. Ventura, Calif.: Regal, 1991.

Bell, Daniel. *The Cultural Contradictions of Capitalism*. 20th anniversary ed. New York: BasicBooks, 1996.

Bellah, Robert N. ". . . Bring Along Your Compass." *Family Therapy Networker* 16 (November/December 1992): 53-55.

———. "Christian Faithfulness in a Pluralist World." In *Postmodern Theology: Christian Faith in a Pluralist World*, edited by Frederic B. Burnham, pp. 74-91. New York: Harper & Row, 1989.

———. "The Invasion of the Money World." In *Rebuilding the Nest: A New Commitment to the American Family*, edited by David Blankenhorn, Steven Bayme and Jean Bethke Elshtain, pp. 227-36. Milwaukee: Family Service America, 1990.

Bellah, Robert N., Richard Madsen, William M. Sullivan, Ann Swidler and Steven M. Tipton. *Habits of the Heart: Individualism and Commitment in American Life*. New York: Harper & Row, 1985.

Bennett, William. ed. *The Book of Virtues: A Treasury of Great Moral Stories*. New York: Simon & Schuster, 1993.

———. *The Children's Book of Virtues*. New York: Simon & Schuster, 1995.

———. *The Moral Compass*. New York: Simon & Schuster, 1995.

Berger, Brigitte, and Peter Berger. *The War over the Family: Capturing the Middle Ground*. Garden City, N.Y.: Doubleday/Anchor, 1984.

Berger, Peter, Brigitte Berger and Hansfried Kellner. *The Homeless Mind: Modernization and Consciousness*. New York: Vintage, 1974.

Berger, Peter, and Thomas Luckmann. *The Social Construction of Reality: A Treatise in the Sociology of Knowledge*. Garden City, N.Y.: Doubleday/Anchor, 1967.

Blankenhorn, David. *Fatherless America: Confronting Our Most Urgent Social Problem*. New York: BasicBooks, 1995.

———. "The Possibility of Civil Society." In *Seedbeds of Virtue*, edited by Mary Ann Glendon and David Blankenhorn, pp. 271-82. Lanham, Md.: Madison, 1995.

Blankenhorn, David, Steven Bayme and Jean Bethke Elshtain, eds. *Rebuilding the Nest: A New Commitment to the American Family*. Milwaukee: Family Service America, 1990.

Boorstin, Daniel J. *The Americans: The Democratic Experience*. New York: Vintage, 1974.

Borgmann, Albert. *Crossing the Postmodern Divide*. Chicago: University of Chicago Press,

1992.

Borrowdale, Anne. *Reconstructing Family Values*. London: SPCK, 1994.

Boszormenyi-Nagy, Ivan, and Geraldine Spark. *Invisible Loyalties*. Hagerstown, Md.: Harper & Row Medical, 1973.

Brockelman, Paul. *The Inside Story: A Narrative Approach to Religious Understanding and Truth*. Albany: State University of New York Press, 1992.

Brown, William P. *Character in Crisis: A Fresh Approach to the Wisdom Literature of the Old Testament*. Grand Rapids, Mich.: Eerdmans, 1996.

Brueggemann, Walter. *Hope Within History*. Atlanta: John Knox, 1987.

Bruner, Jerome. *Acts of Meaning*. Cambridge, Mass.: Harvard University Press, 1990.

———. *Actual Minds, Possible Worlds*. Cambridge, Mass.: Harvard University Press, 1986.

Burke, Phyllis. *Family Values*. New York: Random House, 1993.

Carter, Stephen. *Integrity*. New York: BasicBooks, 1996.

Cherlin, Andrew J. *Public and Private Families: An Introduction*. New York: McGraw-Hill, 1996.

Clapp, Rodney. *Families at the Crossroads: Beyond Traditional and Modern Options*. Downers Grove, Ill.: InterVarsity Press, 1993.

Clifford, Paul Rowntree. *The Reality of the Kingdom: Making Sense of God's Reign in a World like Ours*. Grand Rapids, Mich.: Eerdmans, 1996.

Clift, Eleanor. "The Murphy Brown Policy." *Newsweek*, June 1, 1992, p. 46.

Coontz, Stephanie. *The Social Origins of Private Life*. London: Verso, 1988.

———. *The Way We Never Were: American Families and the Nostalgia Trap*. New York: BasicBooks, 1992.

———. *The Way We Really Are: Coming to Terms with America's Changing Families*. New York: BasicBooks, 1997.

Cushman, Philip. *Constructing the Self, Constructing America: A Cultural History of Psychotherapy*. Reading, Mass.: Addison-Wesley, 1995.

———. "Why the Self Is Empty: Toward a Historically Situated Psychology." *American Psychologist* 45 (1990): 599-611.

Dearborn, Tim. *Taste and See: Awakening Our Spiritual Senses*. Downers Grove, Ill.: InterVarsity Press, 1996.

DeVries, Mark. *Family-Based Youth Ministry*. Downers Grove, Ill.: InterVarsity Press, 1994.

Dillard, Annie. *An American Childhood*. New York: HarperPerennial, 1987.

Dizard, Jan, and Howard Gadlin. *The Minimal Family*. Amherst, Mass.: University of Massachusetts Press, 1990.

Doherty, William J. "Family Therapy Goes Postmodern." *Family Therapy Networker* 15 (September/October 1991): 37-42.

———. *Soul Searching: Why Psychotherapy Must Promote Moral Responsibility*. New York: BasicBooks, 1995.

Dostoyevsky, Fyodor. *The Brothers Karamazov*. Translated by Constance Garnett. Edited by Manuel Komroff. New York: New American Library, 1957.

Dulles, Avery. *The Assurance of Things Hoped For: A Theology of Christian Faith*. New York: Oxford University Press, 1994.

Efran, Jay, Robert Lukens and Michael Lukens. *Language, Structure and Change*. New York: W. W. Norton, 1990.

Ells, Alfred H. *Family Love*. Nashville: Thomas Nelson, 1995.

Fackre, Gabriel. *The Christian Story: A Narrative Interpretation of Basic Christian Doctrine*. Vol. 1. 3rd ed. Grand Rapids, Mich.: Eerdmans, 1996.

Falwell, Jerry, ed. *The New American Family: The Rebirth of the American Dream*. Dallas: Word, 1992.

Fancher, Robert T. *Cultures of Healing: Correcting the Image of American Mental Health Care*. New York: W. H. Freeman, 1995.

Fay, Martha. *Do Children Need Religion?* New York: Pantheon, 1993.

Featherstone, Mike. *Consumer Culture and Postmodernism*. London: Sage, 1991.

Fineman, Howard. "The Virtuecrats." *Newsweek*, June 13, 1994, pp. 30-36.

Fishburn, Janet. *Confronting the Idolatry of Family: A New Vision for the Household of God*. Nashville: Abingdon, 1991.

Fowl, Stephen E., and L. Gregory Jones. *Reading in Communion: Scripture and Ethics in Christian Life*. Grand Rapids, Mich.: Eerdmans, 1991.

Frei, Hans W. *The Eclipse of Biblical Narrative: A Study in Eighteenth and Nineteenth Century Hermeneutics*. New Haven, Conn.: Yale University Press, 1974.

Gallagher, Maggie, and Barbara Dafoe Whitehead. "End No-Fault Divorce?" *First Things* 75 (August/September 1997): 24-30.

Gergen, Kenneth J. "The Healthy, Happy Human Being Wears Many Masks." In *The Truth About the Truth: De-confusing and Re-constructing the Postmodern World*, edited by Walter Truett Anderson, pp. 136-44. New York: Tarcher/Putnam, 1995.

———. "The Saturated Family." *Family Therapy Networker* 15 (September/October 1991): 26-35.

———. *The Saturated Self: Dilemmas of Identity in Contemporary Life*. New York: BasicBooks, 1991.

Getzen, Robin, and Erik Bruun, eds. *The Book of American Values and Virtues*. New York: Black Dog and Leventhal, 1996.

Gillis, John R. *A World of Their Own Making: Myth, Ritual and the Quest for Family Values*. New York: BasicBooks, 1996.

Glendon, Mary Ann. *Rights Talk: The Impoverishment of Political Discourse*. New York: Free Press, 1991.

Glendon, Mary Ann, and David Blankenhorn, eds. *Seedbeds of Virtue: Sources of Competence, Character and Citizenship in American Society*. Lanham, Md.: Madison, 1995.

Goesel, Elizabeth. *Courtship and Marriage of the 1700s*. Williamsburg, Va.: Bicast, 1993.

Goolishian, Harold, and Harlene Anderson. "Human Systems as Linguistic Systems: Preliminary and Evolving Ideas About the Implications for Clinical Theory." *Family Process* 27 (1988): 371-93.

Gottlieb, Beatrice. *The Family in the Western World: From the Black Death to the Industrial Age*. New York: Oxford University Press, 1993.

Grenz, Stanley J. *A Primer on Postmodernism*. Grand Rapids, Mich.: Eerdmans, 1996.

Hafen, Bruce C. "Individualism in Family Law." In *Rebuilding the Nest: A New Commitment to the American Family*, edited by David Blankenhorn, Steven Bayme and Jean Bethke Elshtain, pp. 161-77. Milwaukee: Family Service America, 1990.

Harak, G. Simon. *Virtuous Passions: The Formation of Christian Character*. New York: Paulist, 1993.

Hauerwas, Stanley. *A Community of Character: Toward a Constructive Christian Social Ethic*. Notre Dame, Ind.: University of Notre Dame Press, 1981.

———. "The Family as a School for Character." In *Perspectives on Marriage: A Reader*, edited by Kieran Scott and Michael Warren, pp. 146-57. New York: Oxford University Press, 1993.

——. *Unleashing the Scripture: Freeing the Bible from Captivity to America.* Nashville: Abingdon, 1993.

Hauerwas, Stanley, and William Willimon. *Where Resident Aliens Live.* Nashville: Abingdon, 1996.

Hays, Richard B. *The Moral Vision of the New Testament: A Contemporary Introduction to New Testament Ethics.* San Francisco: HarperSanFrancisco, 1996.

Hendrix, Harville. *Getting the Love You Want: A Guide for Couples.* New York: HarperPerennial, 1990.

Herman, Arthur. *The Idea of Decline in Western History.* New York: Free Press, 1997.

Himmelfarb, Gertrude. *The Demoralization of Society: From Victorian Virtues to Modern Values.* New York: Vintage, 1994.

Hochschild, Arlie Russell. *The Second Shift.* New York: Avon, 1989.

——. *The Time Bind: When Work Becomes Home and Home Becomes Work.* New York: Metropolitan, 1997.

Hunter, James Davison. *Culture Wars: The Struggle to Define America.* New York: Basic Books, 1991.

——. *Evangelicalism: The Coming Generation.* Chicago: University of Chicago Press, 1987.

Jewett, Robert. *Saint Paul at the Movies: The Apostle's Dialogue with American Culture.* Louisville, Ky.: Westminster John Knox, 1993.

Johnson, Luke Timothy. *Scripture and Discernment: Decision Making in the Church.* Nashville: Abingdon, 1996.

Kain, Edward L. *The Myth of Family Decline: Understanding Families in a World of Rapid Social Change.* Lexington, Mass.: Lexington, 1990.

Kemp, Jack. Foreword to *The New American Family: The Rebirth of the American Dream,* edited by Jerry Falwell, pp. xi-xv. Dallas: Word, 1992.

Knight, Robin. "An Unmarried Woman and a Political Fight." *U.S. News & World Report,* June 1, 1992, p. 10.

Kotva, Joseph. *The Christian Case for Virtue Ethics.* Washington, D.C.: Georgetown University Press, 1996.

Kozol, Jonathan. *Amazing Grace: The Lives of Children and the Conscience of a Nation.* New York: HarperPerennial, 1996.

Kreeft, Peter. *Back to Virtue: Traditional Moral Wisdom for Modern Moral Confusion.* San Francisco: Ignatius, 1992.

Kuhn, Thomas S. *The Structure of Scientific Revolutions.* Rev. ed. Chicago: University of Chicago Press, 1962.

Lasch, Christopher. *The Culture of Narcissism: American Life in an Age of Diminishing Expectations.* New York: W. W. Norton, 1979.

——. *Haven in a Heartless World: The Family Besieged.* New York: BasicBooks, 1977.

——. "Misreading the Facts About Families." *Commonweal* 22 (February 1991): 136.

Lee, Cameron. "Parenting as Discipleship: A Contextual Motif for Christian Parent Education." *Journal of Psychology and Theology* 19 (1991): 268-77.

Leo, John. "A Pox on Dan and Murphy." *U.S. News & World Report,* June 1, 1992, p. 19.

Lewis, C. S. *The Abolition of Man.* New York: Macmillan, 1947.

——. *The Four Loves.* New York: Harcourt Brace Jovanovich, 1960.

Lewis, Robert. *Real Family Values.* Gresham, Ore.: Vision House, 1995.

Lloyd-Jones, D. Martyn. *Studies in the Sermon on the Mount.* Vol. 1. Grand Rapids, Mich.: Eerdmans, 1959.

MacIntyre, Alasdair. *After Virtue.* 2nd ed. Notre Dame, Ind.: University of Notre Dame

Press, 1984.

Marshall, I. Howard. *The Gospel of Luke: A Commentary on the Greek Text*. Grand Rapids, Mich.: Eerdmans, 1978.

Maturana, Humberto, and Francisco J. Varela. *Autopoiesis and Cognition: The Realization of the Living*. Boston, Mass.: D. Reidel, 1980.

May, Elaine Tyler. *Homeward Bound: American Families in the Cold War Era*. New York: BasicBooks, 1988.

McAdams, Dan. *The Stories We Live By: Personal Myths and the Making of the Self*. New York: William Morrow, 1993.

Medved, Michael. *Hollywood vs. America: Popular Culture and the War on Traditional Values*. New York: HarperCollins/Zondervan, 1992.

Meilaender, Gilbert. *Faith and Faithfulness: Basic Themes in Christian Ethics*. Notre Dame, Ind.: University of Notre Dame Press, 1991.

———. *The Theory and Practice of Virtue*. Notre Dame, Ind.: University of Notre Dame Press, 1984.

Mellman, Mark, Edward Lazarus and Allan Rivlin. "Family Time, Family Values." In *Rebuilding the Nest: A New Commitment to the American Family,* edited by David Blankenhorn, Steven Bayme and Jean Bethke Elshtain, pp. 73-92. Milwaukee: Family Service America, 1990.

Middleton, J. Richard, and Brian J. Walsh. *Truth Is Stranger Than It Used to Be: Biblical Faith in a Postmodern Age*. Downers Grove, Ill.: InterVarsity Press, 1995.

Miller, James B. "The Emerging Postmodern World." In *Postmodern Theology: Christian Faith in a Pluralist World,* edited by Frederic B. Burnham, pp. 1-19. New York: Harper & Row, 1989.

Mintz, Steven, and Susan Kellogg. *Domestic Revolutions: A Social History of American Family Life*. New York: Free Press, 1988.

Minuchin, Salvador. *Families and Family Therapy*. Cambridge, Mass.: Harvard University Press, 1974.

Moltmann, Jürgen. *Theology of Hope*. Translated by James Leitch. London: SCM Press, 1967.

Moore, R. Laurence. *Selling God: American Religion in the Marketplace of Culture*. New York: Oxford University Press, 1994.

Morgan, Edmund S. *The Puritan Family: Religion and Domestic Relations in Seventeenth-Century New England*. Rev. ed. New York: Harper & Row, 1966.

———. *Virginians at Home: Family Life in the Eighteenth Century*. Williamsburg, Va.: Colonial Williamsburg Foundation, 1952.

Morrow, Lance. "But Seriously, Folks . . ." *Time,* June 1, 1992, pp. 29-31.

Mouw, Richard, and Sander Griffioen. *Pluralisms and Horizons*. Grand Rapids, Mich.: Eerdmans, 1993.

Navone, John. *Seeking God in Story*. Collegeville, Minn.: Liturgical Press, 1990.

Neuhaus, Richard John, ed. *Virtue—Public and Private*. Grand Rapids, Mich.: Eerdmans, 1986.

Newbigin, Lesslie. *The Gospel in a Pluralist Society*. Grand Rapids, Mich.: Eerdmans, 1989.

———. *The Light Has Come: An Exposition of the Fourth Gospel*. Grand Rapids, Mich.: Eerdmans, 1982.

———. *Proper Confidence: Faith, Doubt and Certainty in Christian Discipleship*. Grand Rapids, Mich.: Eerdmans, 1995.

———. *Truth to Tell: The Gospel as Public Truth*. Grand Rapids, Mich.: Eerdmans, 1991.

Noonan, Peggy. *Life, Liberty and the Pursuit of Happiness.* New York: Random House, 1994.

Nygren, Anders. *Agape and Eros: A Study of the Christian Idea of Love.* 3 vols. New York: Macmillan, 1932.

O'Hara, Maureen, and Walter Truett Anderson. "Welcome to the Postmodern World." *Family Therapy Networker* 15 (September/October 1991): 18-25.

Parry, Alan, and Robert E. Doan. *Story Re-visions: Narrative Therapy in the Postmodern World.* New York: Guilford, 1994.

Pieper, Josef. *About Love.* Translated by Richard Winston and Clara Winston. Chicago: Franciscan Herald, 1974.

———. *Belief and Faith: A Philosophical Tract.* Translated by Richard Winston and Clara Winston. New York: Pantheon, 1963.

———. *Hope and History.* New York: Herder & Herder, 1969.

———. *On Hope.* Translated by Mary Frances McCarthy. San Francisco: Ignatius, 1986.

Pipher, Mary. *The Shelter of Each Other: Rebuilding Our Families.* New York: Ballantine, 1996.

Plantinga, Cornelius. *Not the Way It's Supposed to Be: A Breviary of Sin.* Grand Rapids, Mich.: Eerdmans, 1995.

Polanyi, Michael. *Personal Knowledge: Towards a Post-critical Philosophy.* Chicago: University of Chicago Press, 1962.

Polkinghorne, Donald E. *Narrative Knowing and the Human Sciences.* Albany: State University of New York Press, 1988.

Popenoe, David. "American Family Decline, 1960-1990: A Review and Appraisal." *Journal of Marriage and the Family* 55 (August 1993): 527-42.

———. *Disturbing the Nest: Family Change and Family Decline in Modern Societies.* New York: Aldine de Gruyter, 1988.

———. "Family Decline in America." In *Rebuilding the Nest: A New Commitment to the American Family,* edited by David Blankenhorn, Steven Bayme and Jean Bethke Elshtain, pp. 39-51. Milwaukee: Family Service America, 1990.

———. *Life Without Father.* New York: Free Press, 1996.

———. "The National Family Wars." *Journal of Marriage and the Family* 55 (August 1993): 553-55.

———. "The Roots of Declining Social Virtue: Family, Community and the Need for a 'Natural Communities Policy.' " In *Seedbeds of Virtue: Sources of Competence, Character and Citizenship in American Society,* edited by Mary Ann Glendon and David Blankenhorn, pp. 71-104. Lanham, Md.: Madison, 1995.

———."Scholars Should Worry About the Disintegration of the American Family." *Chronicle of Higher Education* 14 (April 1993): A48.

Post, Stephen G. *Spheres of Love: Toward a New Ethics of the Family.* Dallas: Southern Methodist University Press, 1994.

Postman, Neil. *Amusing Ourselves to Death: Public Discourse in the Age of Show Business.* New York: Penguin, 1985.

Quayle, Dan, and Diane Medved. *The American Family: Discovering the Values That Make Us Strong.* New York: HarperCollins, 1996.

Ramsey, Paul. *Basic Christian Ethics.* Louisville, Ky.: Westminster John Knox, 1993 (1950).

Rasmussen, Larry. *Moral Fragments and Moral Community: A Proposal for Church in Society.* Minneapolis: Fortress, 1993.

Ricouer, Paul. *Time and Narrative.* Vol. 1. Translated by Kathleen McLaughlin and David

Pellauer. Chicago: University of Chicago Press, 1984.

Rieff, Philip. *The Triumph of the Therapeutic: Uses of Faith After Freud*. Chicago: University of Chicago Press, 1987 (1966).

Roof, Wade Clark. *A Generation of Seekers: The Spiritual Journeys of the Baby Boom Generation*. San Francisco: HarperSanFrancisco, 1993.

Shea, John. *Stories of Faith*. Chicago: Thomas More, 1980.

Shorter, Edward. *The Making of the Modern Family*. New York: Basic Books, 1975.

Skolnick, Arlene. *Embattled Paradise: The American Family in an Age of Uncertainty*. New York: BasicBooks, 1991.

Stacey, Judith. *Brave New Families: Stories of Domestic Upheaval in Late Twentieth Century America*. New York: BasicBooks, 1990.

———. "Good Riddance to 'The Family': A Response to David Popenoe." *Journal of Marriage and the Family* 55 (August 1993): 545-47.

———. *In the Name of the Family: Rethinking Family Values in the Postmodern Age*. Boston: Beacon, 1996.

Strasser, Susan. *Satisfaction Guaranteed: The Making of the American Mass Market*. New York: Pantheon, 1989.

Sykes, Charles J. *A Nation of Victims: The Decay of the American Character*. New York: St. Martin's, 1992.

Taylor, Charles. *The Ethics of Authenticity*. Cambridge, Mass.: Harvard University Press, 1991.

Tocqueville, Alexis de. *Democracy in America*. Translated by George Lawrence. Edited by J. P. Mayer. Garden City, N.Y.: Doubleday/Anchor, 1969.

Tolkien, J. R. R. *The Hobbit*. New York: Ballantine, 1965.

———. *The Return of the King*. New York: Ballantine, 1965.

———. *The Two Towers*. New York: Ballantine, 1965.

Veroff, Joseph, Elizabeth Douvan and Richard A. Kulka. *The Inner American: A Self-Portrait from 1957 to 1976*. New York: Basic Books, 1981.

Wallerstein, Judith S., and Sandra Blakeslee. *The Good Marriage: How and Why Love Lasts*. Boston: Houghton Mifflin, 1995.

———. *Second Chances: Men, Women and Children a Decade After Divorce*. New York: Ticknor & Fields, 1989.

Walsh, Brian J., and J. Richard Middleton. *The Transforming Vision: Shaping a Christian World View*. Downers Grove, Ill.: InterVarsity Press, 1984.

Waters, H. F. "Fractured Family Ties." *Newsweek*, August 30, 1993, pp. 50-52.

White, Michael, and David Epston. *Narrative Means to Therapeutic Ends*. New York: W. W. Norton, 1990.

Whitehead, Barbara Dafoe. "Dan Quayle Was Right." *The Atlantic Monthly*, April 1993.

———. *The Divorce Culture*. New York: Alfred A. Knopf, 1997.

Willimon, William. *The Service of God*. Nashville: Abingdon, 1983.

Wilson, James Q. "The Family-Values Debate." *Commentary* 95, no. 4 (1993): 24-31.

Woodward, Kenneth L. "What Is Virtue?" *Newsweek*, June 13, 1994, pp. 38-39.

Wuthnow, Robert. *God and Mammon in America*. New York: Free Press, 1994.

Wylie, Mary Sykes. "Consumer-Driven Therapy." *Family Therapy Networker* 21 (July/August 1997): 34-41.

Yancey, Philip. "Neat! Way Cool! Awesome!" *Christianity Today*, April 7, 1997, p. 72.

Index of Names & Subjects

abortion *32-33, 69-70, 87, 95, 124, 155, 231*
adultery *127-28, 203*
advertising *97-101, 193-94, 199, 205*
Ahrons, Constance *113, 117, 244, 254*
Alderman, Ellen *243, 254*
Allen, Diogenes *146, 156, 246, 254*
Alter, Jonathan *236, 254*
American dream *24, 200*
Amnesty International *96*
Anderson, Harlene *241, 256*
Anderson, Walter T. *72, 83, 240, 242, 259*

baby boomers *48*
Barna, George *73, 118, 123, 126, 238, 240, 245, 254*
Bayme, Steven *237, 238, 242, 243, 245, 254*
Beatitudes *154*
Bell, Daniel *74, 97, 100-101, 108, 241, 243, 254*
Bellah, Robert *87, 89, 100, 113, 152, 206-7, 212, 242, 243, 244, 247, 251, 252, 254*
Belloc, Hilaire *162*
Bennett, William *8-9, 150-52, 162, 236, 247, 248, 254*
Berger, Brigitte *68, 238, 239, 240, 242, 250, 254*
Berger, Peter *68, 238, 239, 240, 242, 248, 250, 254*
Blackmun, Harry *95*
Blankenhorn, David

115-16, 143, 236, 237, 238, 242, 243, 244, 245, 246, 254
blended families *29*
Boorstin, Daniel *100-103, 243, 254*
Borgmann, Albert *193, 197, 250-51, 254-55*
Borrowdale, Anne *146, 246, 255*
Boszormenyi-Nagy, Ivan *251, 255*
Bowers v. Hardwick *94-96*
Brandeis, Louis *94, 96*
Brockelman, Paul *176, 248, 249, 255*
Brothers Karamazov, The *222, 228, 255*
Brown, Murphy *7, 19*
Brown, William *179, 249, 255*
Brueggemann, Walter *181, 184, 192, 194-95, 250, 251, 255*
Bruner, Jerome *165, 247, 248, 255*
Bruun, Erik *236*
Burke, Phyllis *9, 236, 255*
Burnham, Frederic *240, 242*

capitalism *97, 101, 117*
Carter, Stephen *9, 144, 151, 236, 246, 255*
character *157, 161, 186-87*
Cherlin, Andrew *116, 245, 255*
Christmas, commercialization of *103*
Chronicles of Narnia, The *181*

civil rights *96*
Clapp, Rodney *65, 240, 242, 255*
Clifford, Paul Rowntree *249, 255*
Clift, Eleanor *8, 236, 255*
Clinton, Bill and Hillary *8, 151*
cohabitation *29-30*
Cold War, the *23*
colonial families *45, 50-55, 57-60, 69, 208*
consumerism, consumption *24, 49, 60, 74, 97-104, 193, 197*
  as moral horizon *12, 97, 116-17, 125, 131, 153, 194, 195, 229*
Coontz, Stephanie *9, 23-24, 48-49, 236, 237, 238, 239, 240, 244, 248, 255*
credit, consumer *101-2, 196*
crisis, family *20-22, 26, 37-42, 67, 76*
crisis markers *40, 113*
Crosby, Bing *103*
culture war *13, 68*
Cushman, Philip *193-94, 251, 255*

Dearborn, Tim *58-59, 239, 255*
decline, family. *See* crisis, family
demography, family *45*
DeVries, Mark *66, 240, 255*
Dillard, Annie *172, 249, 255*
discipline, parental *51*
diversity, family *22,*

27
divorce *13, 23, 28-29, 36, 40, 90, 113-39, 151, 208*
  culture *13, 114-18,137-39*
  no-fault *116*
Dizard, Jan *56, 63, 77, 239, 243, 255*
Doan, Robert *75, 78-83, 106, 241*
Doherty, William *80, 148-50, 246, 255*
domestic revolutions *45, 48-57*
domesticity, cult of *60-61*
Dostoyevsky, Fyodor *222, 228, 253, 255*
Douvan, Elizabeth *244*
Dulles, Avery *160, 247, 248, 249, 255*

Eastman, George (Kodak) *98*
economic factors in family life *6, 76-77, 84, 114, 138*
education, parent *46, 177-78*
Efran, Jay *241, 255*
Ells, Alfred *207-13, 223-24, 255*
Elshtain, Jean Bethke *237, 238, 242, 243, 245, 254, 256*
empty self *193*
Enlightenment, the *72, 80, 86, 92, 145*
Epston, David *241*
evangelicalism *104, 207*

Fackre, Gabriel *247, 255*
faith *13, 32, 63, 107, 151, 156, 160-73, 229*

and hope
   184-85,
   195, 230
Falwell, Jerry 22,
   237, 256
familism *56, 63, 71,*
   77, 96, 102
Fancher, Robert *147-*
   50, 246, 256
Father Knows Best
   23
Fay, Martha *164,*
   175, 248, 256
Featherstone, Mike
   240, 243, 256
feminism *23-24, 76*
Fineman, Howard
   151, 246, 256
Fishburn, Janet *62-*
   63, 240, 256
"floating family"
   (Gergen) *81-85*
Ford, Henry *101*
Fowl, Stephen *170,*
   179, 249, 256
Frei, Hans *246, 256*
Friedan, Betty *49-50*

Gadlin, Howard *56,*
   63, 77, 239, 243
Gallagher, Maggie
   244, 256
general social survey
   14-15
Gergen, Kenneth *73-*
   75, 80-85, 86,
   241, 242
Getzen, Robin *236,*
   256
Gillis, John *42, 62,*
   146, 238, 240, 256
Glendon, Mary Ann
   93, 237, 242, 243,
   246, 256
Goesel, Elizabeth
   239, 256
Goolishian, Harold
   241, 256
Gottlieb, Beatrice
   52-55, 239
Gray, John *129*
Great Depression,
   the *48*
Grenz, Stanley *73,*
   241, 256
Griffioen, Sander

238

Hafen, Bruce *93,*
   242, 243, 256
happiness, marital
   and family *32, 61-*
   62, 125
Harak, G. Simon
   253, 256
Hauerwas, Stanley
   47, 65-66, 143.
   151, 157, 176,
   200-201, 236, 238-
   39, 246, 247, 249,
   251, 256-57
haven, family as *41,*
   55, 60, 98, 109,
   153, 176-77, 206-7
Hays, Richard *69,*
   88, 138-39, 240,
   242, 245-46, 249,
   252-53, 257
Hendrix, Harville
   207, 252, 257
Herman, Arthur
   240, 257
heterosexuality/
   homosexuality *28-*
   29, 34, 48
Himmelfarb, Ger-
   trude *10-11, 144-*
   45, 236, 246, 257
Hobbit, The 182
Hochschild, Arlie
   102-3, 238, 241,
   243, 257
Hoffmann, Heinrich
   162
hope *13, 111, 135,*
   159, 181-203
   and faith *184-*
   85, 195
Hunter, James Davi-
   son *104, 146, 238,*
   243, 246, 257
hyperindividualism.
   See individualism
hypermodernity. *See*
   modernism, mod-
   ernity

idolatry, family *48,*
   63
individualism *24,*
   34, 59, 78, 89-93,
   106, 111-12, 117,

121, 125, 148, 154
   commodious
      individualism
      193
   expressive indi-
      vidualism
      100, 116,
      120, 220
   hyperindividual-
      ism *90-91,*
      95, 123, 144,
      154
industrialization *45,*
   55, 60, 72, 97, 206
indwelling *170-73*

Jewett, Robert *167,*
   248, 257
Johnson, Luke Timo-
   thy *137-38, 236,*
   245, 248-49, 257
Jones, L. Gregory
   170, 179, 249
Jordan, Michael *105*

Kain, Edward *26,*
   238, 257
Kellner, Hansfried
   250
Kellogg, Susan *45,*
   238, 239, 252
Kelly, Walt (*Pogo*)
   42
Kemp, Jack *22, 237,*
   240, 257
Kennedy, Caroline
   243
Khruschev, Nikita *49*
Knight, Robin *7,*
   236, 257
Kotva, Joseph *218,*
   247, 252, 257
Kozol, Jonathan *24-*
   25, 238, 257
Kreeft, Peter *247,*
   257
Kuhn, Thomas *147,*
   246, 257
Kulka, Richard *244*

Lasch, Christopher
   75, 106, 107, 238,
   241, 244, 257
Lazarus, Edward *30,*
   31, 238, 245
Leave It to Beaver 23

Lee, Cameron *249,*
   257
Leo, John *7, 236,*
   257
Lewis, C. S. *181,*
   222-25, 253, 257
Lewis, Robert *22-*
   23, 237
lifestyle enclave *152*
Lloyd-Jones, D. Mar-
   tyn *247, 257*
Lord of the Rings,
   The 181-84
love *13, 58, 109,*
   159, 204-28, 230
   vs. faith and
      hope *216, 225*
   need-love vs.
      gift-love *223-*
      25
   neighbor love
      216-20
Luckmann, Thomas
   242, 248
Lukens, Michael *241*
Lukens, Robert *241*
Luther, Martin *186*
Lyotard, Jean-Fran-
   cois *78, 241*

MacIntyre, Alasdair
   12, 145, 158-59,
   236, 245, 246,
   247, 257
Madsen, Richard *242*
Malone, Karl *105*
marketplace, influ-
   ence of. *See* con-
   sumerism
Marshall, I. Howard
   64-65, 240, 258
Marxism *58-59*
Mather, Cotton *50-*
   51, 58, 239
Maturana, Hum-
   berto *241, 258*
May, Elaine Tyler
   49, 238, 239, 258
McAdams, Dan *247,*
   258
McLaughlin, Kath-
   leen *248*
media *7-8, 20, 35,*
   81-82, 86, 114,
   207
Medved, Diane *236,*

259
Medved, Michael
114, 244, 258
Meilaender, Gilbert
67, 157, 186-87,
240, 247, 249,
250, 258
Mellman, Mark 30,
31, 35, 42, 119,
238, 245, 258
metanarratives 78-
80, 83-85, 90,
105, 158-59, 192
Middleton, J. Richard 166-67, 187,
248, 250, 258
Miller, James 240,
258
ministry, family 47,
66, 177, 230
Mintz, Steven 45,
238, 239, 252, 258
Minuchin, Salvador
252, 258
modernism, modernity 10-11, 45, 71-
75, 85-87, 97,
112, 148, 154,
192-95, 229
hypermodernity 86
Moltmann, Jürgen
181, 201, 225-26,
250, 251, 253, 258
Moore, R. Laurence
103, 243, 258
Morgan, Edmund
51, 58, 239, 258
Morrow, Lance 7-8,
10, 236, 258
Mouw, Richard 39,
238, 258
Mrs. Doubtfire 114-
15

narrative, elements
of 166-73
Navone, John 250,
258
Neuhaus, Richard
John 247
Newbigin, Lesslie
89, 169-73, 188,
201, 242, 249,
250, 251, 258
Nietzsche, Friedrich

144-46
Nixon, Richard 49
Noonan, Peggy
151, 246, 259
nostalgia, family 50,
76
Nygren, Anders
253, 259
O'Hara, Maureen
72, 83, 240, 242,
258
Oldham, Margaret
106, 108
Ozzie and Harriet 23

Parry, Alan 75, 78-
80, 106, 241, 259
Passover 174
Pellauer, David 248
permanence, marital 32, 36, 48, 123-
24, 136-39
culture of 118-
23
Pieper, Josef 193,
223, 247, 249,
250, 251, 253, 259
Pipher, Mary 213,
252, 259
Plantinga, Cornelius
250, 259
pluralism 39
Polanyi, Michael
171, 249, 259
Polkinghorne, Donald 161, 248, 259
Popenoe, David 21-
22, 25-26, 75,
237, 238, 241, 259
Post, Stephen 220,
253, 259
Postman, Neil 194,
251, 259
postmodernism,
postmodernity 11-
13, 20, 71-87, 90-
91, 146, 154-57,
180, 192-95, 229-
31
postmodern
family 75-85
postwar families
(World War II) 48-
50, 55
poverty, inner-city
24-25

prayer in school 32-
33, 124
pregnancy, teenage
69-71
privatization of family life 53-55, 60-
61, 136, 153,
177-78, 212, 220,
229-31
Protestant work
ethic 97, 101, 152
psychotherapy 77-
85, 109-10, 147,
161
as moral horizon 12, 105-
10, 117, 125,
129, 131-39,
149-50, 199,
206-13, 223,
229
therapeutic,
triumph of
106, 128
Puritan families. *See*
colonial families

Quayle, Dan 7-9,
19, 116, 236, 259

Ramsey, Paul 216-
17, 252, 253, 259
Rasmussen, Larry
68, 97, 111, 240,
241, 243, 244,
249, 251, 259
Reagan, Ronald 74
recovery movement
207-213
Revolution, American 60, 72, 206
Ricouer, Paul 248,
259-60
Rieff, Philip 105-6,
244, 260
Riesman, David 49
rights 138
as moral horizon 12, 91-
96, 117, 125,
153, 229
Bill of 93
to privacy 70-71
Rivlin, Allan 30, 31,
238, 245
Roe v. Wade 94

Roof, Wade Clark
249, 260

Schiffren, Lisa 8
Scott, Kieran 246
Shea, John 160,
170, 247, 249,
250, 260
"Sheilaism" (Sheila
Larson) 107, 168
Shorter, Edward 75,
241, 260
"siege mentality"
40, 43, 58, 69
single parenthood
7, 29-30
sitcoms, television
23, 48
Skolnick, Arlene
239-40, 260
sloth *(acedia)* 193
Smith, Adam 97
social saturation 74,
80-81
Spark, Geraldine 251
Stacey, Judith 23,
75-77, 80, 85,
237, 238, 241, 260
*Star Trek: Deep
Space Nine* 165-66
Star Wars 167
Stockton, John 105
Strasser, Susan 98,
243, 260
subculture, church
as 30, 33, 43, 48,
68, 153
suburban family
ideal 48-50
Sullivan, William
242
Swidler, Ann 242
Sykes, Charles 111,
243, 244, 260

Taylor, Charles 108,
112, 145-46, 244,
246, 260
Teresa, Mother 205
Tocqueville, Alexis
de 89, 93, 242-43,
260
Tolkien, J. R. R. 181-
84, 250, 260
traditional families
21, 24, 27-30, 48

transmission of values 37, 85, 152, 163

Veroff, Joseph 244, 260

Wadsworth, Benjamin 239
Wallerstein, Judith 115, 244-45, 260

Walsh, Brian 166-67, 187, 248, 250, 260
Warren, Michael 246
Warren, Samuel 93
Waters, H. F. 239, 260
White, Michael 241, 260
Whitehead, Barbara Dafoe 8, 13, 116-18, 236, 244, 245, 260
Whyte, William 49
Williams, Robin 114
Willimon, William 70, 239, 250, 260
Wilson, James Q. 75, 143, 241, 246, 260
women, changing role of 45, 62, 75

Woodward, Kenneth 246, 260
Wuthnow, Robert 103-4, 120, 238, 243-44, 245, 260
Wylie, Mary Sykes 110, 244, 260

Yancey, Philip 88-89, 242, 260

Index of Scripture References

Exodus
12:24-27 174
13:8 174
13:14-15 175

Leviticus
19:18 205

Deuteronomy
5:1-3 163
6:4-9 175, 205
8:11-19 177
8:12-14 194

Joshua
4:21-24 175

1 Kings
19:19-21 65

Proverbs
1:7 173-74
2:1-16 173-74

Isaiah
25:8 226

Matthew
5:6 198
5:13 153
5:31-32 128
5:43-48 217
5:44 218
6:10 218

10:34-39 220, 230
11:4-5 198
13:33 153
13:34-35 214
15:12 214
19:3-9 128
22:23-30 64
22:37-40 205, 213
22:39 216
25:1-13 188-90

Mark
12:29-30 213
12:31 216

Luke
9:59-60 64
9:61-62 65
10:25-37 216-17
10:27 213
14:26 65, 230
15:11-32 226
17:11-19 198

John
2:13-25 169
3:16 213
4:46-54 169
5:1-15 198
6:5-9 202
11:3 213
11:21-27 191
11:32 191
11:36 213

11:39 191
13:34-35 204
15:9 213
15:12-13 227

Acts
16:7 219

Romans
4:18 185
4:20-21 185
5:1-5 198
5:8 213, 219
7 96
8:9 219
8:16-26 186, 227
8:29 218

1 Corinthians
1:12 214
11:24-25 174
12:31 215
13:1-3 215
13:4 218
13:8-10 215
13:13 204, 214
14:1-5 215
14:12 215
15:49 218

2 Corinthians
3:18 218
5:7 168

Galatians
4:6 219
5:19-23 218-19

Ephesians
5:1-2 219

Philippians
1:19 219
2:1-4 56
2:1-8 219, 231
2:5-11 57

1 Timothy
6:10 104

Hebrews
11:1 169, 185
11:6 185
11:8 185
11:10 185
11:13-16 169, 185

1 Peter
1:11 219

1 John
3:2 218
4:8 216
4:10-21 220
4:16 216